EVALUATION OF ALTERNATIVE CURRICULA

T5-ADP-873

EVALUATION OF ALTERNATIVE CURRICULA

Approaches to School Library Media Education

Robert N. Case
Director

Anna Mary Lowrey
Associate Director

C. Dennis Fink
Harold Wagner
Project Evaluators

SCHOOL LIBRARY MANPOWER PROJECT
Funded by the KNAPP FOUNDATION OF NORTH CAROLINA, INC.
Administered by the AMERICAN ASSOCIATION OF SCHOOL LIBRARIANS
A Division of the AMERICAN LIBRARY ASSOCIATION

AMERICAN LIBRARY ASSOCIATION
Chicago 1975

Library of Congress Cataloging in Publication Data

School Library Manpower Project.
    Evaluation of alternative curricula.

    1. School Library Manpower Project. 2. Instruction-
al materials personnel. 3. Library education--United
States. I. Case, Robert N., 1931-   II. Lowrey,
Anna Mary. III. Title.
Z675.S3S356 1975   027.8'07'1173   74-34592
ISBN 0-8389-3165-0

Copyright © 1975 by the American Library Association

  All rights reserved. No part of this publication
  may be reproduced in any form without permission
  in writing from the publisher, except by a reviewer
  who may quote brief passages in a review.

         Printed in the United States of America

CONTENTS

Advisory Committee — vii

Preface — ix

Acknowledgements — xi

Chapter 1 SCHOOL LIBRARY MANPOWER PROJECT — 1
    Phase I — 2
    Phase II — 3
    Phase III — 8
        Goals and Objectives — 9
        Evaluation Philosophy — 9
        Evaluation Topics — 10
        Dissemination of Information — 11

Chapter 2 METHODOLOGY — 13
    Design — 13
    Participants — 13
    Instrumentation — 14
        Behavioral Requirements Analysis Checklist — 14
        Interview Questionnaires — 15
    Survey Procedures — 19
        Questionnaire Administration — 19
        Interviews — 20
    Data Processing and Analysis — 22
        BRAC Questionnaire Data — 22
        Interview Responses — 25

Chapter 3 FINDINGS — 26
    Questionnaire Data — 26
        Program Graduates — 26
        Supervisors of Program Graduates — 32
        Program Students — 32
        Program Directors — 32
    Program Graduate Interviews — 33
        BA-Level Graduates — 33
        MA-Level Graduates — 35
        Sixth Year Level Graduates — 36
        All Graduates: Work-Related Questions — 37
    Supervisor Interviews — 38
        Supervisors of BA-Level Graduates — 38
        Supervisors of MA-Level Graduates — 39
        Supervisors of Sixth Year Level Graduates — 40
        All Supervisors: Work-Related Questions — 41
    Interview Discrepancies — 42

Chapter 4	PROGRAM STATUS REPORTS	43
	Program Goals and Objectives	43
	Program Participants	44
	Program Components	46
	Program Results	48
	Program Impact	49
	Conclusions and Recommendations	50
Chapter 5	BRAC SURVEY PROCEDURES	53
	Use of Questionnaire Data	53
	BRAC-Related Interview Questions	54
	Program Graduates	55
	Supervisors of Program Graduates	56
	Improvement of Survey Procedures	56
	Improvement of BRAC	57
Chapter 6	CONCLUSIONS	59
	Fieldwork as a Program Component	59
	Role of a Program Director	61
	Program Costs	62
	Program Transportability	63
	Program Goals and Job Requirements	63
Chapter 7	FINAL ASSESSMENT	65
	Project Accomplishments	65
	Program Characteristics	67
	Interdisciplinary Approach	67
	Course Material Duplication	67
	Occupational Relevancy	68
	Individualization of Programs	69
	Program Evaluation and Quality Control	70
	Educational Impact for the Profession	72
	Unresolved Issues	74
	Further Research	76

Appendices   77

Tables

  I. Sample Page from the Behavioral Requirements Analysis Checklist   16

 II. Sample Page from the "BRAC Survey Questionnaire and Response Form for the GRADUATES of the School Library Media Educational Program"   17

Tables

III.	BRAC Survey Questionnaire for the GRADUATE of the School Library Media Education Program	18
IV.	Job Status of 1972 and 1973 Graduates Immediately Following Graduation	20
V.	Comparison of Responses to BRAC Questionnaire by Graduates of BA-Level and MA-Level Programs	31

Figures

1a	Summary of Graduate Responses for BRAC Question A -- Percentage of Respondents Who Performed Task for Competency Areas A, B, and C	27
1b	Summary of Graduate Responses for BRAC Question A -- Percentage of Respondents Who Performed Task for Competency Area D	28
1c	Summary of Graduate Responses for BRAC Question A -- Percentage of Respondents Who Performed Task for Competency Areas E, F, and G	29

ADVISORY COMMITTEE

Leslie H. Janke, Chairman 1968-74
University of California at San Jose
San Jose, California

Eleanor E. Ahlers, 1968-74
University of Washington
Seattle, Washington

Thomas Buchta, 1970-71
Skokie School District #68
Skokie, Illinois

Richard L. Darling, 1968-70
Columbia University
New York, New York

Ruth M. Ersted, 1970-74
Minnesota Department of Education
St. Paul, Minnesota

Sara I. Fenwick, 1968-74
University of Chicago
Chicago, Illinois

Bernard Franchowiak, Ex Officio 1973-74
Wisconsin Department of Public
 Instruction
Madison, Wisconsin

Margaret H. Grazier, 1972-74
Wayne State University
Detroit, Michigan

Frances Hatfield, Ex Officio 1971-72,
 Member 1972-74
Broward County Board of Public
 Instruction
Ft. Lauderdale, Florida

Phyllis Hochstettler, Ex Officio 1968-69
Portland State College
Portland, Oregon

Virginia Owens, 1971-74
Oklahoma Department of Libraries
Oklahoma City, Oklahoma

Miriam E. Peterson, 1968-74
Chicago Board of Education
Chicago, Illinois

Elnora M. Portteus, Ex Officio 1972-73
Cleveland Public Schools
Cleveland, Ohio

John Rebenack, 1968-74
Akron, Public Library
Akron, Ohio

John Rowell, Ex Officio 1969-70
Case Western Reserve University
Cleveland, Ohio

Alice C. Rusk, 1968-72
Baltimore City Public Schools
Baltimore, Maryland

Russell Shank, 1968-70
Smithsonian Institution Library
Washington, D.C.

Lu Ouida Vinson, Ex Officio 1968-74
American Association of School Librarians
Chicago, Illinois

Carolyn Whitenack, Ex Officio 1967-68
Purdue University
LaFayette, Indiana

Edward A. Wight, 1968-70
University of California
Berkley, California

Roberta Young, Ex Officio 1970-71
Colorado Department of Education
Denver, Colorado

PREFACE

This publication is the final report of the School Library Manpower Project and brings to conclusion the evaluation study conducted during Phase III.

The School Library Manpower Project, initiated in 1968, was designed to "study vital questions leading to the redefinition of the concept of school librarianship and to support the effective utilization of professional school library media personnel through the implementation and evaluation of a variety of new and innovative educational approaches".

As originally conceived the Project was to be conducted in two phases. Phase I, completed in 1970, was concerned primarily with identifying the tasks performed by school library media personnel, developing job descriptions for such personnel, developing suggestions for how such persons should be educated, and developing plans for supporting experimental educational programs for school library media personnel. A detailed report of Phase I findings and activities has been presented in School Library Manpower Project, Phase I -- Final Report, published in 1970.

The primary goal of Phase II of the project was to "provide six experimental program models in school library media education which could be a relevant and intelligent response to the needs identified in Phase I." Support for the development and conduct of these six experimental programs was provided by the Project during the 1971-72 and 1972-73 academic years. The nature of these programs, their developmental problems and their status as of the Summer of 1973 is described in Curriculum Alternatives -- Experiments in School Library Media Education, a 1974 publication.

During the early stages of Phase II of the Project it was recognized that a complete evaluation of the Project should include a follow-up survey of program graduates after they had worked on a job for at least six months. For this reason the study was extended to a sixth year. This extension was designated as Phase III of the Project. This report describes the survey procedures and instruments used during Phase III. Also, the survey findings are presented and discussed as are the Program Status Reports prepared by the six Program Directors during the third year of their programs.

This publication brings to a close the School Library Manpower Project. This Project was proposed by the American Association of School Librarians

Preface

and conducted under the auspices of the American Library Association. The Project was funded in its entirety by the Knapp Foundation of North Carolina, Inc.

The findings of this study are based on comments of graduates and supervisors associated with the six experimental programs only. These findings therefore may not be representative of the professional work activities of graduates of other school library media education programs.

The data collected throughout the Project, and especially during Phase III, will be stored at least through 1979. Researchers interested in obtaining access to this data should contact the Research Office of the American Library Association.

ACKNOWLEDGEMENTS

Throughout the six years of the Project many persons have played a significant role in contributing to the work of the Project which led to the realization of its goals. An appreciation to all the special study committees, individuals and institutions was cited in the Phase II report, Curriculum Alternatives -- Experiments in School Library Media Education.

During the Phase III evaluation study the Project staff continued its close relationship with the members of the Project's Advisory Committee and the Program Directors and staffs of the six Phase II experimental programs. The Project staff is most appreciative of the opportunity to have worked with each of these persons individually. The staff was happy for the opportunity to have known and worked with the graduates of the six experimental programs, for it is through their educational and work experience that the data for Phase III and this publication was obtained. The willingness of the graduates and their supervisors to cooperate in the Phase III study was greatly appreciated. We extend to them our best wishes in the future and are assured that they will make a positive contribution to the school library media field.

A special appreciation is extended to Dr. C. Dennis Fink and Dr. Harold Wagner who with the Human Resources Research Organization have provided the Project Advisory Committee and staff with insight and direction to bring Phase III to its fruition. Their knowledge of research techniques and evalution of competency-based education programs was invaluable. Their abilities to lead us through the various assessment steps of Phase III was both a personally and professionally rewarding experience.

Finally, appreciation is extended to the Knapp Foundation of North Carolina, Inc. whose generous grant of $150,000 provided the Project with the resources to extend the original School Library Manpower Project into an additional one year Phase III evaluation study. Without their support and commitment to the final goals of the Project, this report to the library and education profession would not have been possible.

Robert N. Case
Anna Mary Lowrey

Chapter 1

SCHOOL LIBRARY MANPOWER PROJECT

The School Library Manpower Project, funded by the Knapp Foundation of North Carolina, Inc. and administered by the American Association of School Librarians, a Division of the American Library Association, was originally a five-year study of task analysis, education, and utilization of school library media personnel. The $1,163,718 initial grant provided not only the school library profession, but the total field of librarianship with an opportunity to study vital questions and seek new solutions through the implementation and evaluation of a variety of new, relevant, and innovative approaches in school library media education. Midway through the Project a need for a summative evaluation study was identified and additional grant funds of $150,000 were obtained by the Knapp Foundation of North Carolina, Inc. to implement a third phase of the project.

The School Library Manpower Project was originally developed in two distinct phases. During the two years of Phase I, (1968-1970) the Project was concerned with societal and educational change and its effect upon the future of school librarianship. The first purpose of Phase I was to study the roles and job functions of school library personnel to support the development of new occupational definitions. The second purpose was to provide recommendations for implementing six experimental school library media education programs in Phase II. The primary purpose of Phase II, (1970-1973) was to implement six job relevant, innovative experimental programs for professional school library media personnel based on the responsibilities identified in Phase I. At the conclusion of Phases I and II in August, 1973 an evaluative and summary report, _Curriculum Alternatives: Experiments in School Library Media Education_[1] was published by the American Library Association. The reports of the six experimental programs and the findings of the School Library Manpower Project included in this publication provide new directions for recruitment, curriculum change, and methodology to prepare school library media personnel for their roles in the continually changing process of education.

---

[1] School Library Manpower Project, _Curriculum Alternatives: Experiments in School Library Media Education_ (Chicago: American Library Association, 1974).

2　The Project

Phase I

The initial activity in Phase I which led to the development of new definitions for school library media personnel was the Task Analysis Survey, conducted under contract by the Research Division of the National Education Association. Guidelines established by the Project, including the "Criteria of Excellence Checklist",[2] were used to identify the 694 outstanding school library media programs used in the national purposive sample. The Task Analysis Survey Instrument[3] developed for the research study was used in the survey to identify the tasks performed in a wide variety of staff positions in school library media centers throughout the country. In October 1969, the published report School Library Personnel: Task Analysis Survey[4] was made available and served as a working paper to advance Phase I toward the development of new definitions for school librarianship.

The results of the research study were analyzed in depth by a special Task Analysis Committee. The work of this committee effected a second publication, Occupational Definitions for School Library Media Personnel.[5] The four basic definitions included in this publication are: School Library Media Specialist, Head of the School Library Media Center, District School Library Media Director, and School Library Media Technician. These definitions manifest the functional tasks in which school library media personnel should be skilled, the need for both vertical and horizontal mobility, and a branching pattern for specialization beyond the core position of the school library media specialist. They are presented as models for adaptation to the functions and objectives of a variety of school library media center organizational patterns.

A Curriculum Content Committee, appointed by the Project's Advisory Committee, had the next task of objectively scrutinizing the competencies, the educational background, and the experience necessary for the newly defined functions delineated in the Occupational Definitions for School Library Media Personnel.[6] The committee analyzed the occupational definitions and identified essential competencies in its report "Major Areas of Competencies for the Education of the School Library Media Specialist."

---

[2]SLMP, "Criteria of Excellence Checklist", School Library Personnel: Task Analysis Survey, (Chicago: American Library Association, 1969, p.8).
[3]SLMP, Task Analysis Survey Instrument, (Chicago: American Library Association, 1969).
[4]SLMP, School Library Personnel: Task Analysis Survey, (Chicago: American Library Association, 1969).
[5]SLMP, Occupational Definitions for School Library Media Personnel, (Chicago: American Library Association, 1971).
[6]SLMP, "Major Areas of Competencies for the Education of School Library Media Specialists", School Library Manpower Project, Phase I - Final Report, (Chicago: American Library Association, 1970) pp. 37-52).

The work of the Curriculum Content Committee was further detailed in its report "Suggestions for Curriculum Content Within Major Areas of Competencies."[7] The seven major areas of competencies identified were: Media, Human Behavior, Development and Interaction, Learning and Learning Environment, Professionalism, Planning and Evaluation, Management, and Research. Each major area of competency was supported by a series of behavioral objectives essential to the foundation position of the school library media specialist.

In the spring of 1970 the School Library Manpower Project sponsored three regional conferences in San Francisco, Pittsburgh, and New Orleans. The purpose of the regional meetings was to present the findings of the Task Analysis Survey, the Task Analysis Committee, and the Curriculum Content Committee. A study of the reports by the participants at the regional conferences led to specific recommendations for the Phase II experimental programs. Reactions from the field were instrumental in refining the work of the Project study committees.

The 105 participants at the regional conferences represented a wide variety of disciplines. Their combined contributions and the recommendations from the regional meetings served as a milestone in providing the national direction for school library media education from the grass roots level. In addition to the reactions to Phase I activities, the regional conferences provided an opportunity for leaders in special fields related to school librarianship to meet face to face in a full discussion of the future direction for the roles and education of school library media personnel. Current education demands for redefined job functions led to discussions on needed innovations in school library media education. Discussions of national trends in certification incorporated aspects of recruitment and manpower needs. The outcome of all three regional meetings emphasized the need for innovative practices in school library media education to meet the mandates for change.

Recommendations from the regional conferences encompassed the following broad areas: the education of the school library media specialist; entry levels for education; education program financial support; and certification. Each broad category included many recommendations specifically related to the development of the six experimental programs. A special team of consultants, who aided the Project in writing the "Proposal Format and Guidelines"[8] incorporated the recommendations from the regional conferences within the document to foster and encourage innovation in future program development for school library media education.

Phase II

Early in Phase II the Project conducted a second survey to identify all institutions in the United States which offered a minimum of twelve or more semester hours in school library education, an eligibility requirement for

---

[7]SLMP, "Suggestions for Curriculum Content Within Major Areas of Competencies", ibid., pp. 53-69.

[8]SLMP, "Proposal Format and Guidelines for Experimental Programs in School Library Media Education, Phase II", ibid., pp. 98-123.

4 The Project

an experimental program. The 306 institutions which met the eligibility criteria were invited to attend one of three regional planning clinics in the Fall of 1970 in Denver, Cleveland, and Atlanta.

The planning clinics focused on the goals of the Phase II experimental programs. The format and structure of the sessions were designed to encourage a dialogue between the Project staff and representatives from the institutions interested in submitting a proposal. Participants in the planning clinics received copies of the "Proposal Format and Guidelines" and through discussion gained a clearer understanding of the varieties of program change which could be developed in the experimental programs. Recruitment and scholarship programs, integral parts of the Phase II experimentation, were supported by the Project film, At the Center.[9] This film, a twenty-eight minute, color/sound, recruitment film was developed to present the role of school library media personnel as a changing, exciting and dynamic force in the total educational system, and to project the diverse career opportunities within the field of school librarianship.

Forty-six proposals were submitted for award consideration and funding. Evaluated by a team of nine readers appointed by the Advisory Committee, eleven proposals were recommended for committee consideration. The Advisory Committee selected six institutions to receive $100,000 grants each to develop, implement, and evaluate, over a two-year period, new curriculum design and innovative approaches for the education of professional school library media personnel. Each institution also received an additional $2,000 planning grant to support staff development activities prior to program implementation. The institutions selected were: Arizona State University, Tempe; Auburn University, Alabama; Mankato State College, Minnesota; Millersville State College, Pennsylvania; University of Denver, Colorado; and the University of Michigan, Ann Arbor. Each experimental program began some phase of operation in September 1971 concluding their experimentation in August 1973. Millersville State College developed an undergraduate program. Four of the programs were at the fifth year level. A sixth year program was featured at the University of Denver.

The unique focus of each of the six experimental programs was on school library media education and the preparation for one of three distinct positions -- the School Library Media Specialist, the Head of the School Library Media Center, or the District School Library Media Director as defined during Phase I in Occupational Definitions for School Library Media Personnel.[10] The experimental programs adopted the seven major areas of competencies identified during Phase I as the foundation for their programs. The nature of the job relevant competencies required curriculum components in media and their associated technology, management,

---

[9]SLMP, At The Center, 16mm, 28:45 minute color/sound film, (Chicago: American Library Association, 1970).

[10]SLMP, Occupational Definitions for School Library Media Personnel, op. cit.

and guided field experience. The programs reflected a balance of library media content with a strong relationship to the general education component, the teacher education component and other disciplinary fields. The wide range of competencies placed high priority on the provision and management of media for learning. Equally high priority was given to the human aspects inherent in the best utilization of media.

The six experimental programs had some similarities as required by the "Proposal Format Guidelines".[11] Objectives of each program were stated in behavioral terms and encompassed a broad media base. An interdisciplinary approach to the programs fostered articulation among the various departments within the institution and between levels of school library media education. Each program implemented a recruitment and scholarship program to ensure student participation in the two-year experiment. Individual programs were assisted by a local Advisory Board, had at least three full-time faculty members assigned to the program, and included student involvement in program planning and evaluation activities. Staff development activities, prior to program implementation and continuing throughout the two program years, were vital elements in each program. All programs included a fieldwork component which provided students with opportunities to put theory into practice in a variety of field centers representing diverse social, economic and cultural backgrounds. The six experimental programs each received additional institutional support during the two-year period. The parent institutions provided flexible administrative policies to effect the implementation of the unique and innovative aspects of the special programs. Equally important was the provision of facilities, resources, and personnel for the experimental program. In addition, all six programs were given the assurance from the appropriate state education agencies that program graduates would be awarded certification.

Finally, the similarities of each experimental program were reflected in a research and evaluation plan to identify and assess the processes that evolved during the two-year experimentation. Central to all the programs were the innovative and experimental practices employed to meet specified program goals. The primary concern through all evaluation phases was the attention and understanding given to the role of the student and his expected outcomes from the educational experience. Early and continuous interaction between student and faculty identified individual student needs. The flexibilities within the experimental programs made it possible to meet these needs through a variety of organizational structures, teaching strategies and learning methodologies. It was the unique approach to these objectives by each program which identified the experimental and innovative practices being implemented and assessed.

Five elements created an environment within each institution which permitted the experimental programs to develop innovative applications to meet major individual program objectives. These elements were: informality and

---

[11]SLMP, "Proposal Format and Guidelines for Experimental Programs in School Library Media Education, Phase II", op. cit.

flexibility; modular, block or course organization of content; individualization and self-instruction; team teaching and an interdisciplinary approach; and the field work component.

The informality and flexibility within the programs were reflected in the one-to-one relationships developed between a student and a staff member. Through guidance and counselling programs students, singly or in small groups, had an opportunity to contribute to program planning and assist in decisions for program modification. The results of interviews and proficiency testing substantially effected the entry level of a student in an experimental program. A flexible structure of the institution or the program was necessary to ensure the student a wide choice of alternatives and options to meet individual needs.

Restructuring of time periods within most of the experimental programs was best seen in the module-block units. Subject matter deemed irrelevant to performance objectives was eliminated, while other content more closely related to program objectives and student needs was introduced or stressed. Through variations in the modular or course approach, content was acquired in a more individualized way. Long or short term modules offered a high degree of flexibility for students and provided for a better utilization of time within a prescribed curriculum. The experimental programs paid close attention to the sequence of content. The experimental programs encouraged interdisciplinary planning and implementation and provided a flexibility for both students and teachers. The programs supported by seminars, mini courses, case studies, games, simulated field trips and autotutorials offered individual students a variety of options for learning.

The experimental programs were learner-oriented to meet individual needs. Recognition was given to the range of educational and experiential backgrounds of students in program planning and implementation. More discerning students who were able to identify individual strengths and weaknesses expressed a desire to explore their own ideas and grow in self-understanding. The flexible structure of the programs provided self-instruction units and options within the experimental programs to meet these needs. The flexibility of the programs and understanding of staff provided the necessary elements which encouraged a greater freedom for the learner.

The interdisciplinary emphasis incorporated within the program content was vital to the realization of program goals. Staff interaction during initial program planning sessions and staff development activities identified the individual differences of the teaching faculty. Team teaching assignments focused on the strengths individual faculty could bring to the curriculum content and drew upon the special expertise from other disciplines within the total institution.

Finally, program flexibility was continually emphasized in the application of theory into practice through the fieldwork component. Early and continuous fieldwork experiences provided the student with an opportunity to put program content into practice in a variety of settings and school levels. While the fieldwork component was vital for reinforcing content, it was also complex to administer. Flexibility in assignments and time were required if students were to field test their acquired competencies to meet individual needs. The planning and communication processes between the institution and the field centers were essential to the ultimate success of the student's fieldwork experience. Coordinating time, field center personnel, student experiences, evaluations from field center supervisors, and assessing feedback data to the institution for program modification was critical. Assigning and orienting a student or teams of students to field experiences, and relating content objectives to practical experiences were examples of some of the activities the experimental programs implemented and tested to strengthen the total program.

Formative evaluation of the six experimental programs focused on nine evaluation topics identified cooperatively among the six experimental programs, the Project staff, the Advisory Committee, and the Human Resources Research Organization who was under contract with the Project to develop the Phase II evaluation component. The process of identifying and selecting evaluation topics began by building from the three broad categories of general education, program support and education objectives. After an initial compilation of eighty-eight topics, a process was implemented to determine the major importance of each topic. Once the ranking was done and agreement reached, the formative evaluation indices and procedures were identified and selected. An analysis and review were made of the evaluation plans from each experimental program to ensure that each institution would be able to meet the requirements of the experimental program evaluation plans for the Project. The nine evaluation areas were:

1. Preparation of lists of specifically stated job-relevant training/education objectives.

2. Communication of program goals to students, staff, outside institutions, etc.

3. Development of procedures for assessing student proficiency.

4. Development of procedures for implementing individualized and/or modularized instruction.

5. Evaluating effectiveness of methods, media, and special program features.

6. Development of quality control procedures.

7. Development and/or utilization of field experiences and practicums.

8. Determining transportability of experimental programs.

9. Assessing probability of program continuance after end of Project funds.

The Project's final report of Phases I and II, <u>Curriculum Alternatives: Experiments in School Library Media Education</u>[12] was developed in two distinct parts. Part One focused on the processes and procedures utilized by the Project which led to the implementation of the six experimental programs.

---

12 SLMP, <u>Curriculum Alternatives: Experiments in School Library Media Education</u>, op. cit.

8 The Project

Part Two incorporated the formative evaluation processes and the results achieved by each of the six experimental programs during the two year experimentation. The published report also included an assessment of the impact of the total five year study in the areas of task analysis, education and utilization of school library media personnel. It incorporated recommendations for the library profession and for education programs for professional school library media personnel.

Phase III

As the Project was nearing the end of Phase I, it became increasingly clear to the Advisory Committee, Project staff and members of various study committees that a very serious time limitation at the conclusion of Phase II would directly affect the total impact of the School Library Manpower Project. The original Project proposal provided only a three-month time period from the end of the experimental programs to the completion of the Project. This brief period did not provide enough time for a detailed study and analysis of each experimental program. While each experimental program was to develop its own formative evaluation report, the Project itself needed a plan, along with time and means, to develop a comprehensive research study to test the validity of all the experimental programs. As a result of the Advisory Committee's investigations and discussions, a subcommittee was appointed to work with the Project staff, ALA staff liaison and with research consultants from the Human Resources Research Organization to initiate such a plan. An exploration was made of the time, method, manpower and cost to support an immediate extension of the Project into a Phase III. The proposal, A Summative Evaluation of Six Experimental School Library Media Education Programs[13] to extend the Project into a sixth year Phase III study was approved by the Advisory Committee, the American Association of School Librarians, and the American Library Association in the Winter and Spring of 1972.

The heavy investment by the Knapp Foundation of North Carolina, Inc. and the six colleges and universities resulted in the development of occupationally-relevant education programs. The Foundation, recognizing the value of the proposed summative evaluation process and its broad application to the total field of education, awarded a grant of $150,000 to fund the Phase III extension. Though the Phase III funding did not commence until the end of Phase II in August 1973, the Advisory Committee, Project staff, experimental Program Directors and consultants from the Human Resources Research Organization already had prepared a plan for the methodology to be utilized.

---

[13]A Summative Evaluation of Six Experimental School Library Media Educational Programs, (Chicago: School Library Manpower Project with the assistance of Human Resources Research Organization, 1972).

GOALS AND OBJECTIVES

The purpose of the Phase III extension was to provide an assessment of the validity of the experimental programs and to give guidance for the future direction of school library media education programs. A second, and equally important goal, was to demonstrate the value of a quality control system for the continued evaluation and improvement of education programs. Utilizing a variety of techniques the summative evaluation study would give special emphasis to the following evaluations of the experimental programs: (1) the degree to which the education programs prepared students to perform those activities which they were actually required to perform on the job, and (2) the degree to which the graduates could capably perform in the field those activities which were covered in the experimental programs.

The major objectives of Phase III were to perform a summative evaluation of the six experimental programs and to develop and field test survey procedures for obtaining information from the experimental program directors and staff, in-program students, and from experimental program graduates and their supervisors on the job. Procedures were developed for using survey information to evaluate and modify educational programs on a continuing basis. The six Phase II experimental programs, utilizing the survey information for program modification and revision, prepared status reports of their experimental programs three years after their inception.

EVALUATION PHILOSOPHY

A necessary part of a summative evaluation is the "quality control" activity exemplified by a field follow up of program graduates. One purpose of an instructional program is to produce graduates who can capably perform a selected specifiable list of tasks. These tasks must bear a clear relation to job activities required in the field. Quality control procedures are needed both at the school and in the field. Information from both locations must be "fed back" so that the instructional program can be adjusted appropriately.

Schools require several types of feedback information: the first type deals with an assessment of the ability of a graduate to perform acceptably those tasks which the program claims to teach. In most instances this assessment can be made at the school. In addition, the administrative characteristics and problems associated with conducting a given program can be identified within the school setting. Another type of feedback information deals with the discrepancies between the program graduates' performance and field requirements. This type of information assesses whether or not the program teaches the appropriate subjects or tasks, and whether or not graduates can transfer these competencies to the field. Such field feedback information can be obtained from program graduates who can identify changing field requirements and provide more precise descriptions of job activities.

The foregoing philosophy led to the assumption that Program Directors and former students of a program are the best source of information about the success of that program. Furthermore, it was assumed that information obtained from former students should be as job-related as possible. Finally, it was assumed that information obtained from Program Directors should be especially related to administrative problems. During Phase II of the Project the individual programs were evaluated in terms of whether or not they achieved their original objectives. Phase III was concerned with whether the programs had been greatly modified since the end of Phase II, if they were occupationally relevant, and especially if the programs were apt to be in existence in future years.

In keeping with the forementioned philosophy, much of the evaluative information collected during Phase III was obtained from program graduates. In addition to obtaining detailed information about the tasks they performed, program graduates were interviewed to obtain information regarding such things as how they obtained their jobs and the settings of their jobs. Every effort was made to determine whether or not the graduates had been prepared to perform effectively in a job related to a school library media center.

A second major source of evaluative information was the Program Directors. They were asked to prepare status reports describing what had happened to their programs during the Phase III time frame, and what they expected to be the future of their programs.

EVALUATION TOPICS

The evaluation topics addressed in Phase III were quite similar to the nine evaluation topics addressed in Phase II. Those topics were listed on a prior page of this report. Based on those nine topics, a series of questions were developed and the Program Directors were requested to address these questions in their Phase III Status Report. These reports are summarized in Chapter 4 of this report. In these Status Reports considerable emphasis was placed on: (a) providing evaluative information about the field work component of each program; (b) describing what changes were made to the program after the completion of Phase II; (c) describing what happened to the program after Project support funds were withdrawn; and (d) commenting on the prospects for continuance of the program, including whether or not the program had been or would be approved for certification of its graduates.

The evaluation plan for Phase III was based on the philosophy that any educational program should have a mechanism for continually obtaining information about how well its graduates can perform in the field. For this reason the Behavioral Requirements Analysis Checklist (BRAC)[14] was developed for use as the major data collecting instrument during Phase III. A portion of the evaluative information obtained during Phase III pertained to the use of the BRAC instrument as a data collecting instrument. This information was collected from the various groups of persons who were asked to complete a BRAC questionnaire. Also, members of the

---

[14]SLMP, Behavioral Requirements Analysis Checlist: A Compilation of Competency-Based Job Functions and Task Statements for School Library Media Personnel, (Chicago: American Library Association, 1973).

Project staff, through their familiarity with the problems in administering a BRAC questionnaire, provided their own self-engendered evaluation of the BRAC document and its associated procedures. A critique of the BRAC survey technique is presented in Chapter 5 of this report.

DISSEMINATION OF INFORMATION

One of the objectives for the summative evaluation of the six experimental programs was to disseminate the Phase III findings to the experimental programs and also to the general field of library education. The procedures for the disbursement of information consisted of four types: (1) reports to the Program Directors of the six experimental programs, (2) regional workshops for library education personnel, (3) written reports in professional publications, and (4) presentations at professional meetings.

As outlined in the Phase III proposal, the Program Directors received feedback through the provision of print-outs of the data resulting from the completion of the BRAC by program graduates and their supervisors in the field. The data are displayed and discussed in more detail in other sections of this report. The findings of the follow-up interviews were compiled and also served as an indicator for the validity of the school library media education programs funded during Phase II.

The major dissemination focus during Phase III was three regional workshops conducted by the Project staff during the Spring of 1974 in San Francisco, Atlanta, and Chicago. The objectives of these workshops were:

1. To disseminate the results of the six experimental programs.

2. To report and interpret the results of the Phase III evaluation to date.

3. To explore the implications of the Behavioral Requirements Analysis Checklist (BRAC) which was the data collecting instrument used during Phase III.

4. To share ideas about new and innovative changes in the education of school library media personnel.

Invitations to attend one of the workshops were issued to all institutions preparing professional school library media personnel at both the undergraduate and graduate levels, to directors of audiovisual and educational technology programs and to all state school library supervisors. The participants who attended the three workshops, numbered 160 and included representatives from ninety-three institutions. Each of the workshops was designed to permit active participation of attendees through formal and informal presentations, simulated experiences in the utilization and interpretation of BRAC and small group work sessions.

The opportunity to share innovative practices from various program representatives was offered to participants. Since the response to this kind of participation was very limited at all three workshops, no effort was made to evaluate this aspect of the workshop.

Participants were encouraged to evaluate the workshop content at the end of each of the three sessions. Approximately half of those in attendance submitted an evaluation form. The total response was overwhelmingly positive in that sixty-two of the participants believed that the workshop format made it possible to achieve their objectives. The objectives most frequently noted were: (1) to achieve an understanding of the content and utilization of the BRAC instrument, (2) to gain information on the status of the School Library Manpower Project and the six experimental programs, (3) to interact with other people in the media education field, and (4) to gain information applicable to the modification and evaluation of their own programs. The participants indicated that the following workshop features helped them to attain these objectives: the presentations of Project staff and Program Directors, and the opportunities for personal involvement and interaction through small group discussions and simulated exercises in the utilization of BRAC.

Seventy-two respondents thought that the BRAC instrument could be of assistance to them in program development. The primary possibilities which were noted were its use in the evaluation of current media education programs and its application during curriculum change and development.

Sixty-nine participants approved of the simulated experience developed around the BRAC instrument. While a large number of respondents replied that it gave them an understanding of the utilization and application of the BRAC instrument, many people also noted that working through the decision making process was a highly valuable experience. A few respondents indicated that the simulated exercise was of little benefit to them.

Throughout Phase III the dissemination of information by the Project staff was carried out primarily through programs at national conferences. Presentations were made at the Association for Supervision and Curriculum Development Conference, the Association for Educational Communications and Technology Conference and the American Library Association Conference. Written reports were confined to the "Library Education Division Newsletter", a publication of the Library Education Division of the American Library Association.

Chapter 2

METHODOLOGY

Design

The Phase III evaluation plan called for obtaining information about each of the six experimental programs from four different information sources -- Program Directors, Program Graduates, Supervisors of Program Graduates, and Students presently attending the programs. This information was separately analyzed for first and second year program graduates. When no inter-year differences were found the findings were combined.

Similar types of information were obtained from each source of information so that a cross-check of the information could be obtained. For example, it was possible to determine if program graduates and their supervisors agreed regarding the tasks performed by the graduates.

The six experimental programs which were developed in Phase II of the Project study consisted of one BA-level program, four programs which essentially were MA-level programs, and one sixth-year program. The information collected from program graduates was analyzed by level. Data for each level are presented separately.

The bulk of the information for Phase III of the study was obtained from program graduates through the use of a survey instrument. To properly interpret such information it is necessary to obtain detailed background information as well as detailed job-related information about each respondent. This was obtained through the use of personal interviews. Also, these interviews were employed to follow-up on and to obtain additional information about the responses provided on the survey instrument.

Participants

As mentioned previously, four groups of respondents participated in Phase III. The program directors of each experimental program prepared a status report at the end of the 1973-74 academic year. Also, each director completed a BRAC survey questionnaire.

Program graduates who were working in a media center or in a related job were asked to complete a BRAC survey questionnaire. In addition, each

14 Methodology

graduate who completed a questionnaire was interviewed, usually by telephone, to obtain a variety of information about his job, how he obtained it, and the nature of the work setting. Information about what happened to program graduates not working in a media center was obtained whenever possible and will be reported later in this report.

The supervisor of each program graduate working in a media center was asked to complete a special version of the BRAC survey questionnaire. In addition, a few supervisors were interviewed during on-site visits or by telephone.

Finally, students presently enrolled in one of the experimental programs were asked to complete a version of the BRAC questionnaire as they progressed through their coursework.

Instrumentation

The data for Phase III were obtained through the use of two basic instruments -- the Behavioral Requirements Analysis Checklist (BRAC) and a structured interview questionnaire. A discussion of these two items follows.

BEHAVIORAL REQUIREMENTS ANALYSIS CHECKLIST

In the early planning stages for Phase III, a study of the literature supported the need for a special inventory of competencies for professional school library media personnel to be used in education program development and assessment. As the Project looked toward summative evaluation plans for Phase III, it recognized the need not only for an instrument to examine the performance of experimental program graduates on the job, but also to assess the capabilities of an education program to produce competent professional school library media personnel. The efforts of the Project staff, with direction and input from the Advisory Committee, the Human Resources Research Organization and the directors of the six experimental programs, resulted in the publication of the <u>Behavioral Requirements Analysis Checklist</u> (BRAC). The BRAC instrument was used during Phase III as the basic data collecting device.

BRAC is a compilation of approximately 700 tasks to be performed by professional school library media personnel. The job functions and task statements were developed not only from the occupational definitions and seven major competency areas identified and described during Phase I, but also from the behavioral objectives developed by the experimental programs during Phase II. Each of the seven major competency areas and its definition is presented as a separate section of BRAC. Each broad competency area is broken down into behaviorally-stated job functions supported by task statements.

During Phase III the BRAC instrument provided the basis for four questionnaires. A separate questionnaire was developed for collecting data from: students in or about to graduate from the experimental programs;

supervisors of recent graduates; program graduates; and experimental program directors and their staffs. The four questionnaires were all based on BRAC, differing only with the respect to specific questions relating to each task activity statement. The value of the BRAC questionnaires was their adaptability to different evaluation purposes. The questionnaires for the school library media educators and the school library media education student permitted an assessment of what was being accomplished or omitted from the school library media education programs. Actual on-the-job performance was evaluated through the use of the questionnaires for the school library media specialists and the school library media directors. The development of the BRAC questionnaires, tabulation of data and the initial analysis was done in cooperation with the Human Resources Research Organization which provided contractual services to the Project during Phase III.

The BRAC task statements represent primarily the required behavior of a school library media specialist who functions as a generalist in a school library media center. However, the BRAC document also contains tasks which might be performed mostly by the head of a media center or by district-level media personnel. Therefore, a school library media specialist would not be expected to be proficient on all the tasks listed in BRAC. Table I contains a reproduction of page 14 of the BRAC document.

A sample page from the "BRAC Survey Questionnaire and Response Form for the GRADUATE of the School Library Media Education Program" is presented in Table II. Each questionnaire page was keyed to the BRAC instrument, and provided space to record the responses to six questions per task statement. To complete the form the graduate was to read a task statement then answer up to six questions about that statement. The six questions on the graduate questionnaire are shown in Table III. For each statement the respondents noted whether or not they had performed the task, and if so how often. If they did perform the task they were instructed to answer the remaining five questions about the task.

The questionnaire and response form for the other Phase III participants was identical to that for the program graduate except that each participant group responded to a different set of questions. The BRAC questionnaire questions for program directors, supervisors, and students are located in Appendix A.

INTERVIEW QUESTIONNAIRES

The BRAC survey instrument was used to obtain information about individual tasks. A variety of additional information is needed to interpret such data. Also, other types of information were needed to determine more fully just what happened to program graduates. For these reasons a structured interview questionnaire was developed, one for experimental program graduates and one for their supervisors. Both interview questionnaires covered similar topics related to five general areas -- position-related questions, placement-related questions, BRAC-related questions, work-related questions, and program-related questions. These interview forms are contained in Appendix B.

Table I. Sample Page From the
BEHAVIORAL REQUIREMENTS ANALYSIS CHECKLIST

D. Media

Media are the printed and audiovisual forms of communication and their accompanying technologies. The media program provides a totality of services focused on the best utilization of these media to facilitate, improve and support the learning process.

Function 1

  To develop and implement criteria for evaluating and selecting a variety of categories of media and equipment.

    Task 1. Develop rationale to support the selection of appropriate media and equipment.

        2. Develop evaluative criteria to select appropriate media and equipment.

        3. Develop criteria to select information storage and retrieval systems for media.

        4. Develop specifications for the acquisition of media and equipment.

        5. Enlist faculty assistance to formulate selection policies for the acquisition of media and equipment.

        6. Establish selection policies for the acquisition of media and equipment.

        7. Implement selection policies for the acquisition of media and equipment.

Function 2

  To build a collection of bibliographic tools to provide current information about media and equipment.

    Task 1. Develop a system to locate descriptive information and evaluation data about media and equipment.

        2. Develop a system to locate procurement information about media and equipment.

        3. Establish and maintain files to provide reviews of media.

        4. Establish and maintain files to provide evaluations of equipment.

Table II. Sample Page from the "BRAC Survey Questionnaire and Response Form for the GRADUATES of the School Library Media Educational Program"

A. HUMAN BEHAVIOR (BRAC pp. 3-5)

Function 1 (p. 3)

	Question				
	A	B	C	D	E
A.01.01.	—	—	—	—	—
A.01.02.	—	—	—	—	—
A.01.03.	—	—	—	—	—
A.01.04.	—	—	—	—	—
A.01.05.	—	—	—	—	—
A.01.06.	—	—	—	—	—
A.01.07.	—	—	—	—	—

Function 2 (p. 3-4)

	A	B	C	D	E
A.02.01.	—	—	—	—	—
A.02.02.	—	—	—	—	—
A.02.03.	—	—	—	—	—
A.02.04.	—	—	—	—	—
A.02.05.	—	—	—	—	—
A.02.06.	—	—	—	—	—
A.02.07.	—	—	—	—	—
A.02.08.	—	—	—	—	—
A.02.09.	—	—	—	—	—
A.02.10.	—	—	—	—	—
A.02.11.	—	—	—	—	—
A.02.12.	—	—	—	—	—

Function 3 (p. 4-5)

	A	B	C	D	E
A.03.01.	—	—	—	—	—
A.03.02.	—	—	—	—	—
A.03.03.	—	—	—	—	—
A.03.04.	—	—	—	—	—
A.03.05.	—	—	—	—	—
A.03.06.	—	—	—	—	—
A.03.07.	—	—	—	—	—
A.03.08.	—	—	—	—	—
A.03.09.	—	—	—	—	—

18 Methodology

Table III. BRAC Survey Questionnaire for the GRADUATE of the School Library Media Education Program

A. How frequently do you perform this task in your job?
   0 – Never (I do not perform this task).
   1 – Seldom (I perform this task less than once a month).
   2 – Monthly (I perform this task at least once, but less than four times a month on the average).
   3 – Weekly (I perform this task at least once, but less than five times a week on the average).
   4 – Daily (I perform this task at least once each day on the average).

B. How would you judge your capability to perform this task when you first began working on your job immediately after graduation?
   0 – Unsatisfactory (I needed constant guidance to perform this task).
   1 – Below Average (I needed fairly close guidance to perform this task).
   2 – Average (I could perform this task adequately with only some general supervision).
   3 – Above Average (I performed this task competently without any supervision).
   4 – Excellent (I was an expert at performing this task).

C. How would you judge the importance of this task to your overall job?
   0 – Minor Importance (Little if any importance).
   1 – Less Than Average Importance.
   2 – Average Importance.
   3 – More Than Average Importance.
   4 – Major Importance (One of the most important tasks of my job).

D. How would you judge the appropriateness of this task to your job as a professional school library media specialist?
   0 – Inappropriate (Task should be performed by aides or persons other than a professionally educated school library media specialist).
   1 – Somewhat Inappropriate (Although this is not a task for professionally educated school library media personnel, it is all right to perform it on occasion).
   2 – Somewhat Appropriate (Although this is a proper task for professional school library media personnel, it can at times be performed by other professionals or by aides).
   3 – Highly Appropriate (This is a task which should be performed by professionally educated school library media specialists).

E. What emphasis did this task receive in your recent school library media education program?
   0 – Not Covered (I received no preparation).
   1 – Slight (I received some preparation, but it was inadequate).
   2 – Average (I received adequate preparation).
   3 – Heavy (I received more than adequate preparation).

F. In your judgment, where is the best place to learn this task?
   0 – In formal classes, instruction.
   1 – In internships, practicums.
   2 – On the job.
   3 – Self-study, when the need arises.

Survey Procedures

QUESTIONNAIRE ADMINISTRATION

Following the development of the survey questionnaires to be used with the BRAC instrument, the BRAC package was field-tested in August of 1973 for final recommendations prior to its use as the data collecting device for Phase III.

The field-test participants were selected to represent a variety of positions and to test the four survey questionnaires in the field. This group included a library educator, a state school library supervisor, an audiovisual educator, a recently graduated practicing media specialist, a district level media supervisor and a library education program student.

Participants were asked to respond from the particular point of view of the questionnaire assigned. No one participant completed the entire BRAC instrument, but rather each one was assigned specific sections of the BRAC. All respondents, however, did complete the questions for a similar number of task statements. Respondents were requested to give their reactions and comments, as well as the amount of time necessary to complete the assigned sections of the questionnaire. Approximately 160 tasks were completed by each participant requiring an average completion time of six hours. In recognition of the contribution made by the participants, a small honorarium was given.

Following changes recommended during the pretest of the BRAC questionnaire, procedures were established to contact all graduates of the experimental programs for the purpose of soliciting their assistance in the Phase III evaluation study. Those individuals who had graduated no later than August, 1972 from the first year of the programs and those who had graduated no later than August, 1973 from the second year of the programs were contacted. One exception was made in the case of the University of Michigan graduates. Because that program started in mid-year, those who graduated by December, 1973 were included. The initial contact requested information on the job status of the graduate and the identification of the immediate supervisor of the position. A breakdown of the graduates' job status for each year is represented in Table IV.

The 103 graduates who qualified for participation in the BRAC study all held positions directly involved with media services. The majority of supervisors were either school administrators or district library supervisors. At the time of their participation in the Phase III evaluation all graduates had been on the job for a minimum of six months. The first year graduates and supervisors were sent the BRAC instruments and the response forms in September of 1973 while the second year graduates received the material no later than May of 1974. One month was established as a completion time for the response and each respondent received a small honorarium for his contribution to the study.

Methodology

Table IV. Job Status of 1972 and 1973
Graduates Immediately Following Graduation

Position Status	1972	1973	Total
Media Center			
Elementary	10	31	41
Secondary	11	32	43
Jr. College	2	2	4
College	2	2	4
District	2	3	5
Public Library	2	2	4
Graduate Work	1	3	4
Other Educ. Setting	11	13	24
Unemployed	1	7	8
Unable to Locate	0	7	7
Other	0	4	4
Total	42	106	148

In addition to graduates and supervisors in the field, two other groups participated in the study during the Phase III evaluation: (1) the directors of the six experimental programs and (2) students enrolled in those programs for the academic year 1973-1974.

In the Fall of 1973 the experimental Program Directors all received response forms developed for the use of directors and staff of school library media education programs. Their responses were returned and tabulated in the Fall of 1973. During the academic 1973-1974 year all students in the continuing experimental programs participated in an evaluation of their in-program competency attainment. In two institutions, Millersville State College and Auburn University, the students responded to the questionnaire in a continuous process throughout the year. In the four other institutions: Arizona State University, University of Denver, Mankato State College, and the University of Michigan, students completed their questionnaire during the last month of the program year.

INTERVIEWS

For the purpose of ascertaining the settings in which the graduates were working and for gaining information about the working conditions and environment, two follow-up questionnaires were devised as a basis for

Methodology 21

interviewing the survey participants. These questionnaires are displayed in Appendix B to this report. The original decision to interview 25% of the graduates and their supervisors on-site was modified to include some on-site interviews plus telephone interviews with as many of the graduates and supervisors whose replies were usable for this purpose. All interviews were set up through an initial telephone call to the interviewee to establish the date and time most acceptable for a thirty to fifty minute interview either on-site or by telephone. The majority of the telephone interviews took place during the working day and averaged thirty-five minutes in length. A comparison between on-site and telephone interviews disclosed that telephone interviews were as satisfactory in the search for information as were the on-site interviews. In many instances, the telephone interviews made it possible to maintain a closer adherence to the specific topics of the questionnaires. The on-site interviews had a tendency to cover more extraneous topics which, while interesting, were not always relevant to the job at hand.

All 148 graduates from the six programs during the two years of experimentation were located, with the exception of five graduates from Airzona State University and two graduates from Auburn University. It should be noted also that the fourteen graduates from the first year of the Arizona program were not included in the evaluation study, since that program was still in the developmental stage.

Of the initial 148 graduates, 103 or 70% were eligible to participate in the Phase III evaluation. There were originally fifty-one graduates who were excluded from participation because they were not employed in media centers. However, six of the 1972 graduates not qualified to participate in the first evaluation survey did move into media center positions the second year following their graduation and were then included with the 1973 graduates. A breakdown of the reasons for non-qualification of the fifty-one graduates noted above were:

Type of Position	Number of Graduates
Graduate Work	4
Public Library	3
Other Educational Settings	24
Unemployed	8
Unable to Locate	7
Did not Respond	1
Death	1
Other	3

Of the eight graduates who were unemployed, four reported that for personal reasons they were not seeking employment.

The BRAC instrument was sent to the 103 eligible graduates. The instrument was returned by ninety-five of the graduates representing a 92% response. However, twenty-one response forms were not usable because they were incomplete, had been completed incorrectly, or were returned too late to incorporate into the data analysis. The remaining seventy-four usable response forms represented an 85% return of valid data.

22   Methodology

Follow-up interviews by the project staff were conducted with both graduates and supervisors of graduates. Fourteen interviews were done on-site and eighty-one interviews were accomplished by phone for a total of ninety-five follow-up interviews.

Data Processing and Analysis

BRAC QUESTIONNAIRE DATA

The data processing and analysis procedures were designed to serve two purposes -- to provide information to each Program Director and to obtain information to be included in this report.

BRAC questionnaire data obtained from program graduates were processed by program and by year of graduation. Thus, for any particular school, a printout was prepared summarizing the BRAC questionnaire responses for graduates of that program for 1972, for 1973, and for both years combined. These printouts were forwarded to the Program Directors. These printouts showed how graduates responded to the six questions on their BRAC questionnaire. A sample printout page is shown in Appendix C.

An examination of the data for 1972 and 1973 graduates revealed little difference between the two sets of data. Therefore, they were combined and the results discussed in this report are based on the combined responses of 1972 and 1973 graduates.

As mentioned previously, of the six experimental programs four were MA-level programs, one (Millersville) was a BA-level program, and one (Denver) was a 6th-year program. Therefore, the BRAC survey findings for the MA-level programs were combined and then compared with those of the BA-level and 6th year programs. In this way a determination could be made of whether or not graduates of these different levels of programs might be performing different tasks on their job.

In this report data will be presented only for Questions A, B, and C as shown in Appendix D. For program graduates these questions were:

    A. How frequently do you perform this task in your job?

    B. How would you judge your capability to perform this task when you first began working on your job immediately after graduation?

    C. How would you judge the importance of this task to your overall job?

It was judged that these three questions were the ones most directly germane to the evaluation objectives of Phase III, namely, were program graduates suitably prepared and were they able to perform tasks which were important and which were an integral part of their job?

The BRAC questionnaire responses first were summarized by task. That is, a determination was made of the percentage of respondents who chose each alternative response for each question. If the respondent did not perform a task (Question A) then he did not answer the other questions for that task. As an illustration, for the Millersville Program the responses of all of the graduates showed that:

- for Question A, Task A.01.03, only one of sixteen persons reported never performing the task. Five of sixteen reported performing it about monthly and ten of sixteen said they performed the task "seldom".

- for Question B, Task A.01.04, one person said they first performed the task in a "below average" manner; ten reported first performing it in an "average" fashion; four reported performing it in an "above average" fashion; and one reported first performing it in an "excellent" fashion. Each of these response options had a scale number (see Table III and Appendix A), and the Mean value for these numbers in the above illustration would come to 2.31. Referring again to Table III, the average response of 2.31 lies a third of the way between "average" and "above average".

- for Question D, Task A.01.05, eight respondents said the task was of "more than average importance" and the remaining eight respondents judged the task to be of "major importance". The average of the values represented by these sixteen responses is 3.50.

Printouts containing the above information for each program were forwarded to the appropriate Program Director. Similar printouts were prepared to summarize supervisor BRAC responses. However, for most programs the supervisor returns were too few to be analyzed by program. Therefore, all supervisor responses were combined and a single printout prepared of the summary data. Copies of these printouts were sent to each Program Director. Supervisor questionnaire data will not be discussed in detail in this report because it was found that most supervisors of the program graduates were not too familiar with the tasks performed by school library media personnel.

The BRAC questionnaires completed by Program Directors were not processed. These were prepared for use by the Program Directors themselves. It allowed them to compare their responses with those provided by graduates of their programs.

BRAC questionnaire data provided by students of the experimental programs were not processed. Such questionnaires are useful primarily to allow students to keep a record of those tasks they have learned to perform, and to provide them with an overview of the various tasks which may be performed by school library media personnel.

The previous section describes the printouts prepared for the Program Directors. These printouts summarized BRAC questionnaire data by task. Summaries of these data for Questions A, B, and C are presented in Appendix D. Summaries are provided for the BA-level program, the four MA-level programs combined, and the 6th-year program. To make these data more compact and manageable they have been summarized further by function and competency area. These summaries are contained in Appendix E and in Figures 1A through 1D (see Chapter 3). The following paragraphs explain how these summaries were obtained.

With reference to Appendix D, for each task (e.g., A.01.01) the first row of numbers pertains to BA-level graduates; the second row to MA-level graduates; and the third row to 6th-year program graduates. For Question A the number refers to the percentage of persons who reported that they did perform the task. For this analysis it was assumed that if the task was performed at all it was performed at an appropriate frequency. Thus, for Competency Area A (Human Behavior), Function 1, 93.8 percent of the BA-level program respondents said they did perform tasks 01, 03, and 07. All the other four tasks listed under that function were performed by all BA-level graduates -- a total of 16 persons.

For each function the task data have been summarized and reported in Appendix E. Thus, the number 97.3 which appears under Q-A (Appendix E) for Function 1 of Competency Area A represents the degree to which graduates of the BA-level program were involved with that function. The figure of "100" would represent maximum involvement. It would mean that 100% of the respondents said they performed all seven tasks listed under Function A.01 at least once per year.

A figure of "90" would mean that most respondents reported performing most tasks listed under a function. There are a variety of ways in which the number "90" might be obtained. For example, within a function containing 10 tasks all persons might perform nine tasks and never perform the tenth task. This would work out to an "involvement" figure of 90. As a second example, ninety percent of the respondents might perform all ten tasks.

Referring to Appendix D one can see that there are seven tasks listed under Function 1 of Competency Area A. For the BA-level program 15 of 16 graduates performed Tasks 01, 03, and 07. All graduates performed all of the other four tasks. Therefore, out of a possible 112 (16 x 7) "Yes, I perform this task" responses, 109 "yes" responses were obtained. That works out to be an involvement factor of 97.3% for the total function. That is the number reported for Function 1, Competency Area A, Appendix E.

By procedures similar to those just described one can combine percentages at the Function level to calculate the amount of Task involvement at the Competency Area (CA) level. These are the figures listed after the heading "C.A. Av." (Appendix E). These percentages are weighted in that they take into account the number of tasks listed under each function.

The numbers shown under Columns Q-B and Q-C of Appendix D represent the average of the response values selected for each task for those respondents who indicated they performed the task. When the average values for each task are combined, one can calculate an average response value at the function level. These values are shown in Columns Q-B and Q-C of Appendix E. The number listed after "C.A. Av." is the weighted average of the alternatives selected for an entire function.

Methodology 25

To interpret the numbers of Columns Q-B or Q-C of Appendices D and E the reader should refer to Table III. For example, an average value of 2.00 for Question C means that a Task (or a Function or a Competency Area) was judged to be of "average importance".

INTERVIEW RESPONSES

The interview form shown in Appendix B was used to interview the graduates of the experimental programs. Paragraph summaries of the replies obtained from the graduates of each program then were prepared. In addition, the interview responses obtained from graduates of MA-level programs were combined to produce paragraph summaries. In Chapter 3 the interview findings are presented separately for BA-level graduates, MA-level graduates and for graduates of the sixth year level program. Interview responses pertaining to ways to improve the BRAC document and questionnaire are discussed in Chapter 5. Paragraph summaries of the interview responses obtained from the graduates of each MA-level program are contained in Appendix B.

Supervisor interview responses were summarized as described above for graduate interview replies. These too are found in Appendix B.

Chapter 3

FINDINGS

Questionnaire Data

PROGRAM GRADUATES

The BRAC Survey Questionnaire was completed by former graduates of an experimental program who were working in a media center or in a related job. A total of 103 persons met this criterion. The discussion that follows is based on an analysis of 74 returns. The distribution of these returns across experimental programs is shown in the following table.

Experimental Program	No. of Useable Returns
Arizona State University	6
Auburn University	17
University of Denver	5
Mankato State College	12
University of Michigan	18
Millersville State College	16

As described in Chapter 2 the data for each program were summarized and returned to the Program Director. For purposes of this report the data were combined by academic level -- BA-level, MA-level, and 6th year level. The combined data for each task for survey Questions A, B, and C are contained in Appendix C. A discussion of how to interpret this data was presented in Chapter 2. The data in Appendix C were further summarized by Function and by Competency Area. The summarized data are displayed in Appendix D. The data contained in Appendix D for Question A also are shown in Figures 1A through 1C.

Of particular interest are the comparisons between the BA-level and MA-level graduates. These persons essentially compete for similar jobs at the building level. The 6th year level graduates, on the other hand, were prepared for and eventually expected to be employed in district-level jobs.

Figure 1A shows the BRAC Survey results for Competency Areas A, B, and C for Question A -- How frequently do you perform this task? The numbers represent the percentage of persons reporting that they did perform the tasks

Findings 27

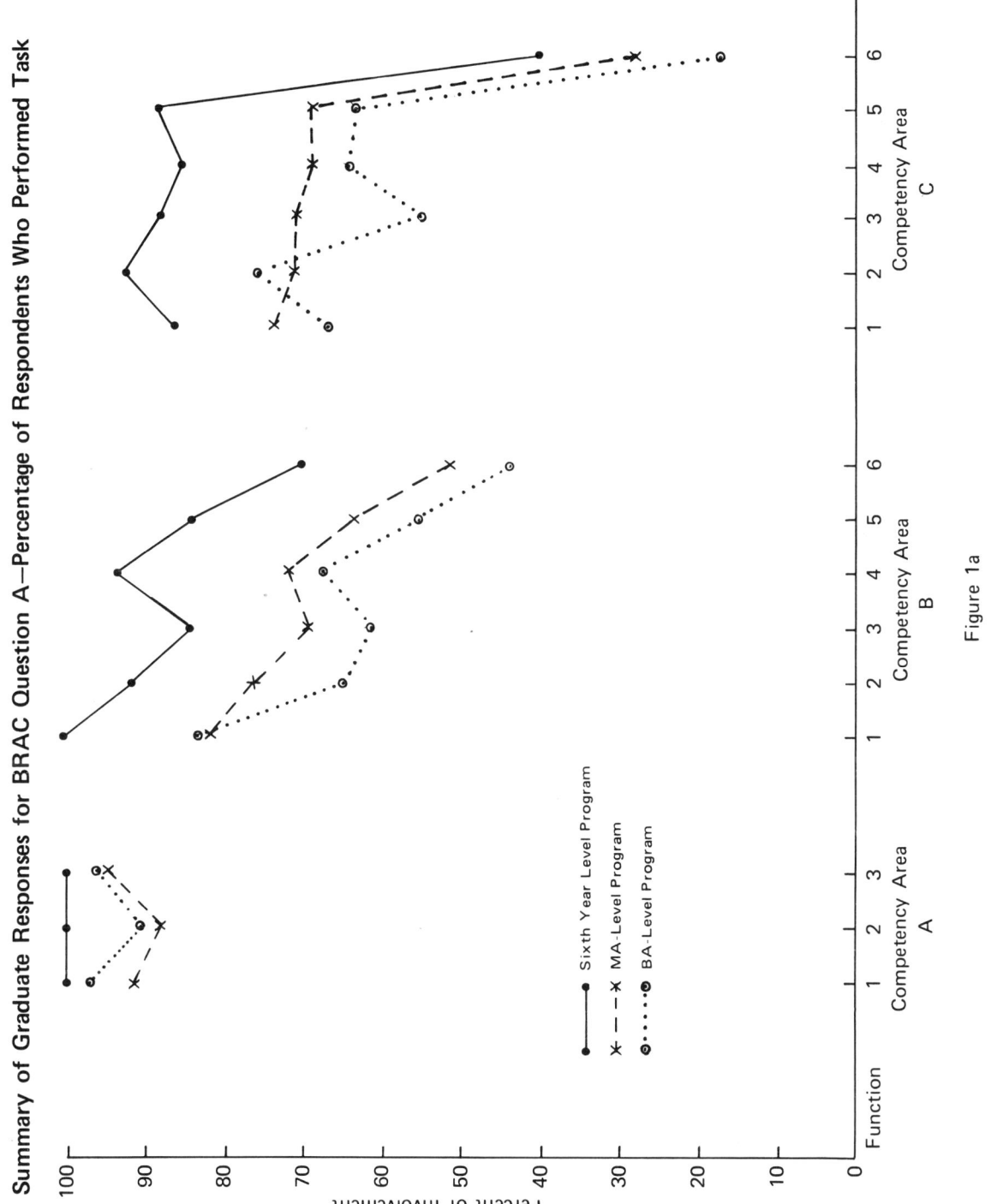

Figure 1a

28 Findings

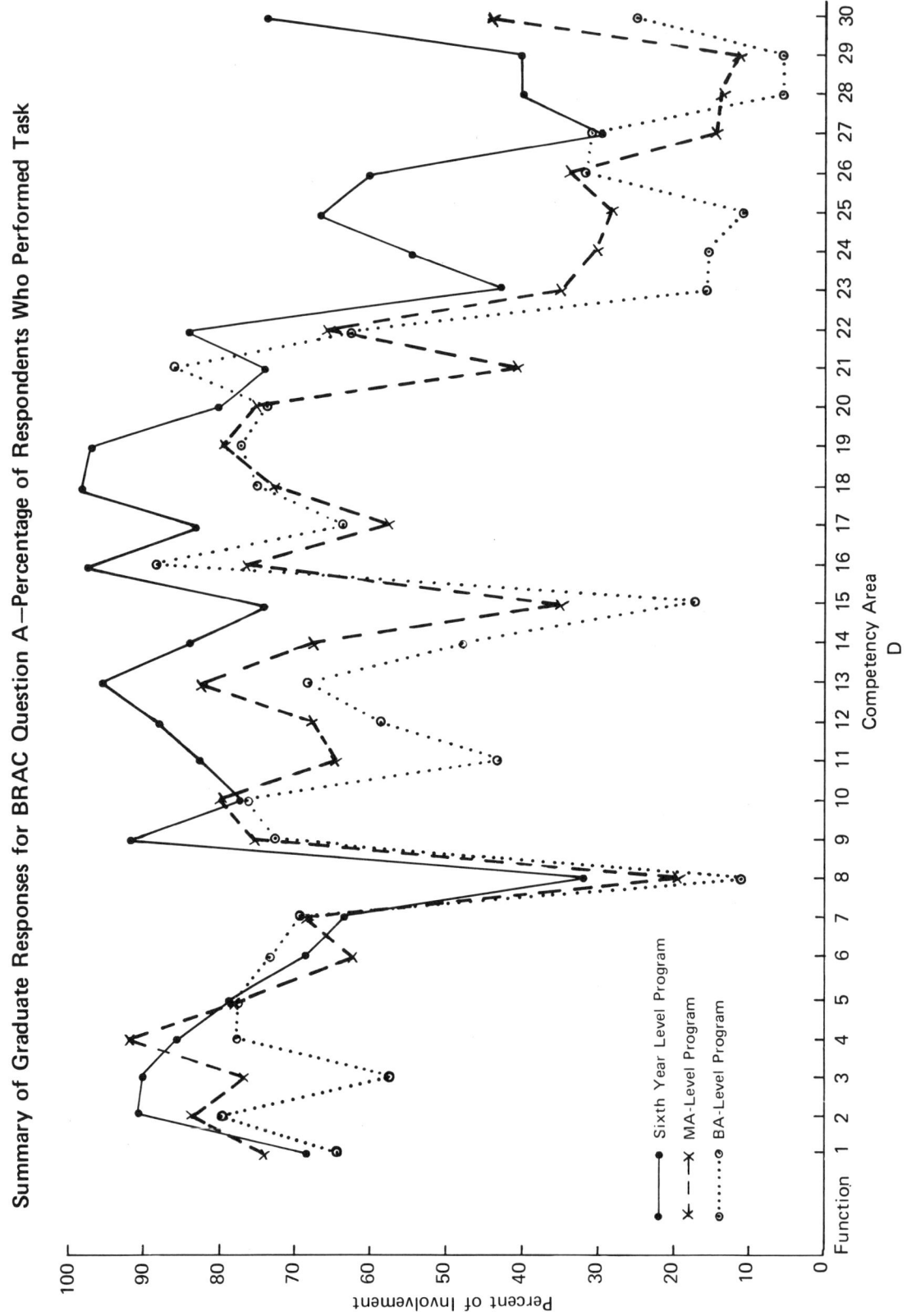

Figure 1b

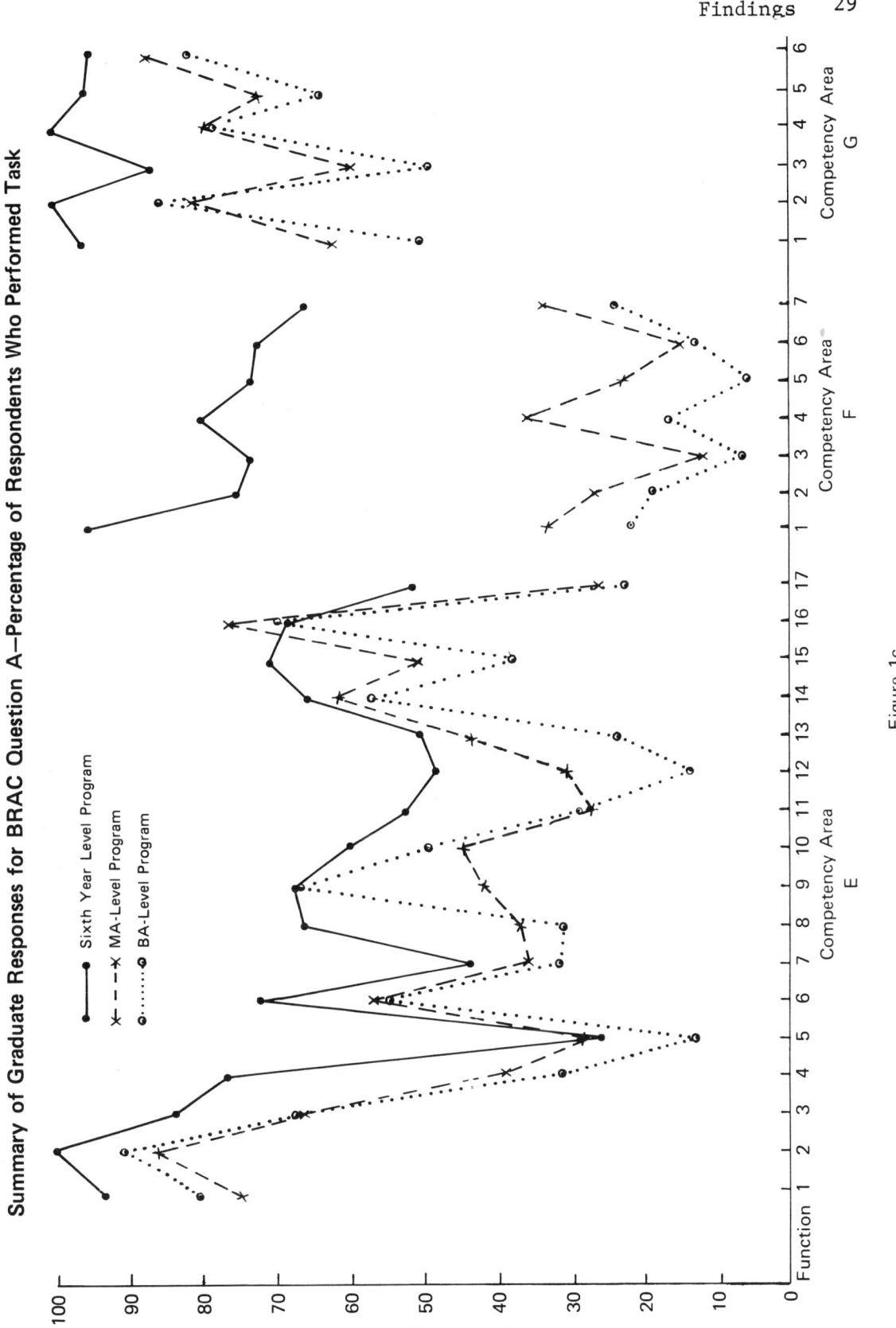

Figure 1c

30 Findings

associated with a function at least once per year. For the first three Competency Areas there were consistent differences between the BA-level, MA-level and 6th year level graduates. Notice that the 6th year level graduates had a much higher rate of involvement with Competency Areas A, B, and C. Also, the MA-level graduates had a slightly higher level of involvement with these three Competency Areas than did the BA-level graduates. However, these differences were not significant statistically.

A statistical comparison (t-test) between BA-level and MA-level graduates was made by comparing their rate of involvement in each overall area. The results of this analysis are presented in Table V. As an illustration, for Competency Area C the MA-level graduates had an involvement rate of 61.17 percent; the BA-level graduates had an involvement rate of 53.50 percent. While this difference might seem large enough to be statistically significant, it was not, primarily because of the variability between respondents.

On the other hand, an inspection of Table V and Figure 1B might suggest that there were no significant differences between BA and MA-level program graduates in terms of their involvement with media-related tasks. The statistical analysis however revealed that this difference was significant at the .05 percent level of confidence. All other Question A comparisons between BA and MA-level program graduates were not significant. Note however that the MA-level graduates reported a slightly higher level of involvement with Competency Areas B through G (Table V). The detailed questionnaire data suggested that the MA-level graduates, either because of their jobs or because of their preparation, performed a slightly greater variety of tasks.

Before leaving Figures 1A through 1C it should be noted that for certain functions the rate of involvement was low for all graduates. For example, notice Function 6 of Competency Area C, Function 8 of Competency Area D, and Functions 23 through 29 of Competency Area D. By looking up these functions in the BRAC document it will be seen that the functions cover tasks that have a low probability of being performed in the field. For example, Functions 27, 28 and 29 of Competency Area D deal with radio and television. These are topics which might be covered at certain large high schools, but seldom at the K-9 level, the level at which most of the respondents of this study were employed.

Question B of the BRAC Questionnaire for graduates asked the respondents to record how competent they felt themselves to be the first time they had to perform a task on the job. The results are summarized by Task in Appendix D, and by Function and Competency Area in Appendix E. A statistical comparison between BA and MA-level graduates was made at the Competency Area level. Table V contains the results of these comparisons. For Competency Areas D, F, and G the BA-level graduates reported a significantly lower "first try" task capability than did the MA-graduates. However, even for Competency Area F the BA-level graduates reported a slightly above average capability to perform (2.00 would represent "average" capability). It might be expected that BA-level graduates would feel less confident than MA-level graduates when first performing research tasks (Competency Area F)

Table V. Comparison of Responses to BRAC Questionnaire by Graduates of BA-Level and MA-Level Programs

Competency Area	Mean Response to BRAC Questions			BA vs MA-Level Programs p-values		
	Q-A	Q-B	Q-C	Q-A	Q-B	Q-C
A Human Behavior	94.00[1] 90.96	2.65[2] 2.69	3.33[3][4] 3.26	---[5]	---	---
B Learning & Learning Environment	63.50 70.28	2.57 2.50	2.98 3.05	---	---	---
C Planning and Evaluation	53.50 61.17	2.49 2.49	2.99 3.02	---	---	---
D Media	50.05 56.72	2.57 2.64	2.93 2.89	.05	.05	---
E Management	44.50 48.34	2.50 2.50	2.94 2.85	---	---	.05
F Research	16.20 28.44	2.26 2.52	2.41 2.57	---	.05	---
G Professionalism	64.10 70.30	2.59 2.74	2.96 2.95	---	.05	---

[1]Number represents percentage of respondents who performed tasks listed under Competency Area.
[2]Number represents judged capability to perform a task the first time it had to be performed. Judgments based on a five-point scale from "0" (Unsatisfactory) to "4" (Excellent).
[3]Number represents judged importance of Competency Area to overall job. Judgments based on a five-point scale from "0" (Minor Importance) to "4" (Major Importance).
[4]For each Competency Area the number on the top row is for the BA-level program.
[5]Comparisons were not made between 6th year level graduates and graduates of the other levels.

32   Findings

and tasks where they had to interact with their community or profession (Competency Area G). These are tasks one becomes familiar with during advanced training and through experience.

Question C of the BRAC Questionnaire for graduates asked the respondents to judge the importance of the tasks they performed. Both BA-level and MA-level graduates tended to report that the tasks they performed were of "above average" in importance. BA-level graduates rated their management tasks (Competency Area E) significantly higher in importance (Table V) than did the MA-level graduates. Although of statistical significance, this difference does not seem to be of practical significance.

SUPERVISORS OF PROGRAM GRADUATES

Thirty-three supervisor questionnaire returns were analyzed. All data from these respondents were combined, summarized on a computer printout, and copies provided to each Program Director.

One usually expects supervisors to be one of the best sources of information about the work capabilities of persons employed under their supervision. This assumes that supervisors have considerable direct contact with employees, and considerable knowledge about employee work requirements. In this study this was found not to be the case. In most instances, school library media personnel worked in one-professional-person media centers, even those who were newly graduated, and they received general supervision from the building principal.

Most supervisors who completed a BRAC Supervisor Questionnaire were building principals who often admitted that they were not very knowledgeable about the duties and responsibilities of school library media personnel. Many supervisors, primarily those who were principals, declined to complete the BRAC questionnaire because of their unfamiliarity with the tasks performed by school library media personnel. For this reason supervisor data were not analyzed. The manner in which supervisory data might be used, assuming knowledgeable supervisors, is discussed in Chapter 5.

PROGRAM STUDENTS

Questionnaire returns were received from 25 students in the program. Students attending the experimental programs during the third year of the program were requested to complete a student questionnaire as they went through their coursework. It was hoped that this would provide another source of information regarding what was covered in each experimental program, and how extensively it was covered. However, because of administrative oversights many students did not complete the questionnaire until the school year had terminated. Many students did not complete the questionnaires. For these reasons student questionnaires were not analyzed.

PROGRAM DIRECTORS

Each Program Director and the key staff members for each program completed a BRAC questionnaire. This allowed those involved with the program to identify what, in their judgment, was covered in the program, and where

Findings   33

it was covered. These data were prepared for future use by Program Directors and will not be discussed in this report. It was reported, however, that completing this questionnaire played a very useful role in helping the staff of each program to identify the gaps and duplications in their program.

Program Graduate Interviews

As described in Chapter 2, telephone or on-site interviews were held with as many program graduates as could be contacted. The form used to structure these interviews is located in Appendix B. The interview questions dealt with five general topics -- nature of the job position; how the job was obtained; opinions about the experimental program; the nature of the work required on the job; and problems in completing the BRAC questionnaire. The interview data have been summarized in terms of the academic level of the experimental program attended by the respondent, and in terms of the topics covered. The job status of the 1972 and 1973 graduates immediately following graduation has been shown in Table IV.

BA-LEVEL GRADUATES

A total of 16 graduates were interviewed. These all were graduates of the Millersville State College program.

The majority of all graduates of the Millersville State College experimental program were employed in elementary schools. Most of the graduates carried a position title of librarian. The majority of the graduates identified their building principal as their immediate supervisor, though some were not aware of any direct formal supervision. Less than half of the graduates did identify district level library or audiovisual coordinators as their supervisors.

The majority of the graduates were placed in small town rural or suburban, middle class communities. Three-fourths of the graduates were employed in schools whose enrollments were between 500-1,000 students. The remaining quarter of the graduates were placed in smaller schools with enrollments below 500 students.

All graduates except one were employed as the only professional in a media center. The majority of graduates had support from volunteer aides, part-time clerks or paid aides. Many of the graduates indicated a large number of mothers were used in the volunteer aide program. The majority of the graduates were employed in districts where district level support services were provided. For the most part, the nature of these district services were film libraries and audiovisual equipment or software services. Few of the districts where Millersville graduates were employed provided centralized processing services. All but two graduates were employed on a full-time basis and the majority had no additional responsibilities assigned to them outside the scope of the media program. Most graduates did not think their media program was sophisticated.

34   Findings

The majority of the graduates had a choice of positions. Most of the graduates learned about the position vacancy through the college placement bureau of through personal knowledge or contact with a school district. The majority of graduates were offered positions they could not take primarily because they had already signed a contract with another district. The main reason graduates accepted their positions was because of the geographical location. A few graduates accepted the first position offered to them, but for the most part graduates primarily identified the quality of the education program and the philosophy of the school administration as the main reasons for accepting a position. Several graduates accepted an assignment because they believed the position offered the challenge of starting a new media program with future potential. The majority of the graduates felt their experimental training program was helpful to them in getting their positions. All but one graduate felt they had made an impact on the school during their first year, citing greater utilization of media and rapport with teachers and students as the major evidence for this impact. Almost all graduates felt they could relate this impact to the type of media education program they had experienced. Though the graduates were not in total agreement on how the experimental program helped them to make an impact in their first year position, many did identify the program's emphasis on the total media concept, awareness of educational change and the stress on human relationships as they apply to working with students and teachers. Almost all the graduates believed the fieldwork experience was a key factor in giving them the opportunity to see the total scope of their education as it related to realistic situations in the field.

The Millersville graduates felt the experimental program's modularized approach and the opportunity to do fieldwork at a variety of levels were most useful to them. Many identified the independent study projects and the emphasis on practical application of knowledge as most important. All graduates believed more time should be given to internship and observation in the field and that these experiences should be continued to be offered at all three education levels. A few graduates felt that the modules were not comprehensive enough. The graduates identified the content areas they felt needed more emphasis. Administration, including budget and personnel, audiovisual presentation and production skills were the content areas cited most frequently as needing greater emphasis. The majority of graduates felt a lack of time in the modularized program was the main reason they did not receive more background in these areas. The graduates liked most the fieldwork practice at all levels and the opportunity to work at their own pace in a modularized program. They were also in agreement in their positive feeling of the close human relationships they had with program faculty and fellow program students. For the most part, the graduates had no overall criticism of the experimental program, though some stated that at times early in the program year they were not certain where they were going in the total program. A few graduates found a split fieldwork schedule difficult to manage. Several graduates stated that there was not enough use made of the case study, problem solving method of instruction. This led a few graduates to believe that the experimental program was too idealistic, in that they were not made aware of the problems they would face in the real world.

MA-LEVEL GRADUATES

The following information is based on interviews with 51 graduates of the programs at Auburn University, Arizona State University, University of Michigan and Mankato State College.

The majority of graduates from both years of all MA-level experimental programs were employed in elementary schools. The majority of position titles were that of media specialist and the building principal was most often designated as the immediate supervisor. The majority of graduates were placed in middle class, semi-urban communities in schools with student enrollments between 500-1,000. Almost all graduates worked as the sole professional on the media center staff and most indicated they had clerical or volunteer aide support. All graduates were employed on a full-time basis though several were assigned to serve two or more media centers on a part-time basis.

Over half of the graduates were employed in school districts where there was a district level media supervisor and where a district media center provided services to the building level media center. The majority of these district media centers provided services through film libraries and media production centers. Less than half of the graduates had access to centralized processing services from the district media centers. For the most part, graduates were not assigned additional responsibilities outside the scope of the media program. The majority of the graduates did not believe their media programs were sophisticated at either the building or district level.

The majority of the graduates had a choice of more than one position. Over half the graduates stated they used the services of their college or university placement bureau to identify position openings. The geographical location of a position was most cited by graduates as the reason they accepted the position. Reasons for taking a position which were cited next in frequency were the challenge of the position and the philosophy of the building principal. Almost all graduates believed their educational media program was helpful to them in finding a position.

Nearly all graduates stated they had made an impact on the school during their first year on the job. For the most part the graduates cited increased use of media and the media center on the part of students and teachers as reasons they believed this impact had been made. A large majority of graduates stated that their attitude and background of media philosophy was a key element in the progress made in changing a traditional service program into a unified media program.

The majority of the graduates stated they felt their media education programs had given them a good background in media philosophy, production, administration and organization. The graduates felt their training programs emphasized media utilization, involvement with staff, and a good knowledge of curriculum materials. For the most part the graduates believed their media education program stressed flexibility. The graduates expressed self-confidence in the use of media. They believed they were open to new ideas and were able to articulate the media philosophy with confidence.

36 Findings

The fieldwork component and internship experience were cited by almost all graduates as the most favorable instructional feature of their media education program. The flexibility of the program, program individualization and the close and informal relationship with fellow students and program faculty were also frequently mentioned as instructional features the graduates liked about their educational media program.

The majority of graduates were highly satisfied with their media education program. However, many graduates believed program modification should include more emphasis on media production, increased opportunities for individualization and opportunities for flexibility and choice in the development of their own course of study within the program.

The majority of graduates of MA-level media education programs stated they least liked the idealistic approach to content. Most of the graduates cited they would have profited by a more realistic approach to the curriculum and many graduates stated that the time factor was their greatest barrier in providing the opportunities and flexibility for them to plan and complete a course of study to meet their individual needs.

SIXTH YEAR LEVEL GRADUATES

The majority of the five University of Denver graduates interviewed were employed in building level positions. Other program graduates were employed in other educational settings including higher education and state departments of education. Most of the graduates' position titles were media specialist and most of them reported to a district director of media services rather than a principal. Their assignments were in suburban communities and the schools were mainly large, having 1,000-1,500 students. Only one graduate worked as the only professional on the media center staff. The other graduates worked in centers where there were two or more professionals. All graduates had clerical support staff. All graduates worked in districts where district level support services were provided. The nature of these services included centralized processing, film libraries, professional libraries and media production centers. All graduates were employed full-time. None of the graduates had additional responsibilities outside the scope of the media program. Most graduates felt their media programs were sophisticated.

Most graduates had a choice of positions. The remaining graduates were on leave from the district to attend the Denver program and returned to their district after completing the program, though then did not, for the most part, assume a position at a higher level of responsibility. All graduates stated that they had had an impact on the school in moving the district toward a total media program. The majority of graduates related this impact to their training program at Denver citing the confidence they had gained in writing program goals and objectives and developing a total program through the case study method as reasons for this impact. Most graduates agreed that the educational program at the University of Denver gave them the insight to think in broader, system-wide terms.

All graduates cited the utilization of the case study method and the independent study approach as the most useful instructional practices at

Denver. They also identified the mini courses and the interdisciplinary approach as useful. The graduates all felt they needed more time to complete their course at Denver. They would like to see longer mini courses, less theory and to be sure that the program flexibility is not lost in any future modification. As the Denver program was highly idividualized there was no total agreement on what instruction the graduates felt they should have. Some areas that were mentioned, however, were: more simulated problem solving, opportunity to review other case studies, more supervision, administration and management skills and a broader understanding of other types of budgeting procedures besides PPBS. There was the expression on the part of some graduates that more emphasis on the future and trends in education would have been valuable. One graduate felt the content was all there in the experimental program, but some friction and communication barriers hindered opportunities for content to be explored in depth. Lack of time was stated by most graduates as reasons this instruction was not always available. The graduates all liked the case study and mini courses best, as well as an opportunity to learn from their fellow students. All graduates identified aspects of the program they liked least. Again, lack of time was the most identified concern. As the case studies began to generate more data the time factor became even more paramount. Several graduates expressed the desire to have had some clerical support through graduate assistants to help them handle the data and details of the case study. The graduates also identified that communication procedures within the program on an individual and group basis could have been more refined. The graduates found themselves redoing some aspects of their study because of lack of clarity in instructions or diversity in faculty opinion.

ALL GRADUATES: WORK-RELATED QUESTIONS

The majority of graduates from each program worked at the building level. Furthermore, answers provided to work-related questions were similar for most program graduates even though they may have graduated from a different level of program. For these reasons the answers to work-related questions have been summarized for all graduates.

The majority of the graduates identified their building principal as their direct supervisor. Most of the graduates stated that they received almost no supervision in any of their activities. All but a very few graduates did have supervisory responsibilities. For the most part graduates supervised student assistants, library aides, clerks and volunteers.

The majority of the graduates served as the only professional on the media center staff. Most graduates did not consider this a handicap citing that their media education program had prepared them to work alone, delineate functions, adapt and make decisions. While the graduates liked the freedom, there was concern for the feeling of isolation they had in making judgments with no previous experience. A few graduates stated they expected someone to be there to confer with, to help in making decisions and that they would have liked more supervision during their first year.

Most of the graduates cited too little time as the reason they did not perform the tasks identified in the BRAC instrument. A lack of budget, personnel, equipment and inadequate facilities were also frequently mentioned as reasons some tasks were not performed. Graduates who worked in schools where there were district level media services indicated that many tasks identified as not performed at the building level were provided through a district media center.

The majority of graduates stated that there were barriers to their desire to perform functions related to media center activities. The most cited barriers were related to time and people. For the most part, being the only professional on the media center staff with responsibility for developing the media program with minimal support staff did not provide the time for the graduates to advance the program. The majority of the graduates stated their greatest barrier was reflected in the attitude of the administration and faculty. The lack of understanding of the philosophy of the media center on the part of the faculty and administration greatly diminished the opportunities for the graduate to develop and integrate the media program into the total school program.

Supervisor Interviews

Supervisors of program graduates were asked questions similar to those asked of program graduates. Their responses are summarized on the following pages.

SUPERVISORS OF BA-LEVEL GRADUATES

The five supervisors of the Millersville State College program graduates who were interviewed reflected a variety of position titles. Over half of the supervisors were employed as heads of a building level media center. The remaining supervisors held district level positions either as a library supervisor or audiovisual coordinator. The districts in which these supervisors were employed provided some degree of media support to the building level media programs. For the most part this support was in the nature of film libraries and audiovisual equipment distribution. Only one district provided centralized processing services for the building level media centers. All media centers in the school districts where supervisors were interviewed were staffed with professionals, however, in one district all elementary level media personnel were assigned two or more centers on a part-time basis. The size of the school districts ranged from the largest with thirty-nine schools to the smallest with nine schools. One supervisor was employed in a private country day school.

The supervisors identified specific criteria for the candidates for the vacant position. For the most part this criteria stressed a strong background in a unified media concept and a knowledge of curriculum materials. The position also required candidates with the personal characteristics which would permit the media specialists to work closely and effectively with students and teachers. The candidate's personal characteristics were particularly important in one district which was interested in employing a media specialist who could function in an open concept, student-centered school. For the most part the candidate made an application to the school district. The second most cited method of identifying candidates for a position was through contact with the college placement bureau.

The majority of supervisors agreed that the graduates had met the expectation for the position and had made an impact upon the school. All stated that the graduates had developed excellent rapport with students and teachers. In only one district did the supervisor feel the graduate was not able to develop the desired program. While the supervisor felt the graduate did not take the initiative expected, nor did the graduate show evidence of audiovisual skills, further questioning did reveal that the graduate was responsible for developing three different programs in three different schools on a part-time basis in each school.

The supervisors of the Millersville graduates felt the graduates had been trained very well in the experimental program, especially citing their training in the selection and organization of media. For the most part, the supervisors agreed the graduates had been given a solid background in the media field and could not identify any area in the media education program in which more instruction was required. Several supervisors, however, did state that the graduates needed more emphasis in program development, media utilization, and production skills. One supervisor felt the graduates should have a broader background in vocational education. The majority of the supervisors felt that the status of the current media education programs was excellent. They believed programs were becoming more relevent to educational practices in schools. The supervisors also believed that media education programs would have to communicate more with local school districts in order to continue to assure program relevancy.

SUPERVISORS OF MA-LEVEL GRADUATES

Interviews were held with 24 supervisors of MA-level graduates. The majority of direct supervisors of all graduates of the MA-level experimental programs were district media coordinators with a library background. These supervisors were employed in school districts which provided district level media services to the media programs at the building level. For the most part these services were in the nature of film libraries and media production services. Few districts provided centralized processing services and few districts employed media technicains at the district level. The majority of supervisors were employed in districts where building level media centers were staffed by media professionals, though some districts did have media professionals serving two or more schools. The majority of supervisors stated the type of media services available in their districts was unsophisticated. The school districts ranged in size from a one-school district to sixty-four schools.

All supervisors of graduates from MA-level media education programs stated they had specific criteria in mind for candidates to fill a position. All supervisors were looking for candidates with a broad media background. In addition to the media competencies, the supervisors sought candidates with a good knowledge of curriculum who could work effectively with students

40   Findings

and teachers and who were able to bring a new image to the traditional program. Most of the supervisors indicated they did not use college or university placement bureaus to identify candidates. For the most part, supervisors learned of the candidates through school district personnel offices or knew of the candidates through the graduate internship assignment in the school district's media program.

All supervisors of graduates of MA-level programs stated the graduates had come up to their expectations the first year on the job and were a positive asset to the school's program. Evidence of this impact most cited by supervisors was through the graduate's ability to integrate the media program into the school curriculum and the graduate's ability to work effectively with students and teachers.

Few of the supervisors were able to identify skills or competencies that were lacking in the graduate's training program. For the most part they were impressed with the graduate's broad media background and his abilities to bring about positive relationships with students and teachers.

The opinion of the supervisors on the current status of media education programs was for the most part favorable. Many did believe that the programs weren't broad enough nor did they reflect a balance of content. Some supervisors felt more emphasis should be placed on theory and philosophy. The majority of supervisors stated that the expanding content of the media education curriculum may require longer than one year to complete the training. Almost all supervisors of graduates from MA-level programs believed it would be increasingly necessary to expand and provide continuing education programs for the media specialist.

SUPERVISORS OF SIXTH YEAR LEVEL GRADUATES

Three supervisors of the University of Denver graduates were interviewed. All held positions as district media coordinators. They were employed in districts where district level services were provided. The nature of the services included processing centers, film libraries, professional libraries, and media production centers. None of the supervisors believed his district had a sophisticated media program. All building media centers in the school districts were professionally staffed. Only one district employed technicians. The districts had an average of thirty-six schools.

Since most of the Denver graduates serving under these supervisors were previously employed in the district, placement-related questions did not apply. All supervisors, however, agreed that the graduates did come up to their expectations in job performance. Examples of their success were their ability to implement new curriculum policies, to plan and conduct in-service programs, and to work cooperatively with teachers, principals, and higher administration offices in promoting the media program. No supervisor identified specific problems the graduates had, although some stated that the graduates, upon returning from their leave of absence, were not able to move into positions of higher responsibility. The supervisors agreed that the graduates had made a positive impact on the school.

The supervisors agreed that the training program at Denver had done an excellent job in preparing graduates, though it was unfortunate that graduates were not able to be placed in responsible district level assignments that would provide them with the opportunities to put this newly gained knowledge to work. The supervisors agreed that the graduates were well prepared in problem solving techniques, communication skills, and with the ability to see the total objectives of a media program. One supervisor felt that the graduate needed more management skills and that the graduate had difficulty in narrowing problems down to a manageable size.

The supervisors of these graduates had definite opinions on the current status of media education programs. Most of the supervisors felt too little emphasis was given to the day to day organization procedures of a media program, there being too much theory taught and not enough stress put on management reality. Goal setting and evaluation techniques need to be stressed more in education programs. On the positive side, these supervisors believed library media education programs were doing a find job in promoting high standards in materials selections, in teaching reference skills and the use of the tools of librarianship. The supervisors believed library media education programs were devoted to the ideals of freedom of information and intellectual freedom and in instilling a high enthusiasm toward working with students and teachers.

One supervisor believed library media education programs were not doing their job, citing that they are too concerned about hiring Ph.D.'s to teach who have little if any practical knowledge or experience about school libraries. This supervisor believed that students were coming out of their education programs with strange philosophies not applicable to school libraries and that much content taught in today's library media education programs is not relevant to realities in the school library field.

ALL SUPERVISORS: WORK-RELATED QUESTIONS

Approximately one-third of the supervisors of all program graduates indicated they provided direct supervision. For the most part, however, supervisors stated that they had no direct supervision or that they were on call all of the time for frequent informal communication with the program graduates. A few supervisors stated they discussed monthly reports with the program graduates and some indicated they met with the program graduate in a supervisory or consultative capacity about three times a year.

The majority of supervisors of program graduates were building principals. In addition to the direct supervision of the program graduates, these principals also supervised the total school faculty and administrative and support staff. Supervisors who were identified as district level library supervisors stated that in addition to supervising building level media specialists, they also supervised the staff positions at the district level media center.

The majority of the supervisors stated that tasks not performed by the program graduate at the building level media center were either not applicable due to the size of the school and media program or that these tasks were performed elsewhere within the district. Some supervisors stated that

42   Findings

the low media center budget had an effect on why the program graduate did not perform some tasks. Only a few supervisors cited a lack of staff or lack of time as reasons the program graduates did not perform tasks included in the BRAC instrument.

Most the the supervisors stated that the program graduates were performing as the supervisors expected them to, citing the graduate's conscientiousness and willingness to expand the media program. A few supervisors stated they felt the program graduate could initiate more media program activities through increased communication and in-service programs with the faculty.

Interview Discrepancies

The summary results of the Phase III interviews show a high level of agreement between graduates and supervisors in almost all categories of questions. There were, however, two areas where the respondents were not consistent in their responses. In one instance there was a discrepancy in the graduates' responses between a placement-related question and a work-related question. In addition to citing the geographical location as a reason for accepting the position, most of the graduates also stated that the philosophy of the school administration and building principal was a key factor in their position choice. However, when graduates were asked to identify the barriers which prevented them from doing "more on the job", most cited the attitudes of the administration and faculty. The graduates felt this lack of understanding of the philosophy of the media center on the part of the faculty and administration greatly diminished the graduates' opportunity to develop and integrate the media program into the total school program.

In another instance there was a discrepancy between graduates' and supervisors' responses to a work-related question. Most of the graduates cited a lack of time and staff as the major reason BRAC activities were not performed. However, supervisors, for the most part, indicated the reasons BRAC activities were not performed were due to the size of the school, the media program, a lack of budget or that the activities were performed at the district level. Only a few supervisors cited a lack of staff or time as reasons graduates did not perform tasks included in the BRAC instrument.

Chapter 4

PROGRAM STATUS REPORTS

Phase II of the School Library Manpower Project provided for a two year period during which new or improved programs for school library media personnel were to be developed and implemented. The extent to which this effort was successful can be determined in part by what happened to the programs during their third year, the year when Project support no longer was available. Did the programs continue to exist? Did they obtain offsetting support from their parent institution? Did they become the approved program for school library media personnel? These and other questions were addressed in Status Reports prepared by each of the Program Directors at the end of the third year of their programs. Twenty-two specific questions organized under six topic areas were covered in these reports. The questions are listed in Appendix F. The verbatim Status Reports also are contained in Appendix F. What follows is a summary of these reports for each of the twenty-two questions addressed in the reports. The reader is urged to read each of the individual reports since they contain information not summarized in this section.

Program Goals and Objectives

At the beginning of the third year of the experimental programs the goals and objectives of four programs were essentially the same as those of the prior two years. Significant revisions were made to the Michigan and Millersville programs prior to the third year. After reviewing the core objectives of the Michigan program, the objectives were re-emphasized to cover the essential beginning level competencies of the school library media specialist. One core objective was completely revised. At Millersville the objectives of the program were more concretely and precisely defined, resulting in an increased emphasis on preparing the beginning school library media specialist.

At Auburn a concentrated effort to revise the curriculum got underway following the third year of the program. Apparently it was felt that after three years of experience with the program enough information was available to identify program weaknesses and how they might be improved. The other five programs planned no major changes prior to the fourth program year.

43

Minor changes, however, were noted. Arizona, for example, added a new course during the third year. During the fourth year they plan to try out procedures for identifying those students who probably do not have the interest or ability to effectively interact with teachers and students. An effort would be made to counsel these students out of the program. Other programs, especially Auburn, noted the usefulness of fieldwork as a screening device for identifying those persons who probably cannot be effective media specialists. Most programs noted that while they planned no major changes in course goals, specific course objectives were constantly under review and subject to minor revision.

The loss of Project funding at the end of the second year had a substantial impact on the Mankato program and some impact on the Denver program. The other four programs in one way or another were able to adjust for the loss of Project funds. New faculty positions plus increased support were awarded to the Auburn and Michigan programs. The Arizona and Millersville programs were developed so that new faculty positions would not be required to continue the program once the new course material had been developed.

The Denver program was incorporated into the University's Advanced Study Program. However, since the program only had one student in 1973-74, one faculty member had a part-time assignment to the program. In addition, the program lost its full-time media consultant. As a consequence the 1973-74 Denver program placed less emphasis on media production, the student had to pay for multi-media materials, and there was less time to devote to recruiting activities.

At Auburn a lesser amount of free materials was available to the students. At Arizona, funds had to be re-allocated to support faculty requests for non-print training material. The program at Mankato received no support to offset the loss of Project funds. Therefore, the extensive travel component of that program -- attendance at professional meetings and conventions, visiting media centers, and so on -- had to be eliminated.

Program Participants

The third year enrollment trend for each of the experimental programs varied widely. However, it would appear that for at least four of the six experimental programs, enrollment held up well. The Auburn and Michigan programs had a slight increase in enrollment; the Arizona program had almost a seventy percent increase; and at Millersville third year enrollment was similar to that of previous years.

At Mankato there was no experimental program as such during the third year. Rather, it was absorbed into the regular MS-level media program. Apparently the number of students in that media program was similar to those formerly enrolled in the experimental program.

At Denver enrollment went from seven during the second year to one during the third year. Denver found it difficult to recruit students for a sixth year program. Many of the possible reasons for this are listed in the Denver Status Report.

Three programs, Denver, Millersville and Mankato, anticipated no marked increase in enrollment in future years. One program, Auburn, expected a steady increase of 5 to 10 percent per year. Arizona anticipated a rather large, but steady increase in enrollment over the next several years.

Michigan was not sure that the size of its enrollment could be increased. The reason given is applicable also to the other programs and bears repeating. As reported in the Michigan Status Report, "In the future, the potential for internship placement during a single term may cause limits to be placed on enrollment in the school library media program. Thirty students were placed in cooperating schools for either an internship or student teaching experience during the Winter, 1974 term. This proved somewhat difficult for the core faculty members who supervised these students and the cooperating school system through which they were placed".

Each experimental program was required to establish an Advisory Board. That Board reviewed program activities and was supported by Project funds. Following termination of Project funding, five programs disbanded their Advisory Board. The Michigan Advisory Board was maintained during the third year and did review the Project Phase II report and the revised Michigan program objectives. The Denver Advisory Board was replaced by the Advanced Studies Program Committee of the Graduate School of Librarianship.

Most programs had to adjust their staffing pattern to account for the loss of Project funds. For the most part this was accomplished in such a way that the loss of funds was offset by additional university support or by a decrease in the need for course developers. Most of the programs used Project monies to secure course developers. After the course was developed there was a greatly reduced requirement for such persons.

New faculty positions were awarded at Auburn, Arizona and Michigan to offset those lost due to withdrawl of Project funds. Project-supported course developers at Millersville were reassigned to the Division of Education. Staff requirements at Denver were reduced to one-half time faculty positions because of lack of students. Finally, the experimental program at Mankato was discontinued thus the loss of one full-time Project-supported staff position had an inconsequential impact.

Most programs foresaw the need to adjust for the loss of Project support, and they were for the most part successful in obtaining support from other sources, usually their university or college.

Four of six programs had made or planned to make staffing changes prior to the beginning of the fourth year of the program. However, in no instance did these changes appear to be related specifically to planned changes in the experimental program. Rather, the changes were related to the normal termination and replacement activities which most university departments undergo each year. Staffing for the Denver program varies according to student load, and therefore, the size of the fourth year program staff would depend primarily on the success of the program's recruitment efforts.

46 Status Reports

It was hoped that establishment of the experimental programs, to include publicity about these programs, would eventullly lead to a better qualified student entering the programs. It is almost impossible to demonstrate a cause and effect relationship in this area, but three programs did report that recent students seemed better qualified. Arizona opined that recent students seemed better qualified academically; Mankato thought they now were getting better qualified students into their regular MS program; Millersville believed that recent students were more people-oriented. Future students of the Denver program must meet stricter entrance requirements due to the fact that the program was incorporated into the university's Advanced Studies Program. On the other hand, at Auburn early students of the program often were practitioners who returned to school for retraining. The supply of these persons has run out. Program students now usually come directly from an undergraduate program, and have no practical experience.

Program Components

An educational program is successful in part to the extent that is is revised and updated in accordance with the suggestions of former students and new trends in the profession. Five of the programs were quite active during their third year in terms of curriculum revision. A considerable portion of this activity seemed to stem from a more precise understanding of the goals and objectives of the programs, and from suggestions from former students.

The Auburn program underwent several revisions designed to provide a more comprehensive view of technical processing, a more reality-oriented basic practicum, and a more sophisticated production sequence. Both Arizona and Michigan increased their emphasis on audiovisual production. In the future, Michigan hopes to provide each student with some basic skills in video production.

A variety of changes were made in the Denver program during the third year. These included a decrease in the number of hours devoted to field case study, mini-courses, and electives. An increased emphasis was placed on research methodology, library architecture, and current theories and issues in library and information science and technologies.

At Millersville the curricular outline was revised and now is divided into five contexts representing subject content for: Communication Behavior, Learning Processes, Media, Administration, and Professionalism.

As the programs developed it was expected that changes would be made in certain instructional practices. These changes did occur, but for the most part were not considered to be major in nature. Michigan reported an increased use of newer media and of self-instructional material.

Major changes did occur at Mankato and at Denver. The Mankato program was essentially eliminated during the third year but reinstated during the fourth year. At Denver there was a substitution of regular library courses for special classes developed for the experimental program. As a result of this students, while on their field work assignment, had to be given special assignments by the instructors of their regular campus-based courses.

At Michigan a major change in student counseling practices was adopted. Formerly, a faculty member had provided each student with extensive pre-program counseling. For the third year student planning guides were used extensively, thus lessening the amount of time required for counseling by the faculty.

All programs in some fashion or another increased the emphasis placed on field work. This increased emphasis was obtained at a price to the faculty--it takes considerable time to properly manage practicums and internship programs. Thus, by a variety of methods most programs reduced the amount of time required to conduct the field work component of their program.

At Auburn a committee was established to manage the field work component, thus spreading the workload among the staff. At Denver the field survey was reduced from five to three weeks. At Michigan, in addition to preparing a revised "Guidelines for Internship Experience", they conducted a special field work program for three students who already had considerable media center experience. This special program for experienced students proved to be too time-consuming for the faculty, and probably will not be repeated.

At Arizona the emphasis on field work might possibly have increased. At any rate, interns were placed in a wider geographic and socio-economic range of schools. In addition, several interns were provided experience at both the elementary and secondary level, instead of at one level.

Throughout the entire Project it was obvious that all programs had to devote considerable effort to maintaining a viable field work component. As valuable as this component was judged to be, most Program Directors and their staff seemed to wonder about the degree to which the time and expense involved in this type of component could be justified in future years.

For four experimental programs their interdisciplinary aspects either remained the same as for prior years, or were extended. At Arizona the addition of new courses in educational technology and audiovisual education increased the interdisciplinary aspects of the program. At Millersville these aspects were expanded due to the development of a new secondary certification program in communications. This program was developed in collaboration with the Departments of English, Speech, and Drama.

At Denver the cut back in the number of mini-courses presented probably decreased the interdisciplinary nature of that program.

For the five programs which were active during Phase III all reported that they continue to maintain "open communication channels for obtaining information from students, staff and from the field". Auburn found the individualized field experience to provide a good source of student feedback. Arizona reported receiving useful feedback from students, staff, and supervisors through the use of evaluation forms. Michigan and Millersville used a variety of feedback procedures, to include conferences with cooperating school library media specialists and teachers, internship seminars, student evaluation of individual courses and/or course modules. During the past

year at Denver there was only one student. Thus feedback was obtained
through informal discussions and through an end-of-program evaluation
form. The positive feature of all these reports is that by one way or
another information is being obtained which can be used to modify and to
improve the curriculum when the feedback information suggests that the
program should be modified.

Program Results

During the 1973-74 academic year most programs continued to expand as
well as to consolidate the gains of previous years. At Auburn a general
discussion was held throughout the year as to how the program might be improved in future years. At Michigan the program continued to expand with
increased emphasis placed on self-study activities, the use of "trigger
films", and on the internship component of the program. Plans were made
to continue the program, and steps taken to adopt the program as the approved School Library Media Specialist component within the School of
Library Science.

At Arizona the most interesting development was the increased demand
for graduates of the program despite the fact that the market for teachers
was down within the state. The Millersville program was successful in obtaining approval from the State Department of Education for a five-year
period. In addition, selected features of the program were adopted by other
departments within the Millersville Division of Education.

A number of difficulties did come to the fore during the third year of
the programs. Michigan was unable to secure remuneration for the media specialists cooperating in the internship program. At Millersville considerable
discussion occurred regarding how to assess students in a competency-based
program. In addition to the problem of how to assess certain hard-to-define
skills, there arose the problem of how to grade students on essentially a
pass/fail basis and still adhere to the institution's letter-grading system.
Those interested in these problems should read the Millersville Status
Report, comments to Question IV-1.

In at least four programs third year objectives were achieved quite
well. As part of a university-wide evaluation program, Auburn evaluated the
degree to which students, after various amounts of coursework and internship
experience, had increased their knowledge about educational media. The
study findings showed that knowledge about educational media: (a) was related to the number of courses taken in media utilization and instructional
development; (b) was more in evidence for those students who had internship
experience; and (c) was inversely related to the confidence that interns
expressed in their media utilization and instructional development skills.

The Arizona, Michigan and Millersville programs continued with some
expansion. Arizona had an increased enrollment and found it easier to
place program graduates; Michigan acted positively on all Phase II Report
recommendations and achieved all third year objectives save one -- getting
monies to pay for the services of cooperating media specialists in the
internship program; Millersville obtained state approval for their program.

For both Mankato and Denver it must be concluded that their primary objective, that of maintaining a viable program, was not achieved. Because of a cutback in student enrollment and faculty positions at Mankato the program was all but eliminated. At Denver only one student participated in the program and therefore the program had to be re-oriented to more closely align it with the Advanced Studies Program of the University.

With the exception of Mankato, all other programs maintained most of the program quality control procedures developed during the first two years of the program. Some changes however were made. For example, at Arizona they did not employ module-by-module assessment on a program-wide basis; at Denver the requirement for a member of the faculty to visit each student on-site during the student's field study was dropped; and at Michigan special questionnaires developed for use with faculty and students were not used because of the general switch to self-study activities. Auburn continued to employ first and second year procedures, but hoped to develop more comprehensive procedures such as described for Auburn under Evaluation Item IV-2.

The utilization of a variety of evaluation procedures are required and are considered necessary during the developmental stages of a program. Once developed, many faculty members see less need for strict adherence to quality control procedures. One can surmise that this feeling was felt by many of the staff members of the experimental programs during the third year of the program.

Program Impact

In one manner or another five of the six programs seemed to have had an impact on other University or College educational departments. Throughout the first two years of each program an Advisory Board met periodically to discuss and approve features of the experimental programs. Most Program Directors felt that this interdisciplinary review board led to an increased awareness of the field of librarianship.

In addition to a general impression that the programs had a favorable impact, specific instances were cited by some Program Directors. Millersville reported that "other certified programs in the Division of Education have adopted and/or adapted many of the objectives, procedures, formats and activities of the experimental program." Michigan noted the approval of several new media courses and the considerable expansion of the Educational Media Center.

It is extremely difficult to document any impact a new program might have, especially at the state level. However, certain programs undoubtedly did have such an impact. Representatives from two of the programs, Auburn and Michigan, were involved in the development of revised certification procedures for their respective states. The Millersville program was the first within the state of Pennsylvania to be reviewed for program approval with a set of competency-based procedures. This undoubtedly will affect future program reviews throughout the state.

Most of the programs were visited by the staff of other media programs within their state or region. Auburn, in particular, felt that their program had been influential as the result of these visitations.

In recent years media programs have received increased emphasis within many states. Quite probably the experimental programs contributed to this. At Arizona, for example, instructional media centers now are a feature of most new schools; an increased number of audiovisual specialists are cross-training in library science; and an increasing number of requests are being received from school districts for library media specialists.

Conclusions and Recommendations

The ultimate goal of the School Library Manpower Project was to promote the development of improved programs which eventually would replace those formerly employed to educate school library media personnel. With respect to this goal the Project was successful. Four programs already have been adopted as the approved program for school library media education. These are the programs developed at Auburn University, the Arizona State University, the University of Michigan, and at Millersville State College.

At the University of Denver the experimental program "was modified and incorporated, effective September, 1973, as an identifiable area of the Advanced Studies Program of the Library School." The continued viability of the Denver program rests on the extent to which students can be recruited for the program. At this point in time the demand for a sixth year program focused on the position of District School Library Media Director is questionable. It is difficult to provide support for program graduates during their training; it is difficult to find school districts who will participate in a large-scale case study program; and a sixth year of study does not seem to lead to a better job position or to a higher salary.

The program at Mankato was inactive during its third year. However, it was re-instituted for the 1974-75 academic year and had a fall enrollment of fifteen students. Also, the field trip component of the program was re-activated, this time with the students paying for their field trip expenses. Thus, after a year of being in limbo the Mankato program may be on the road to acceptance.

All six experimental programs attempted to combine and/or reorganize courses and course material. As might be expected, considerable opposition to this was encountered at various levels within the university or college. Audiovisual and school library media faculty were not always willing to cooperate initially. Faculty members who specialized in educational technology might not have agreed initially that educational technology should be stressed in a program for school library media personnel. For a variety of similar reasons a number of Program Directors implied that personal and political problems within their institution were a hinderance to the development of improved and/or more innovated programs.

A number of Program Directors alluded to the problem of educating school library media personnel to perform an increased number and variety of tasks. The demands on such persons has increased markedly to the point where it is difficult, during a fifth year of training, to adequately cover the required topics and skills. One Program Director pointed out the need for a more careful articulation between undergraduate and graduate programs.

All six experimental programs tended to be of the competency-based variety. Two issues related to such programs were mentioned. One dealt with the role of fieldwork and practicums in such programs. All programs tended to emphasize either practicums or case studies. The degree to which such program components can be supported is an issue. Also, the problem of how to assess student skills during their fieldwork was an issue of particular concern to all programs.

Finally, all programs were concerned with the recruitment of better students for their programs. In particular, they saw the need for students who were more interested in the acquisition of inter-personal skills as opposed to technical skills. Also, they were concerned with how they could develop better and more interesting programs which in turn might attract a better caliber of student.

The development or improvement of a school library media education program is a considerable undertaking. That it can be successfully accomplished is attested to by the continued existence of the programs developed during Phase II of the School Library Manpower Project.

The development of the programs occurred despite the misgivings of a few persons associated with each program. It must be expected that new programs will be resisted by various members of the department undergoing modification and by members of other departments who may feel that their jurisdictional boundaries are being invaded. The Status Report of Millersville, and to a lesser extent those of Auburn and Arizona, suggest what must be done to assure the success of a program development effort. The following points, discussed more fully in the Millersville Status Report, apply equally well to most other programs. To assure the successful development of a new school library media education program:

a. The staff should be urged to participate during the early stages of conceptualizing and implementing the new program.

b. The competencies to be covered in the program should be identified and specified, and this activity should be a total faculty effort.

c. The program should be developed gradually over a one or two year period. This provides time for adequate staff development which in turn will assure the development of new instructional material supportive of the objectives of the new program.

d. A special effort should be made to coordinate the objectives and the development of the program with those of other departments of education.

e. The program should be based on an occupational task analysis of recent graduates. Furthermore, the program should be periodically updated through the use of additional task analysis surveys.

f. When possible, students should be allowed to design "alternate avenues of learning" to meet their particular interests and be allowed to enter the program at different points.

Other important recommendations made in relation to the development of new programs included: (a) establish a task force from various departments to direct program development; and (b) begin by identifying program goals and objectives and then determine to what extent new courses are required to meet objectives. This may prevent a certain amount of interdepartment controversy and help participants develop a program independent of what they now are doing.

The need for an active public relations and information program to promote program development also was mentioned. This is a part of the whole attempt to gain active support for the new program from both within the university and from the school districts which must support the field component of the program and who eventually will hire program graduates.

Chapter 5

BRAC SURVEY PROCEDURES

Use of Questionnaire Data

The BRAC questionnaires were designed to collect data which Program Directors could use to identify those portions of their program in need of modification.

The BRAC questionnaire for Program Directors revealed what the staff of a particular program believed to be covered and emphasized in their program. The BRAC questionnaire for students provided similar data from the student's standpoint. The BRAC questionnaire for program graduates provided information about the actual tasks performed by recent graduates, and how well they performed those tasks. The BRAC questionnaire for supervisors provided similar data from the standpoint of the supervisor. Thus, using four versions of the BRAC questionnaire, similar types of program related data are provided by four different groups of respondents. The data provided by one group are cross-checked by at least one other group. When discrepancies exist, this identifies a potential problem area which must be studied more intensively. For example, if a Program Director and program students agree that a task is heavily emphasized in a program, and, program graduates and their supervisors agree that this is a relatively unimportant task performed by few employees, then a serious conflict exists between program emphasis and job requirements. The BRAC questionnaires can be used to uncover such conflicts. The conflict then must be further investigated to determine, if possible, why the conflict exists and what might be done about it.

For most readers the task analysis data provided by program graduates should be of special interest. These data, displayed in Appendices D and E, provide an indication of what first and second year graduates do on their first job. Any program that wishes to produce graduates who can be immediately absorbed into a school library media center might do well to emphasize those activities which, according to the respondents of this study, are performed by most school library media personnel.

The BRAC document organized job-related functions and tasks into seven competency areas dealing respectively with Human Behavior (A), Learning and Learning Environment (B), Planning and Evaluation (C), Media (D), Management

(E), Research (F), and Professionalism (G). As one would expect, certain tasks are seldom performed. As revealed by the survey data, school library media personnel continually interact with students and teachers and thus are heavily involved with tasks related to Human Behavior (Competency Area A). Moreover, their job is intimately related to Learning and Learning Environments (Competency Area B). To a considerable extent media specialists are involved with a variety of tasks which can be subsumed under the category of Professionalism (G).

On the other hand, according to the summary data displayed in Appendix E, school library media personnel are not often involved with Research activities (Competency Area F), and recent graduates usually play a junior role in activities related to Management (Competency Area E) and Planning and Evaluation activities (Competency Area C).

Supposedly school library media personnel are heavily involved in Media activities (Competency Area D). However, this area, as represented in the BRAC, covers over 200 tasks many of which would not be performed except in large, affluent schools. Thus, the relatively low involvement of graduates with media-related activities can be accounted for by the large number of specific task statements contained in Competency Area D.

Table V is of particular importance in that the data and analysis suggest that there is relatively little difference in the duties and competencies of graduates of BA and MA-level programs. The interview data substantiate this--the graduates of both BA and MA-level programs tend to be employed at the building level, usually at the elementary level.

Despite differences in prior education and training, persons employed in similar job positions usually will have to perform similar tasks. This suggests that those who wish to advocate the need for BA and/or MA and/or sixth year level programs should: (1) determine whether or not there are distinctly different job markets for graduates of each program level; and (2) actively promote the development and/or restructuring of job positions so that there are identifiable categories of jobs which do require different levels of education and training.

Probably there are certain types of jobs which are most likely to be held by graduates of MA programs. Possibly graduates of MA-level programs advance more rapidly professionally. Because of the nature of this particular study such hypotheses cannot be examined using the data of this study. A longitudinal study which investigated the job and professional activities of persons after 5 or 10 years of work experience might substantiate such hypotheses. However, most longitudinal studies have found it very difficult to demonstrate a relationship between prior education and on the job or professional success.

BRAC-Related Interview Questions

One of the objectives of Phase III was to evaluate the BRAC document and questionnaire as a means of obtaining job-related information. For

Survey Procedures   55

this reason both program graduates and their supervisors were asked questions about the problems they had completing the BRAC questionnaire (see Interview Form, Appendix B).

PROGRAM GRADUATES

The majority of all graduates stated they did not really have problems in responding to the BRAC instrument used during the Phase III summative evaluation study, even though they did identify some concerns. Only a few stated the instructions were not clear or that they had some difficulty with the terminology. Most of the graduates stated it took too much time to complete the evaluation study. Primarily they found it difficult to gauge the frequency scale element in the response form and this slowed their decision-making process. Many graduates indicated that a lot of the task statements were irrelevant or did not apply to their particular school level position. Some graduates felt the instrument was not geared for a media center in a small school and that many of the task statements were directed to media center operations in larger schools or district level centers. During the process of completing responses to approximately 700 task statements, many graduates felt that to some extent the task statements were repetitious.

The most frequently stated suggestions from the graduates to improve BRAC were to shorten the instrument and eliminate the repetition. Many of the graduates felt that it would be beneficial if space were provided for a "not applicable" response. Some graduates suggested that the terminology and instructions should be clearer, and a few believed the instrument format could be improved to make it mechanically easier for the respondents to use. Several graduates stated the instrument should include more people-related tasks, especially those relating to working with students.

Most graduates stated that the process of completing the BRAC questionnaire was of benefit to them. The majority of graduates believed it was a good evaluation tool and helped them to identify areas for self-improvement. Their responses to the BRAC statements helped most graduates to know what tasks they were or were not doing. This they believed was very beneficial for the analysis of their media center programs. A number of graduates stated the BRAC instrument was a good refresher of their media education program and they believed it would be a valuable tool to use with students in media education programs. Many graduates felt the BRAC instrument would serve as a valuable checklist for future use in setting new goals and objectives and rethinking competencies. As a guide to breaking down work areas and job functions, a few graduates felt the BRAC instrument would be helpful to them in developing future job descriptions.

All but one graduate stated that their jobs were adequately covered in the BRAC instrument. Some graduates indicated more tasks should include statements on attitudes and working with students and teachers. A few graduates stated that more task statements should stress the media center activities relating to reading, literature and curriculum development.

SUPERVISORS OF PROGRAM GRADUATES

While most of the supervisors stated they didn't really have problems responding to the BRAC instrument, they did feel the instrument was too long and too time consuming. Some supervisors indicated that many of the tasks did not apply to the graduate's position level or the type of administrative organization of the school system. A few supervisors indicated they had difficulty with the frequency scales and ambiguity of some task statements.

For the most part supervisors suggested eliminating the repetition they sensed in the task statements as the major recommendation for improving the BRAC instrument. Many of the supervisors would like to have the option to indicate "not applicable" as a response to task statements. Some supervisors indicated they would like to see the BRAC instrument shorter, less detailed, and in a simpler format.

All supervisors stated they thought the BRAC instrument was a good evaluation review tool. They believed the instrument would be useful in strengthening their media programs, and its use would give them an overview of the strengths and weaknesses of their programs. They felt the inventory of task statements would be useful in writing job descriptions. Many supervisors indicated their districts would modify and expand the BRAC instrument to use locally in staff and program development. Several supervisors indicated the BRAC instrument gave them a broad scope of understanding of the role of the media specialist and felt the BRAC instrument would be valuable to media education programs.

Almost all supervisors indicated the position of the program graduate they supervised was adequately covered in the BRAC instrument. Some supervisors stated that while the instrument was very comprehensive, it may not always apply to some building or district situations, especially when a program graduate serves two or more schools.

Improvement of Survey Procedures

The BRAC survey procedures were developed for research purposes. However, it was hoped that the procedures would be of use to Program Directors who from time to time might wish to survey graduates of their program. While the comments of the interviewees indicated that the survey procedures were feasible they also revealed that the procedures were cumbersome and the process of completing a BRAC questionnaire too lengthy for some persons to endure. Therefore, to improve the BRAC survey administrative procedures the following suggestions are offered:

1. The BRAC questionnaire should be reviewed with persons presently in a student status. This will alert them to the probability of being asked to complete the questionnaire some time following their graduation. This review also provides an opportunity to clear up questions about how to complete the questionnaire.

Survey Procedures 57

2. To decrease the time required to complete the questionnaire and to process the questionnaire data one of the following alternatives could be adopted:

   a. Ask each respondent to respond to only a portion of the BRAC questionnaire -- the tasks subsumed under one or two Competency Areas. Assign each respondent a particular portion of the questionnaire to complete. Use sampling procedures to obtain responses to the complete BRAC questionnaire; or,

   b. Each year conduct a survey of recent graduates and cover only one or two Competency Areas. On succeeding years cover a different set of competencies until all seven Competency Areas have been covered.

It has been suggested that the respondents might be asked to answer the BRAC questionnaire at the function level as opposed to the task level. This would ease the burden of responding by a factor of seven. However, each function statement is quite broad, subsuming at least three and usually five to ten task statements. Therefore, most persons might have difficulty responding at the function level because they could respond in a variety of ways depending on the specific function-related tasks they had in mind when responding. This problem would lower the reliability of the survey findings. For this reason it cannot be recommended that the BRAC questionnaire be responded to at the function level.

Each group of BRAC questionnaire respondents was asked a different but related set of questions. These are located in Table III and Appendix A. Comments obtained from the Phase III workshop participants, plus the questionnaire respondents themselves, suggested a number of improvements which could be made to these questions. A revised set of questions for each set of respondents is contained in Appendix G. A "not applicable" option has been provided for a number of questions; certain questions have been clarified; and the number of questions for each respondent group has been reduced. Persons interested in conducting a survey using the BRAC questionnaire should consider using these revised sets of questions.

Improvement of BRAC

The Behavioral Requirements Analysis Checklist was not meant to be a static document nor was it claimed to be a highly polished document which covered all aspects of the job of school library media personnel. Comments obtained from the survey respondents and from participants of the Phase III workshops suggested a number of improvements which should be made to BRAC. Unfortunately, the Project had to terminate before these improvements could be undertaken. Improvement suggestions have been deposited with the American Library Association and hopefully in the future these suggestions can be incorporated into a revised edition of BRAC. The more important of these suggestions include:

1. Review all task statements and when possible remove ambiguities.

2. Subdivide all task statements which contain more than one action verb, e.g., "develop and produce a ..."

3. Add a glossary to the BRAC.

4. Emphasize in the BRAC introduction that the list of tasks covers all the tasks which collectively might be performed by many persons in a variety of settings. Therefore, no one job incumbent would be expected to perform all listed tasks or to be competent to perform all listed tasks.

5. Emphasize in the instructions that the list of tasks may not cover all tasks performed by a job incumbent. Therefore, it is important that each respondent add to the BRAC questionnaire those tasks which he or she performs and which are not included in the BRAC.

Chapter 6

CONCLUSIONS

Fieldwork as a Program Component

Fieldwork constituted an important part of all six experimental programs. The Phase II reports of the six experimental programs and the findings of the Phase III evaluation indicate the feeling was universal that the fieldwork experiences were one of the most favored aspects of the programs. Though a difference in terminology existed in the individual programs to designate the fieldwork experiences: such as practicums, internships, field observations, happenings, and field experiences - all made up a sequence of activities to permit students to put theory into practice.

A successful fieldwork component requires careful planning, implementation and evaluation to insure that the experiences are an integral part of the curriculum and are flexible in structure and format to meet individual needs.

A well planned and closely monitored fieldwork experience gives students an opportunity to identify their own strengths and competencies and at the same time permits them to recognize and eliminate any weaknesses which are revealed. One of the great strengths of fieldwork experience is that it places students not only in media centers, but also in close relationship with school students, teachers and the potential value of media to learning. Through an actual application of course content and theory, the media education student is able to reinforce his newly acquired competencies in a realistic setting representing the total school program. Through the use of orientation workshops, fieldwork seminars and individual counseling procedures which include the fieldwork student, fieldwork supervisor and the university supervisor, the community schools and the university are brought closer together. These kinds of activities not only help to develop a team approach to problem solving in realistic situations, but also encourage an individualization of program for each student. Since students in the experimental programs were encouraged to split their fieldwork experiences among different school levels and settings, they were afforded an opportunity to assess a variety of experiences and make more intelligent career decisions. There are also positive attributes for the university staff in the fieldwork component. The selection of field sites, visits to the field center schools and communication within the school districts make it possible to maintain a knowledge of programs

60 Conclusions

in the field. In addition the fieldwork component provides excellent staff development activities for the university supervisors.

To build a strong fieldwork component there are some crucial factors which must be recognized. The lack of any one of these may present a serious constraint to the development and successful implementation of an effective fieldwork program. The following suggestions are made to serve as guidelines for the planning and evaluation of fieldwork components.

1. Planning, initiating and evaluating a fieldwork component is an integral and complex facet of the curriculum which requires coordination and the use of a wide range of communication patterns.

2. The fieldwork component involves extensive time demands on the university staff and its supervision should be analyzed in respect to its acceptance as part of the teaching load.

3. The fieldwork component involves extensive time demands on the field center institutions and the field media supervisor and should be cleared by the appropriate field site authorities.

4. Time should be allotted to the university supervisor to determine which media centers and which practitioners can make the most effective contribution to the goals of the media education program.

5. The numbers and locations of field centers should be identified well in advance of the fieldwork experience.

6. There should be a mutual understanding and commitment between the university and the cooperating school districts.

7. Orientation programs and evaluation seminars for on-the-job supervisors and students in the field should be a part of the fieldwork component.

8. Students should be placed in fieldwork situations at more than one level and in more than one setting.

9. Students should be placed in field centers where the media specialist is eager to accept the responsibility for professional guidance and where the personality and experience of the media specialist can support the objectives of the media education program.

10. Supervision of students in the field, whether the responsibility of one staff member or a team of staff members, should be continually coordinated and highly individualized.

11. Complete and individual files should be maintained on the student in the field, with extensive time for individual and group counseling.

12. The fieldwork component should be supported by a budget which will permit it to meet the defined objectives.

13. Fieldwork, as an integrated part of the curriculum, should be required of all students.

Role of a Program Director

The School Library Manpower Project demonstrated that major program innovations can be accomplished within a fairly short period of time. However, the Project also suggested that success depends on the strong leadership of a single person who: (a) is a Department Chairman or a very senior and respected member of a department; (b) is skilled at organizing the efforts of others; (c) is skilled at obtaining the support of other departments and of the school administration; (d) is willing to spend considerable time and effort to accomplish the goals of the program; (e) is willing and able to provide leadership to the program and in particular to lead by example; and (f) has the authority and inclination to act decisively to further the goals of the program.

Obviously the successful development and implementation of a new educational program depends on the support and actions of many persons. Yet to a considerable extent, success depends primarily on a single person, a person who takes the responsibility for implementing the program and who is determined to overcome the obstacles to implementation. The Project staff and evaluators were impressed with the apparent relationship between the success of each of the six experimental programs and the support, enthusiasm and all around leadership provided by the Program Director of each program. It seemed that each program succeeded to the extent that the Program Director actively guided the development and implementation of the program.

Recent studies of the process of innovation adoption have suggested that innovations are adopted to the extent that an action agent or transfer agent exists. Such an agent, be it a single individual or a small group of people, assume the responsibility for assuring that an innovation is developed, implemented and eventually incorporated into an organizational setting as a standard element of that organization.

In any organization, but especially within large educational organizations, resistance to change is great. Throughout this Project each experimental program encountered a variety of obstacles. In most instances these obstacles eventually were overcome or at least partially circumvented.

Resistance to the experimental programs was partly overcome by the mere fact that the university or college administration and a particular department of education agreed to support the development of an innovative program. The potential for overcoming obstacles to the program was increased by appointing as Program Director either the chairman of a department or a very senior member of a department. These are the persons who, within certain limits, are authorized to make changes or can at least act as a strong proponent for a suggested change.

Department heads, of course, cannot devote their full attention to a single activity. However, it seemed that each of the six experimental programs succeeded to the extent that a Program Director or a key representative devoted a considerable amount of time to overseeing program

62   Conclusions

development and implementation. In particular, these persons had to be
skilled at both gaining support within their own department and obtaining
the required interdisciplinary support from other departments. To obtain
support for the field component of their experimental program these persons
also had to be skilled at obtaining the cooperation of coordinating schools
and instructors.

Finally, it seemed that the programs succeeded to the extent that the
director of that program led by example. For each program new courses had
to be prepared, or existing courses had to be revised. In either case,
considerable attention had to be paid to such things as the identification
of training objectives, new instructional material and the rationale of
existing courses. The techniques for developing a new course or for revising an existing one are not completely obvious and members of a staff
may not know how to completely analyze and restructure a course. The more
successful Program Directors analyzed and revised their own courses first,
in cooperation with other staff members. By doing this they allowed their
own courses to become the vehicle for others to learn how to revise a
course. Initial criticisms from the staff about the need for revising
courses and the need for developing learning objectives were directed at
the Program Director and his courses. While hard on the ego of a Program
Director this usually is a successful way to lead by example.

Program Costs

Educational programs are expensive both to develop and to conduct.
Undoubtedly many program innovations are not adopted because funds are not
available to support the development of new materials and procedures. The
support provided by the Project to each experimental program was primarily
used to pay for the development of program materials. In addition to a
two thousand dollar planning grant, each program was provided $100,000.00
over a two-year period. In all instances additional developmental support
was provided by the college of university, or was diverted from other departmental activities. Although just barely adequate, the developmental
funds provided by the Project did assure that something new was developed.

Once revised, most of the experimental programs did not require additional funds to conduct the programs. That is, they did not require
additional instructors to present course material. However, it did appear
that for all programs the new field component was more costly and required
more instructor effort than did the field component of the pre-revision
programs. This may present a problem in future years. For most programs
the new field component was one of the more innovative features of the program. The Project was deliberately designed to promote the development of
improved fieldwork techniques in the experimental programs. In most cases
however, these new fieldwork components obviously were more costly to conduct both in terms of student and instructor time. Extensive fieldwork
is obtained at a price which students and/or the staff may not always wish
to pay. As a research project it would be interesting to investigate, three
to five years hence, what happened to the fieldwork components of each of
the six programs developed during this Project.

Program Transportability

At the end of Phase II of the Project the six programs were evaluated in terms of their transportability to other educational institutions. By this we mean the extent to which the programs were well documented, had developed materials and procedures which could be adopted by other institutions, and had developed a program which was not closely tied to special features of a particular college or university. After taking a second look at this topic it must be concluded that while each program developed general strategies, objectives and approaches which can be adopted by others, there seems to be no one of the six programs which could readily be adopted by another institution without first being extensively modified.

Each program was developed to fit the needs of a particular institution. Furthermore, each program was developed such as to overcome or to circumvent a particular configuration of obstacles. Therefore, it must be concluded that each program had been tailored such that it probably could not be transported in its entirety to another institution.

On the other hand, some of the programs did develop lists of learning objectives, specific instructional modules, and other rather specific instructional materials and procedures which could be readily transferable to programs at other institutions. More importantly, each program was developed on the basis of a number of good ideas and premises which appear to have wide application. These ideas and premises are discussed in Curriculum Alternatives,[15] the final report for Phase II of the Project.

Program Goals and Job Requirements

During the Phase III workshops there was considerable discussion regarding the merits of matching program objectives to job requirements. One can adopt the philosophy that an educational program, especially a program for educational practitioners, should gear its objectives to job requirements. Usually this is interpreted to mean that the program should prepare persons to perform those tasks which they are apt to be required to perform during their first one or two years on a job. In fact, the survey procedures used in Phase III of this Project are based on this philosophy -- that a school library media program should cover primarily those tasks encountered during the first year or two on the job.

Obviously, educational philosophies counter to the above can be proposed, and in fact may be more acceptable to some in the educational community. Many educators wish to emphasize the theoretical underpinnings of

---

[15]SLMP, Curriculum Alternatives: Experiments in School Library Media Education, op. cit.

64 Conclusions

a profession rather than its practical aspects. Many educators would like to attempt to prepare students for their professional and job duties as they may exist some five to ten years after graduation. Such persons are more interested in estimating the probable requirements of a profession five to ten years hence than in keeping up with the present job requirements of first and second year graduates.

It is not the intention here to suggest that school library media personnel be educated according to a particular educational philosophy. Rather the survey procedures employed in Phase III of this study are of most use to those who feel that an educational program is most relevant when it prepares persons who can be immediately employed in a useful and skillful fashion. Furthermore, the current emphasis on competency-based instruction which is performance oriented is an approach most amenable to those who believe in preparing persons for immediate skillful employment.

Chapter 7

FINAL ASSESSMENT

Project Accomplishments

In this chapter it is appropriate to review the School Library Manpower Project in terms of its accomplishments, its impact on the profession, and some of the issues which the Project was not able to resolve.

To a considerable degree the primary objectives of all three Phases of the Project were accomplished successfully. During Phase I the primary goal was to accurately identify the tasks performed by school library media personnel and to identify the competency areas which should be covered in a school library media education program. During this Phase a job analysis of the positions within the profession was accomplished. This eventuated in the identification of tasks which should be covered in the curricula for professional school library media personnel. Also, Phase I brought forth the development of model occupational definitions for school library media personnel which provided the basis for the development of the <u>Behavioral Requirements Analysis Checklist</u>, the evaluation tool employed during Phase III.

The primary goal of Phase II of the Project was to support the development of six experimental programs to serve as models for those institutions that wished to upgrade their school library media education programs. These programs were developed over a two year period and at termination of the Project they were still in existence. All had been incorporated in some manner into the educational structure of their parent institutions. At least four programs had been accepted as the official programs in school library media education by their institutions. Finally, all programs were judged to be a considerable improvement over those programs which existed at the six respective institutions prior to the Project.

The primary goals for Phase III were to determine the degree to which the programs were capable of producing graduates who could perform acceptably in the field, and, to develop quality control procedures for evaluating programs in school library media education. A secondary goal was to assess the degree to which all or portions of the experimental programs were transferable to other institutions. The survey conducted during Phase III demonstrated that the experimental programs did produce acceptable graduates, and, that satisfactory survey procedures had been developed for evaluating the field-relevancy of professional school library media education programs. Further analysis of the programs suggested that they were not easily transferable to other colleges or universities.

It seems fair to conclude that the major goals of the School Library Manpower Project were accomplished and that these goals, as embodied in job definitions, suggested educational curricula and quality control evaluative procedures will exist and will continue to have an impact on the school library media profession.

In both tangible and intangible ways the Project appears to have had a major impact on the school library media profession. As a result of Phase I, four distinct occupational definitions for the profession were identified. In turn, these were instrumental in getting the profession to think about education in terms of specific job positions and job levels. It is important that the profession continue to think in this manner, since the various degree level programs within the profession can only be articulated when each program is clearly directed toward the education of persons who hold particular job positions and work at particular professional and non-professional levels.

The occupational definitions and professional levels which emerged from Phase I of the Project were not predetermined. Rather, they evolved from an identification of the needs of the profession in the field. This aspect of the Project was important for two reasons -- one, it led to the development of job definitions and associated curricula which were based on the assumption that educational programs should be occupationally relevant. Current efforts to develop competency-based education programs are based on the same assumption. Secondly, it pointed out the necessity to periodically survey persons working in the field to determine their present and anticipated job requirements. This survey information then can be used to upgrade a curriculum and to make it more occupationally relevant.

A subtle, but very important characteristic of the programs developed during the Project was that they were based on the belief that the school library media profession is an amalgamation of skills and knowledges many of which are related to other disciplines. All Project programs were based on an interdisciplinary approach, and the advisability of following this approach seemed to be borne out by the demand in the field for graduates of the experimental programs. It is now recognized that the successful school library media professional must be prepared to bring to the educational setting the application of a variety of subject areas.

Each of the six experimental programs had a strong fieldwork component, and it was this component more than any other that made the programs occupationally relevant. These fieldwork components were quite lengthly, sometimes continuing throughout most of the program. It was the judgment of Program Directors, Program Graduates and the Project staff and evaluators that the experimental programs identified the need for a strong fieldwork component.

Final Assessment   67

This need applies to school media education programs at both the BA and MA level.

Finally, the Project was an example of how seed monies can be used to foster change. The one hundred and two thousand dollars provided to each experimental program was enough only to allow them to plan for a new program and furnish part of the support during program development. In every instance this seed money had to be supplemented by the parent institution. Each program was developed because certain persons were dedicated to its development. Each Program Director had made a commitment to develop a new program, and, the institution had made a commitment to support the development of that program. These commitments to the Project, and the seed funds furnished by the Project, provided the leverage which the Project staff and each Program Director frequently needed to overcome obstacles to program development.

Program Characteristics

There were many features of the experimental programs which could be highlighted, and there were many observations about the development and conduct of these programs which merit sharing with the profession. What follows are some of the more interesting highlights of Phases II and III of the Project. Many of the points addressed in this review have been discussed more thoroughly in the Status Reports for Phase III (see Appendix F) and in the Program Reports contained in the final report for Phase II of the Project entitled Curriculum Alternatives.[16]

INTERDISCIPLINARY APPROACH

All six experimental programs were developed on the assumption that professional school library media education should be brought into closer relationship with related disciplines. To a considerable extent this was accomplished by the development of programs which integrated the subject matter of librarianship, educational technology, and teacher education. Many of the experimental programs employed faculty from other disciplines to cover such topics as research techniques, budgeting, interpersonal relationships, the selection and evaluation of non-print media as well as the more traditional topics covered in a program for teacher education. By following an interdisciplinary approach the programs attempted to produce graduates who could serve as leaders in the instructional environment at the K-12 level.

COURSE MATERIAL DUPLICATION

It is not uncommon to discover that the various courses within an educational program overlap to a considerable extent. During the

---

[16]SLMP, Curriculum Alternatives: Experiments in School Library Media Education, op. cit.

development of the experimental programs course developers were required to work together to formulate overall program objectives, where within the curriculum these objectives should be covered, and where within the present curriculum extensive duplication existed. These meetings, as contentious as they sometimes were, did result in the development of total programs which were much more carefully integrated, and which contained much less duplication. Such a program development effort serves many useful purposes: it allows each instructor to identify more accurately the role of his subject content in the overall program; it leads to the identification of material which can be deleted, and thus providing space for the incorporation of new material into the program; and finally, it can expose the various educational philosophies which may be followed within the same program. As a result of this process major philosophical conflicts can be identified and hopefully resolved.

OCCUPATIONAL RELEVANCY

All experimental programs were based on the assumption that a curriculum should be occupationally relevant. Therefore, as a prelude to program development the first massive task analysis of the school library media profession was undertaken. The assumption that a curriculum should be job relevant and should be based on a task analysis of job positions within the profession is at the heart of the philosophy upon which the concept of competency-based education is based. Educators within most professions will have different views regarding the degree to which program graduates should be prepared to perform immediately and skillfully those tasks most apt to be encountered during the first year or two on the job. Certainly there is a need to prepare persons to perform professional activities which they may encounter five or ten years after graduation. However, it is extremely difficult to anticipate the exact nature of these activities during a one year education program.

It is up to each profession to identify those work-related activities which can be taught specifically during an educational program, and those anticipated activities which can be covered only in a general manner. Graduates of most educational programs have to be, or at least should be, taught two quite different sets of skills and knowledges. One set relates to those specific tasks which they probably will have to perform soon after graduation. These tasks can be identified readily via job analysis techniques. A second set of skills and knowledges relates to the process of identifying new job requirements and preparing oneself to perform these requirements. This may occur on the job, through formal advanced study, or through taking continuing education courses. At present the techniques of educational technology and job analysis are best suited to identifying those tasks which must be performed soon after graduation. Current models of competency-based education programs prepare persons for these types of tasks as opposed to those which may be encountered later on in one's professional life.

The traditional approach to education assumes that persons should be prepared for job activities throughout their lifetime, and the educational emphasis often is placed on providing a student with a set of basic skills and knowledges which can be used to master new sets of job requirements. This philosophy has considerable merit. However, it is based also on the assumption that once a person had acquired a basic set of skills and knowledges he will be able to determine for himself how to apply them to new job-related tasks. There is little evidence to support this latter assumption. It seems, rather, that the techniques for applying basic principles and basic skills and knowledges to new situations is a learned skill which should receive more emphasis in formal education. Unfortunately, present techniques for identifying core skills and knowledges are not well developed. Also, education is just beginning to explore alternative techniques for teaching persons how to identify, on a continuing basis, new job requirements and the appropriate routes to the mastery of these new requirements.

Any attempt to make programs occupationally relevant soon encounters the problem of how to maintain the relevancy of such programs. As the result of this Project there is an increased awareness within the School Library Media profession of the need to conduct field surveys on a continuing basis to determine presently relevant job requirements. These requirements do change from year to year as new technologies are developed and new job positions are created. To develop and maintain an occupationally relevant program the graduates of the program should be followed up in the field. Field surveys will identify new tasks which now are performed in the field, tasks which are no longer performed or are performed at a different professional level, tasks which now receive increased emphasis on the job and tasks which now are de-emphasized. The data from such surveys can be employed to revise a program; tasks can be added to the curriculum, dropped from the curriculum, given increased or decreased emphasis in the program or incorporated into a program for a different professional level.

Within most professions tasks which once were performed by highly trained professionals become more and more to be performed by technicians. This means that professional level programs should be upgraded periodically and technician-level programs should be broadened and/or sub-divided on the basis of findings in the field.

Who within a profession should take the responsibility for upgrading educational programs? Educational institutions do this from time to time for their own programs. It would seem however that this upgrading should be done on a national basis also. Professional societies probably are the organizations best suited to promoting periodically the critical examination of their profession. During this effort the profession's educational goals and programs can be examined with a view towards upgrading those goals and programs if that seems to be required.

INDIVIDUALIZATION OF PROGRAMS

In recent years there has been an increased tendency to allow students considerable freedom to select those courses and learning experiences which seem best suited to their individual needs. This has been accompanied by an increased emphasis on the use of self-instructional materials and procedures. In the programs developed during the School Library Manpower Project an effort was made to provide students with a wide variety of learning options.

70 Final Assessment

Some programs allowed students, in cooperation with a faculty advisor, to plan their own programs of study and to determine how they would be evaluated as they progressed through their internship. During the survey, graduates of these programs commented very favorably on this aspect of their education. However, outside of favorable comments by graduates and some Program Directors there was no evidence that these individualization practices led to a more capable graduate. It should be pointed out, however, that it is extremely difficult to demonstrate that any particular educational practice has a noticeable impact on program graduate capability.

A number of the experimental programs developed individualized learning modules. In some programs enough modules were developed so that students could select from among them those which were most relevant to their interests and anticipated job requirements. Individualization of educational programs requires that both students and staff clearly identify the educational goals of a particular learning experience and the manner in which attainment of these goals will be assessed.

These approaches, while not unique to the field of school library media education, did demonstrate that educational programs for professional school library media personnel can be individualized successfully. Comments from program graduates, their supervisors, and the faculty suggested that this feature of the program was judged to be highly desireable.

Program Evaluation and Quality Control

All six experimental programs developed various procedures for evaluating the effectiveness of the instructional materials developed for the programs. Early in Phase II of the Project each Program Director was provided guidance by the HumRRO Evaluation Team as to the evaluative devices which should be developed for his program. In addition, a transactional evaluation process was undertaken. That is, based on an analysis of the goals of each program, specific guidance was given each Program Director regarding the features of his program about which evaluative information should be collected. For all programs a list of nine general evaluative topics were identified and each Program Director collected information about each of these topics. These nine topics were addressed in the Phase II Program Director Reports in Curriculum Alternatives[17] and most of them again were addressed in the Phase III Status Reports. Early in the development of each program each Program Director knew the types of evaluative information which should be collected about his experimental program. As a result a variety of evaluative practices were developed for each program.

Some Program Directors and members of their staff maintained logs during the developmental activities of their programs. These logs were used to

---

[17]SLMP, Curriculum Alternatives: Experiments in School Library Media Education, op. cit.

Final Assessment 71

evaluate the ease with which the programs were developed, the problems encountered and the solutions to these problems, and the extent to which various program goals were achieved. Most programs developed formative evaluation procedures for obtaining student feedback about the effectiveness of the instructional materials and techniques. Self-instructional packages, for example, contained forms which students used to evaluate instructional modules. Feedback from students, cooperating teachers, and field coordinators were used to modify portions of the practicums and internship programs. Prior to the Phase III field survey most programs had received some feedback from former students and their supervisors. All of this feedback information was used as appropriate to modify the programs.

The entire Phase III effort of the Project was devoted to obtaining quality control feedback from program graduates. This aspect of the Project was unique. Most educational programs do attempt to obtain informal feedback from former students but such attempts usually are abortive for a number of reasons. Often they do not use systematic survey procedures to collect information; with depressing repetity the rate of returns are so low that the obtained data must be viewed as non-representative of program graduates in general.

The Project developed an instrument, the Behavioral Requirements Analysis Checklist,[18] which could be used to identify rather precisely those tasks performed by program graduates. This instrument, coupled with a series of evaluation-related questions, provided the evaluation tool needed to collect information from former graduates and their supervisors about the degree to which the experimental programs had prepared graduates to work in the field. The BRAC document and its associated procedures provides an evaluation tool which can be used by other educational programs preparing professional school library media personnel. Through a series of workshops held during Phase III of the Project information about how to collect and use field feedback information to revise a program was disseminated to the profession.

Relative to the typical library study the evaluation efforts of the Project were unique for two reasons. First, an outside research organization was employed to guide the collection and interpretation of evaluative information during both Phases II and III of the Project. Secondly, contrary to many developmental efforts, the Project _actually did_ evaluate the six experimental programs developed during the Project. Furthermore, the findings of these evaluations have been and are herein reported.

Many highly competent studies have been performed solely by members of a particular profession. However, added credibility often can be added to such studies when they are done with the assistance of an outside organization. Organizations such as the Human Resources Research Organization are full-time research and development agencies which exist in part to

---

[18]SLMP, _Behavioral Requirements Analysis Checklist_, op. cit.

72 Final Assessment

help others conduct and evaluate projects. Such organizations must know how to employ the latest evaluative techniques; how to identify appropriate data to collect; how to collect, process, analyze and interpret data. When examining one's profession and its educational programs there are many advantages to working cooperatively with an outside organization. Sometimes they may insist on highlighting data which the profession might wish to ignore. On the other hand, such organizations also have the responsibility for identifying those strong points of a profession which the profession may tend to overlook.

Through the use of an outside evaluator the latest methods for obtaining field feedback information were employed, and an "arms-length" evaluation of the Project was accomplished. This evaluation effort, in addition to identifying some interesting similarities between graduates of the various programs, demonstrated the usefulness of the survey procedures employed during Phase III. Also, improved procedures (see Chapter 5) were developed for conducting a survey of program graduates.

It is important to note that throughout the Project program evaluation was employed in a positive sense. That is, an attempt was made to identify program strengths and weaknesses so that the weaknesses could be corrected. As with any experimental program development effort, all programs had their successes and failures. However, the most successful features were that they did employ self-evaluative procedures, they did identify and report on their successes and failures, and they did modify their programs on the basis of evaluative information.

Finally, in agreeing to participate in the School Library Manpower Project the six experimental programs committed themselves to exposure at the national level. They knew their programs would be evaluated and publicized. They agreed to make the contents and characteristics of their programs known to others, knowing full well that in so doing they might expose the program staff, their departments and even their institutions to considerable criticism. Their courage in "going public" must be admired. Developing programs in public view is a harrowing experience. However, the criticisms received can help improve the programs. When finally developed, the programs are difficult for the profession to ignore and they do stand as examples which others can emulate.

Educational Impact for the Profession

During the six years of the Project numerous changes occurred in the school library media profession. Some of these changes would have occurred regardless of the existence of this Project. However, it seems fair to conclude that the Project did have a considerable impact on the profession. In many instances the nature of this impact can be readily identified. In other instances the Project seems to have had a catalytic effect on certain activities within the profession.

It is reasonable to assert that the Project did raise the stature of school library media education programs. Certainly at the institutions

Final Assessment 73

where the six experimental programs were developed, both faculty and students became more aware of the unique features of a program in school library media education. The importance of such programs and the important role which school library media personnel can play in the educational setting should now be much more firmly established in the minds of educators. Through publicity efforts, presentations at professional meetings, workshops, a specially developed film, and reports considerable visibility was given to the school library media profession. The impact of the Project's publicity efforts are difficult to measure. However, responses to articles, workshops and queries within and outside of the profession makes one think that many issues were in some way refined and/or accentuated or developed as a result of the publicity process employed by the Project.

At various points throughout the Project guidance material was developed which should be of continuing use to the profession. Occupational definitions for professional and technician-level jobs were developed, new educational programs were developed, procedures for evaluating programs and for surveying program graduates were developed. A variety of information dissemination activities and tools were developed which should continue to be useful in publicizing and promoting the activities of the school library media profession.

A particularly important outcome of the Project was its impact on efforts in some states to revise their certification guidelines for school library media educational programs. As a result of the Project some states began thinking about revising their certification guidelines. Sometimes staff members of the experimental programs were members of the committee established to work on these revisions. The models and materials developed during the Project provided suggestions as to how state certification programs for school library media educational programs should be modified.

The job analysis material developed during Phase I of the Project provided prime resource material for the development of improved standards for the profession. This task analysis effort was instrumental in bringing into focus the various technical and professional activities performed within the profession. Also, this activity helped identify the skills and knowledges which should be covered at various educational levels within the profession. This resulted in the six educational models developed during Phase II of the Project, models which represented BA-level education, MA-level education, and education at the sixth year level.

One of the more influential products stemming from the Project was the Behavioral Requirements Analysis Checklist.[19] This checklist provides a structured view of the job activities of those members of the profession who work in the K-12 educational setting. For the first time one can document the wide variety of skills, knowledges, functions, and tasks which are encompassed by the profession. The survey procedures developed in conjunction with the BRAC document provide a means for the profession to continually monitor its educational programs. The importance of evaluative

---

[19]SLMP, Behavioral Requirements Analysis Checklist, op. cit.

procedures developed during the Project and how to employ them were the topics of three workshops provided for the profession during Phase III of the Project. Utilization of these procedures should continue to be the focus of future discussions and professional association activities and studies.

Many features of the Project demonstrated the interdisciplinary nature of jobs in the school library media profession. The Project also called attention to the interpersonal aspects of the profession. The seven competency areas identified during Phase I illustrated the interpersonal nature of job positions in the school library media profession, and also the need for possessing a wide range of skills and knowledges to function properly in the profession. Many features of the Project demonstrated the broad content base upon which the profession rests. Finally, the interview data obtained during Phase III of the project indicated that school administrators now more fully recognize the desireability of hiring graduates of broad based school library media education programs as an essential leading member of any K-12 educational team.

Unresolved Issues

The work of the School Library Manpower Project raised a number of questions which should be vigorously addressed in future years. One of the more important of these concerns the relationship which should exist between undergraduate and graduate programs of school library media education. As a result of this Project there now is evidence which suggests that at the first professional entry level, graduates of an undergraduate program can successfully compete with graduates of a MA-level program. Most graduates of both the BA-level and MA-level experimental programs were employed at the school level and were most apt to be employed in an elementary or secondary school. With respect to performance on the job and assigned duties, graduates of BA and MA-level programs were very similar. Indeed, they had to be similar since they held essentially the same type of job position. This raises the question of what the relationship should be between BA and MA-level programs. It seems likely that in future years an attempt should be made to make MA-level programs responsible for a higher level of professional education and to establish as a prerequisite to them the requirement for the attainment of basic skills and knowledges at the undergraduate level.

At present there are approximately three hundred undergraduate programs in school library media education. Their quality varies widely and not much thought has been given to the establishment of uniform prerequisites for these programs. Assuming that improved BA-level programs will continue to be developed in the future, there will be an increased need to specify and monitor undergraduate program prerequisites. Also, of course, there will be a need to revise the prerequisites to graduate programs. Efforts to define and adjust program prerequisites will raise many issues which the profession must now begin to resolve if they aspire to offer viable occupationally relevant programs.

Can a fully credentialized person be produced in a one-year graduate program? The Project was not able to provide a definitive answer to this question. But, based on Project findings it seems doubtful that this can be accomplished. Currently many MA programs in school library media education cover subjects which could be covered at the BA-level. Moreover, because of time limitations many MA-level programs contain a number of survey courses; the programs are forced to sacrifice depth for breadth of coverage. Moreover, assuming the importance of a strong internship program, not a great deal of fieldwork can be accomplished during a one-year program which also has to cover all of the content area associated with the profession. It would seem, therefore, that MA-programs will either have to become two years in length, or, they will have to be articulated with improved undergraduate programs. In one manner or another, more time must be provided to cover the wide variety of subject matter with which school library media personnel must be familiar. If undergraduate programs become more uniform and quality conscious, the prerequisites to MA-level programs can be raised. It may then be possible for MA-level programs to be upgraded. In particular they may be able to cover a variety of subjects in depth and still maintain their one year length.

As part of this Project the University of Denver developed a six-year program. During the first two years of that program it was possible to recruit a suitable number of students. During the third year, however, only one student could be recruited. This raises once more the question of whether or not a six-year program can remain a viable program. At the present there is no particular incentive for a person to attend a six-year program. Advancement in salary or stature seldom depends on such attendance. Obtaining funds to support students of such programs is a problem, particularly since many of the students have families to support. Finally, no degree is associated with such programs and therefore, the academic accomplishment of attending such a program usually is not recognized in the marketplace. Quite possibly there is a need for one or two six-year level programs throughout the country. However, unless clear professional gains can be obtained from attending such programs the need for such programs is doubtful.

One of the ways in which an educational program can be made more occupationally relevant is by incorporating a fieldwork component within the program. Internships, practicums, and other fieldwork experiences were part of all six experimental programs. This Project clearly demonstrated the validity of such field experiences. Graduates and faculty alike thought that these aspects of their programs were most effective and useful.

Fieldwork components clearly convey the relevancy of a program's content. However, such experiences are costly and at times face obstacles to implementation. As support from Project or institutional funds decreased, the Program Directors became concerned about their ability to obtain the funds and time to operate their fieldwork components, <u>in spite of their proven effectiveness</u>. Also, although individuals in the profession were eager and willing to support interns in the field, union problems arose in some instances. Such problems could block widespread adoption of programs which stress fieldwork. The profession should take the lead in attempting to resolve issues which otherwise might prevent the widespread adoption of internship programs.

Further Research

As a sequel to this Project there are a number of research projects which could be conducted in future years. It would be useful to do a longitudinal study of the graduates of the six experimental programs to determine what happened to them professionally after five years and ten years in the field. On the basis of job activities after one or two years on the job, there seems to be no significant difference between the graduates of MA-level and BA-level programs. Possibly differences would begin to appear after a five or ten year span of time. Is it possible that MA graduates eventually secure better jobs? Do they advance more rapidly professionally? Are they more apt to take up teaching positions? Are they more apt to become the leaders in the profession? The Mankato program, for example, exposed its students to a variety of professional activities. As a result of this, is it possible that in future years graduates of that program will become more actively involved in professional activities than graduates of other programs?

As of December 1974, all six experimental programs were still in existence. Four had survived quite well and probably will become even stronger. The Mankato program was not presented during its third year but now appears on the way to becoming firmly established within the institution. The Denver program might not survive because of limited numbers of enrollees. It would be useful to examine, five years hence, the status of the six programs and to identify what they had to do to survive and what they did to improve themselves.

The <u>Behavioral Requirements Analysis Checklist</u> is one of the major products of the Project. Such a checklist is outdated in some respects at the time of its initial publication. Therefore, it should be periodically updated and revised by members of the profession. Suggestions for updating BRAC are on file with the American Association of School Librarians, a division of the American Library Association.

Finally, the Project has provided a massive data bank which can be used in future studies. The task analysis data obtained during Phase I, when compared with new task analysis data, can be used to identify shifts in job requirements. The survey data collected during Phase III provides the baseline data for any future follow-up of graduates of the experimental programs. Access to this data bank can be obtained by contacting the Office of Research of the American Library Association.

In concluding this report one should remember that the School Library Manpower Project set out to produce changes in the profession. It has done that, but at a considerable cost in time and effort. The development of new educational programs is a slow, time-consuming, and often painful process. But it can be done and it is worth doing.

APPENDICES

CONTENTS

A BRAC Survey Questionnaires

    1. BRAC Survey Questionnaire for the DIRECTOR and the STAFF of the School Library Media Education Program ... 78

    2. BRAC Survey Questionnaire for the School Library Media SUPERVISOR ... 79

    3. BRAC Survey Questionnaire for the STUDENT in the School Library Media Education Program ... 80

B Interview Questionnaires and Summaries

    1. Interview Questionnaire: Experimental Program Graduates ... 81

    2. Interview Questionnaire: Supervisor ... 83

    3. Interview Summaries: MA-Level Program Graduates ... 85

    4. Interview Summaries: Supervisors of MA-Level Program Graduates ... 91

C Sample Page from Printout of Program Graduate BRAC Questionnaire Data ... 95

D Summary of BRAC Questionnaire Graduate Responses by Task and by Program Level ... 96

E Summary of BRAC Questionnaire Graduate Responses by Competency Area and Function ... 117

F Phase III Program Status Reports

    1. Phase III Summative Evaluation: Items to Cover in Status Report ... 120

    2. Arizona State University: 1974 Status Report ... 123

    3. Auburn University: 1974 Status Report ... 131

    4. Mankato State College: 1974 Status Report ... 139

    5. Millersville State College: 1974 Status Report ... 143

    6. University of Denver: 1974 Status Report ... 153

    7. University of Michigan: 1974 Status Report ... 165

G Revised BRAC Survey Questionnaires

    1. Graduate Questionnaire ... 180
    2. Supervisor Questionnaire ... 181
    3. Program Director Questionnaire ... 182
    4. Student Questionnaire ... 183

Appendix A-1

BRAC Survey Questionnaire for the DIRECTOR and the STAFF of the School Library Media Education Program

A. Is this task covered in your program?

   0 - No
   1 - In part
   2 - Yes

B. At the time of graduation, what would you judge the capability of a typical student to be on this task?

   0 - Unsatisfactory (Student would require constant guidance to perform this task).
   1 - Below Average (Student would require fairly close guidance to perform this task).
   2 - Average (Student should perform this task adequately with only some general supervision).
   3 - Above Average (Student should perform this task competently without any supervision).
   4 - Excellent (Student should be expert at performing this task).

C. Would you judge this to be an appropriate task for a professionally educated school library media specialist to perform?

   0 - Inappropriate (Task should be performed by aides or persons other than a professionally educated school library media specialist).
   1 - Somewhat Inappropriate (Although this is not a task for professionally educated school library media personnel, they would have to do this under certain circumstances).
   2 - Appropriate (Although this is a proper task for professional school library media personnel, it can at times be performed by other professionals).
   3 - Highly Appropriate (This is a task which should be performed by professionally educated school library media specialists).

D. Is this task covered in your program as a knowledge? (Does the student read about it, talk about it, hear about it, etc.?)

   0 - No
   1 - Yes, slight coverage, slight emphasis
   2 - Yes, fairly thorough coverage
   3 - Yes, extensive coverage, heavily emphasized

E. Is this task covered in your program as a skill? (Does student practice this task in class, practicums, internship?)

   0 - No
   1 - Yes, minimum amount of practice, portions of task are practiced.
   2 - Yes, learning to accomplish this task is emphasized, considerable practice is required.
   3 - Yes, extensive practice, student must know how to do this task.

Appendix A-2   79

BRAC Survey Questionnaire for the School Library Media SUPERVISOR

A. You have under your supervision a recent graduate of a school library media education program. To the best of your knowledge, how frequently does this person perform this task in his/her job?

   0 - Never (Person does not perform this task).
   1 - Annually (Person does this once a year).
   2 - Occasionally (Person does this as required but less often than monthly).
   3 - Monthly (Person performs this task at least once, but less than four times a month on the average).
   4 - Weekly (Person performs this task at least once, but less than five times a week on the average).
   5 - Daily (Person performs this task at least once each day on the average).

B. As best you can recall, how would you judge this person's capability to perform this task when he/she began working for you following his/her graduation?

   0 - Unsatisfactory (Person needed constant guidance to perform this task).
   1 - Below Average (Person needed fairly close guidance to perform this task).
   2 - Average (Person could perform this task adequately with only some general supervision).
   3 - Above Average (Person could perform this task completely without any supervision).
   4 - Excellent (Person was expert at performing this task).
   5 - Unknown (I did not observe this person perform this task at that time and cannot estimate his/her capability to perform it).

C. How would you judge the importance of this task relative to the other tasks performed by this person?

   0 - Minor Importance (Little importance, if any).
   1 - Less Than Average Importance.
   2 - Average Importance.
   3 - More Than Average Importance.
   4 - Major Importance (One of the most important tasks in the job).

D. Would you judge this task an appropriate task for a professionally educated school library media specialist to perform?

   0 - Inappropriate (Task should be performed by aides or persons other than a professionally educated school library media specialist).
   1 - Somewhat Inappropriate (Although this is not a task for professionally educated school library media personnel, they would have to do this under certain conditions).
   2 - Somewhat Appropriate (Although this is a proper task for professional school library media personnel, it can at times be performed by the professionals or by aides).
   3 - Highly Appropriate (This is a task which should be performed by professionally educated school library media specialists).

E. Do you consider this to be a task which a recent graduate of a school library media education program should be able to perform well almost immediately after assuming the job?

   0 - No (Can learn on the job, of minor importance).
   1 - No (But should be familiar with task).
   2 - Yes (Should possess minimally acceptable skills & knowledges and be prepared to acquire other skills/knowledges on the job or through CE).
   3 - Yes (Should possess completely acceptable professional skills and knowledges).

Appendix A-3

BRAC Survey Questionnaire for the STUDENT in the School Library Media Education Program

A. Was this task covered in your program?

0 – No
1 – No, but I learned it elsewhere
2 – In part
3 – Yes

B. How would you judge your present capability to perform this task?

0 – Unsatisfactory (I would need constant guidance to perform this task).
1 – Below Average (I would need fairly close guidance to perform this task).
2 – Average (I can perform this task adequately with only some general supervision).
3 – Above Average (I can perform this task competently without any supervision).
4 – Excellent (I am expert at performing this task).

C. How appropriate do you think this task will be to your job after you graduate as a professional school library media specialist?

0 – Inappropriate (Task should be performed by aides or persons other than a professionally educated school library media specialist).
1 – Somewhat Inappropriate (Although this is not a task for professionally educated school library media personnel it is all right to perform it on occasion).
2 – Somewhat Appropriate (Although this is a proper task for professional school library media personnel, it can at times be performed by other professionals or by aides).
3 – Highly Appropriate (This is a task which should be performed by professionally educated school library media specialists).

D. Was this task covered in your program as a knowledge? (Did you read about it, talk about it, hear about it, etc?).

0 – No
1 – Yes, slight coverage, slight emphasis.
2 – Yes, fairly thorough coverage.
3 – Yes, extensive coverage, heavily emphasized.

E. Was this task covered in your program as a skill? (Did you practice this task in class, practicums, internships?).

0 – No.
1 – Yes, minimum amount of practice, portions of task were practiced.
2 – Yes, obtaining skill at this task was emphasized, practice was required.
3 – Yes, extensive practice was required on this task.

Appendix B-1

SCHOOL LIBRARY MANPOWER PROJECT
PHASE III
EVALUATION STUDY

Interview Questionnaire
Experimental Program Graduates

The following questions will be utilized during the Phase III interview activities as a follow-up to the written responses made on the Behavioral Requirements Analysis Checklist response form.

A. Position related
    1. Level -
    2. Position title -
    3. Supervisor title -
    4. Kind of community -
    5. Number of students -
    6. Number and kind of media center staff -
    7. Are there district support services?   What?
    8. Who and what type of supervision?
    9. Are you full-time in the media center?
       What other responsibilities?
    10. Do you think you have sophisticated services or program in school or district?

B. Placement related
    1. Did you have a choice of positions?
    2. How did you hear about openings?
    3. Were you offered positions you did not take? If so - why not?
    4. What was primary reason for accepting the position you have?
    5. Do you think type of experimental program training was helpful in finding position?
    6. Do you think you have had an impact in the school?
    7. How do you relate this impact to your training?

C. BRAC related
    1. What problems did you have in responding to the BRAC questions?
    2. What suggestions do you have for improving the BRAC as a field feedback instrument?

3. Of what benefit was the completion of the BRAC to you?

4. Was your job adequately covered in the BRAC task statements? If not - what additional task statements would you add?

D. Work related

1. Are you supervised in any of your activities? Which ones? By whom?

2. Do you supervise others? Who? For what activities?

3. If you are only professional staff in the center with little supervision do you find this a handicap? How? Did your training prepare you for this?

4. For those BRAC activities which were never performed - why were they not?

5. Are there things you wanted to do but couldn't? If so - what were the barriers?

E. Program related

1. Which instructional practices in the experimental program do you find most useful to you in your present position?

2. Which aspects of the experimental program do you think should be modified or dropped? Why?

3. What instruction do you feel you should have had? Why?

4. Why didn't you have this instruction?

5. What two features did you like best in the experimental program? Why do you feel this way?

6. What two features did you like least in the experimental program? Why do you feel this way?

Appendix B-2

SCHOOL LIBRARY MANPOWER PROJECT
PHASE III
EVALUATION STUDY

Interview Questionnaire
Supervisor

The following questions will be utilized during the Phase III interview activities as a follow-up to the written responses made on the Behavioral Requirements Analysis Checklist response form.

A. Position related

1. Are there district support services?   What?

2. Do you think you have sophisticated services or programs in the district?

3. Are all media centers professionally staffed? If not - how are they staffed?

4. Do you employ library technical assistants? On what basis?

5. What is the total number of schools in the district?

B. Placement related

1. Did you have specific criteria in mind for the position?

2. How did you find this person?

3. Why did you hire this person?

4. Has this person come up to your expectations? If not - why not?

5. Can you give me two examples where person was successful?

6. Can you give me any examples where person had problems?

7. Did this person have any impact upon the schools since being employed?

C. BRAC related

1. What problems did you have in responding to the BRAC questions?

2. What suggestions do you have for improving the BRAC as a field feedback instrument?

3. Of what benefit was the completion of the BRAC to you?

4. Was the position of the person you supervise adequately covered in the BRAC statements? If not - what additional statements would you add?

Appendix B-2

D. Work related
   1. What is the extent of supervision for this position?
   2. What other positions do you supervise?
   3. For those BRAC activities which were never performed – why were they not?
   4. Are there things you expected this person to do which were not being done? If so – give examples.

E. Program related
   1. In relation to the education of this person – what did you expect that you didn't find?
   2. Can you name two or three skills or knowledges in which person is well prepared?
   3. Can you name two or three areas in which you feel more instruction is needed?
   4. What is your opinion of the current educational programs in your profession? Some good – some bad? Why do you feel this way?

Appendix B-3   85

Interview Summaries:
MA-Level Program Graduates

Arizona State University (2nd year only)

The majority of all Arizona State University program graduates interviewed were employed in positions in elementary schools. The titles of their positions varied from librarian to media specialist. More than half the graduates identified their building principals as their immediate supervisor. Most of the graduates were employed in schools with 500 to 1,000 students in middle class, resort, suburban communities. Half of the graduates interviewed worked in schools where there were two or more professionals in the media center. All graduates had some kind of support through paid clerical or volunteer mothers and/or student assistants. Half of the graduates were employed in districts which provided district level support. All graduates were able to avail themselves of services from intermediate units. Less than half the graduates had services of centralized processing and half the graduates had access to centralized film libraries and audiovisual software. All but one graduate were employed full-time and most had no additional responsibilities outside the scope of the media programs. Most graduates did not think their media programs were sophisticated.

Half of the graduates had a choice of position. Less than half of the graduates used the college placement bureau to identify vacancies. None of the graduates was offered positions they did not take. The primary reason given for accepting the position varied, but geographical location and the challenge of the position were the most mentioned. All graduates felt that their experimental program was helpful to them in getting their positions. Most graduates felt they had made an impact on the school. They based their responses on positive feedback from students and teachers on how the media center had changed from the former traditional center. The graduates related this impact to their training program because of attitudes instilled in them through a unified media program.

The graduates identified fieldwork as the most valuable instruction they had. A few graduates gave high value to the course in materials for children. Graduates also identified observation, individual projects and seminars as useful. A few graduates offered suggestions on what should be modified or dropped. Some were concerned with the overlap of content and some felt their courses could have been more individualized or taught more creatively. One graduate suggested that the use of mini courses be explored for some mechanical skill competencies. Half of the graduates wanted more instruction on the selection and repair of audiovisual equipment. A few graduates wanted more instruction on personnel management and several wanted to get into internship practice in the field center earlier in the program. The reasons why graduates did not have this instruction varied. Some felt the program needed more equipment, some felt that instruction in the above areas was not required and others felt these courses were not included as a part of the experimental program. The graduates had a variety of responses as to what they liked best about their media education program. Many identified their professors, personal counseling sessions, and small group discussions. The majority liked their internship program as well as an opportunity for observation and individual projects. Most graduates felt that the program did not seem well planned the first part of the year and that many instructional objectives and some materials were not ready for them.

Auburn University (1st and 2nd years)

The majority of all graduates from the Auburn University experimental program accepted positions in secondary schools. A few graduates were employed in elementary media centers and other graduates accepted media positions in higher education programs. Their job titles varied from media specialist to librarian to teacher-librarian. Almost all graduates identified their building principal as their immediate supervisor. None of them considered that they had very close supervision from a district or system coordinator.

The majority of the graduates were employed in a school whose enrollment was between 500 and 1,000 students. The majority of these schools were in middle class, semi-urban communities. Almost all of the graduates were employed in media centers as the sole professional and the majority of graduates did have some type of clerical support. All graduates were employed full-time and few had assigned responsibilities outside the scope of the media program. Over half of the graduates were employed in districts which provided district level media services to the building media centers. For the most part, these services were in the nature of film libraries and media production services. Less than half of the district centers provided centralized processing services. The majority of the graduates believed that their media programs and services were not sophisticated either at the building or district level. However, a few graduates did feel their media programs were relatively sophisticated for their area.

About half the graduates had a choice of more than one position. Due to the nature of the experimental program about one third of the graduates returned to the position they held prior to entering the experimental program. Few of the graduates indicated they used the university placement bureau to identify position vacancies. The primary reason for accepting a position was the geographical location or area. Almost half the graduates indicated this reason for their choice of position. The prior knowledge of a school's administrator, and the creative opportunity and challenge to establish a new media program were reasons cited by other graduates for accepting a position offer. Though the graduates for the most part did not use the university placement office, the majority of graduates believed the experimental program was helpful to them in finding employment. Several graduates cited

Appendix B-3   87

the school district's close relationship with the experimental program as a major reason why the school districts knew of the graduate's competencies.

The majority of graduates believed that they had made an impact on the school since taking the position. The development of a more informal, helpful media program for students, organization of the collection for better access, increased use of media and the achievement of a more media conscious attitude were the reasons most cited for causing this impact to be felt. The majority of graduates felt this impact was directly related to their media education program as the program stressed flexibility and emphasized a human approach to learning and media.

The fieldwork component, flexibility and program individualization of the experimental program were cited most frequently by the majority of the graduates as the most useful instructional practices. Other features of the experimental program favored by the graduates were program staff competency and the informal one-to-one communication. The majority of the graduates did not identify any part of the program which should be modified or dropped. A few graduates, however, did indicate that more orientation and guidance to the experimental program would have been helpful. A few graduates also felt more emphasis should be given to reality. While the majority of the graduates were satisfied with the instruction they received, some did cite the need for longer term practicums, case study approaches and more depth in graphics, media utilization and production. A few graduates indicated more emphasis on cataloging and curriculum development. The graduates primarily cited lack of time as the reason they did not receive this instruction, though some graduates believed the course was not offered to them or they did not realize until they started working that they would need more background in a particular area.

The Auburn graduates' responses had no distinct pattern for what they liked least about the experimental program. Such items as writing behavioral objectives, computer course work, research course work and the lack of opportunities to develop instructional materials as a team with other curriculum specialists were noted by the graduates. A few students indicated that it was difficult at first to get used to the amount of freedom and flexibility. Some students felt there was not enough time to cover all 13 global objectives, and suggested a need for more coordination among courses to remove overlap of content.

Mankato State College (1st and 2nd years)

The majority of all graduates from the Mankato State College experimental program found positions in public schools, with an equal number serving in elementary and secondary levels. A few graduates were employed in media positions in higher education. The titles of their positions varied, but all graduates used the descriptor "media" in their titles. Most positions were entitled either media specialist or media generalist. The majority of the graduates worked in a district where there was a district level media supervisor, though most graduates identified their building principal as their immediate supervisor.

Almost all graduates were employed in middle class, suburban or semi-urban school districts. The majority of schools had enrollments between 500 and 1,000 students. In these schools all the graduates worked as the only professional in the media center. In the few positions graduates held in schools whose enrollments were over 1,000, the graduate was not the sole professional on the media center staff. All graduates, regardless of the size of the school or media program had some degree of clerical support, either paid or volunteer. All graduates employed in school districts received media support services from the district level. For the most part the district level provided centralized book processing services. A few districts did provide a film library and media production services to the building level media centers. The majority of the graduates felt their media programs, either at the building or district level, were not very sophisticated.

The majority of graduates had a choice of positions ranging from one to three job offers. The graduates learned about position vacancies primarily through the college placement bureau, through their internship assignments to a particular school district, or by attendance at national professional conferences. Only two graduates chose their position because of the geogaphical location. The majority of graduates chose their position because they knew the school program from their internship assignment and liked the challenge the position offered or they liked the idea of working in an established media program their first year. The fact that a school district provided district level services and supervision was also a deciding factor for choosing a position for all graduates. The majority of graduates believed their experimental program was helpful to them in getting the position. Almost all graduates felt they had made an impact on the school during their first year, citing increased use of media and a greater flexibility on the part of teachers and administrators to incorporate media into their teaching methods and curriculum. The majority of graduates felt their training program gave them the capability to be flexible in coping with a changing environment. They believed their knowledge of curriculum materials and media production skills helped them to bring an enthusiasm and new image to the school in changing the program from a traditional library to an open media center concept. The graduates expressed a self-confidence in the use and production of media. They believed they were open to new ideas and were able to articulate the media philosophy with assurance.

All graduates identified the open, free and relaxed atmosphere of their media education program and the opportunity for visitations and observation as the most valuable instructional practices. There was little agreement from the graduates on what aspects of their training program should be modified or dropped. Graduates' responses to this query reflected strong personal reactions related to their own individual background and feelings. Only a few graduates felt nothing should be modified or deleted from the program. Personal background and differences were also reflected in their responses to what aspects of the program they felt should be strengthened. Some graduates expressed the need for more training in media production, while others wanted more background in curriculum development, facilities and techniques for developing in-service programs.

The Mankato graduates were in agreement on what features they liked best in their media education program. Cited most frequently were attendance at professional conferences, school visitations, field observations and internship. The graduates also rated media production work and the block structure as favorable aspects. The graduates did not agree on what aspects of the program they liked least. A few graduates thought the program was too idealistic. Some graduates expressed a displeasure with the encounter sessions and with the education courses. Again, the individual backgrounds and personalities of the graduates were greatly reflected in these responses, but the general response from the graduates indicated they were very satisfied with their media education program.

University of Michigan (1st and 2nd years)

The majority of all graduates from the University of Michigan experimental program were employed in elementary schools. Most of their position titles were media specialist. More than half the graduates identified their building principal as supervisor, though the majority of the schools in which they worked were in districts which had a district level library supervisor. The majority of graduates were employed in small urban, middle class communities. The schools where most of the graduates were employed had enrollments between 500 - 1,000 students.

The majority of the graduates were employed as the sole professional on the media center staff. Nearly all the graduates had some type of paid clerical support in addition to student assistants. The majority of the graduates were employed in districts where the district or intermediate units provided media support services to the building media centers. This type of service was primarily central processing, film libraries and audiovisual production services. All graduates were employed full-time in their positions and none of them was assigned responsibilities outside the scope of the media program. Most of the graduates did not feel their media programs were sophisticated. The majority of the graduates indicated they did have a choice of positions. A few graduates learned of a position vacancy through direct personal contact with a school district, but the majority of the graduates stated they used the university placement bureau to identify position vacancies. The geographical location and the challenge of a position were most cited as reasons for taking a position. Knowledge of a school's curriculum or the principal's philosophy were also determining factors in taking a position. Almost all the graduates believed their experimental program was helpful in finding a position.

Nearly all graduates stated they had made an impact on the school during their first year. The graduates supported this statement most often by mentioning positive feedback from students, teachers and administrators who spoke

Appendix B-3

of the graduates' ability to change the traditional library to a media center. A number of graduates cited their attitude and the increased involvement with students and teachers as reasons they believed this impact had been made. For the most part the graduates believed they had been given a good background in media philosophy, media production, administration and organization. The majority of the graduates felt their training program stressed utilization of media, involvement of staff, and a positive philosophy to affect change of attitude and leadership skills.

All graduates identified their internship experience as the instructional practice most useful to them. Many graduates further identified field trips, media production courses, and the close relationship with the experimental program faculty as being very helpful. Other helpful practices or content areas identified by some students were experiences in developing objectives, education courses, and the emphasis given to media utilization.

Many of the graduates were in agreement on what they would like to see modified in the experimental program. They wanted to spend more time in media production, they desired an emphasis in the reference, cataloging and classification courses toward a school environment, and they also expressed a desire to have the opportunity for more flexibility to choose their own program. Several graduates wanted more time for special interest courses. While some graduates expressed a concern for a content overload, others wanted shorter sessions in more depth. A number of graduates felt the approach to some content was too idealistic and they would like to have had more practical application to theory based on realistic situations. The time constraints in fulfilling the internship experience was a concern for many graduates.

The graduates were in almost total agreement as to the features they liked best in their media education program. The internship, fellowship with students and the relationships with faculty were cited most. Almost all of the graduates cited the high degree of professionalism and enthusiasm of the program faculty. Other favorite program features mentioned by many students were the curriculum materials course taught with a total media point of view, the evaluation sessions, media and production courses, and the opportunity to take courses in the school of education.

Over half of the graduates identified the reference course and cataloging and classification course as features they liked least, primarily because these courses were taught with emphasis on the public and university library field. Some students believed the classes were too traditionally structured and could have employed better use of media in instruction. Some graduates were concerned with the lack of realism and flexibility of the program. All graduates, even with time pressures, felt their media education program was valuable to them.

Appendix B-4

Interview Summaries: Supervisors of MA-Level Program Graduates

Auburn University (1st and 2nd years)

The majority of interviewed supervisors of the Auburn University program graduates had a library background and served as heads of media centers or district level library coordinators. A few direct supervisors interviewed were building level principals. The majority of the supervisors were employed in districts which provided district level services to the building media center. The nature of these services were professional libraries, film libraries and in a few instances media production. Half the districts did employ media technicians at the district centers. The majority of the supervisors stated the type of media services provided to the schools was unsophisticated. The size of the school districts varied from one school district to the largest with sixty-four schools.

All supervisors stated they had specific criteria in mind when interviewing candidates to fill a vacancy in a media position. For the most part they were looking for a candidate with a total media background, but beyond this competency they sought a candidate who could work effectively with students and teachers. The supervisors were looking for someone who could take the initiative to create new excitement in the media program and who was capable of removing barriers of rigid structure. Few supervisors used the university placement bureau to locate candidates. Most stated they identified the candidate because of their knowledge of the Auburn University experimental program, or because the candidate had done intern work in the school district.

All supervisors stated that the graduates had come up to their expectations, although some limitations were mentioned. Evidence of this success was reflected in the graduates' rapport with students and teachers and their ability to integrate the total media concept into the school program. A few supervisors felt the graduates needed to be more aggressive and self-sufficient. All supervisors agreed that the graduates had made a positive impact upon the school through the leadership role played.

Most of the supervisors saw no deficiency in the graduates' media education program. A few supervisors did state the graduates could profit from more depth in cataloging skills. The supervisors believed the graduates were given a good background in organization and administration and were well prepared in the media field. For the most part the supervisors were impressed with the graduates' broad media background and their ability to effect positive relationships with students and teachers.

The supervisors' opinions on the current status of media education programs varied, but they did agree that the programs aren't broad enough, nor do they reflect a balance of content. The supervisors felt that efforts to individualize the programs were necessary, but a few were concerned that education may become so involved in experimentation it will ignore and/or omit what was good in a traditional program. All supervisors did see a trend in the school media program moving to the center of the instructional program.

Mankato State College (1st and 2nd years)

More than half of the interviewed supervisors of the graduates of the Mankato State College experimental program were district level school library supervisors or coordinators. Three of the supervisors who were interviewed were building principals. All districts where supervisors were interviewed provided some type of district level media service to the building media centers. The type of service provided was primarily a district film library and professional library collection. Only one district provided centralized processing services to the building level centers. More than half of the supervisors believed the building media centers provided a relatively sophisticated program. All media centers in all school districts were staffed with media professionals, though a few schools in some districts did have media specialists serving two or more schools. The district media centers also were staffed with at least one technical assistant. The size of the school districts ranged from eight schools to a high of forty schools.

All supervisors had specific job criteria in mind when hiring media specialists to fill positions. All districts were looking for candidates with a strong media background and a good knowledge of the curriculum. The districts were looking for media specialists who could develop good relationships with students and teachers and who were adaptable and able to present a new image to the traditional library program. Only one supervisor indicated a desire for a media specialist to have prior classroom teaching experience. Many of the supervisors identified the candidate for a position through the candidate internship assignment within the district. The majority of supervisors indicated they also used college placement bureaus to identify possible candidates. All supervisors agreed that the graduates had come up to their expectation of performance during the first year. Examples of the success of the graduates varied from district to district, but for the most part the supervisors cited increased student and teacher use of the media center and resources.

There was little agreement on the part of the supervisors in identifying the main problems the graduates had the first year on the job. Some supervisors cited inexperience as the main cause for any of the graduates' problems. Some graduates had problems in accepting their own limitations and recognizing priorities. Further inquiry revealed that some supervisors agreed that if there were any difficulties, they were: a lack of time or problems of the school and not of the media specialist. All supervisors agreed the graduates had made an impact upon the school.

The majority of supervisors agreed that the Mankato media education program provided the graduates with the competencies needed on the job.

Appendix B-4   93

The graduates had the ability to work well with students and teachers and to apply a knowledge of media to the curriculum. One supervisor, only, stated that while the graduate had an excellent theory and philosophy of media, the graduate could profit with more indepth knowledge of children's literature and media management.

The supervisors were quite explicit in their opinion of the current status of media education programs. They suggested more emphasis on management, administration and human relationships. They felt there was an over emphasis on non-print media and called for a balance of emphasis to all media in the education program. They agreed there should be emphasis placed on theory and philosophy and more time for in-program students to know materials. For the most part the supervisors felt the profession needs depth and to get this depth the education program may require more than a year or at least a greater emphasis on continuing education.

University of Michigan (1st and 2nd years)

All interviewed supervisors of graduates of the University of Michigan experimental program were employed as district level library media coordinators in school districts which provided centralized services to the building media center. The majority of them did not believe their media programs, either at the building or district level, were sophisticated. None of the districts employed technical assistants and only two-thirds of the districts had professional media specialists serving full time in all media centers. The sizes of the school districts were small with an average of nine schools.

All supervisors interviewed had specific criteria in mind for candidates for position openings. They were looking for media specialists with a broad media background. The majority of supervisors identified the candidate through the school district's personnel office and not through university placement bureaus. All supervisors agreed that the graduates of the University of Michigan program had come up to their expectations the first year on the job and were a positive asset to the school's total program. They cited increased use of the media center, the graduate's ability to work with students and teachers, and the creativity and enthusiasm of the graduates. All supervisors stated the graduates were especially good at selecting materials and generating action on the part of teachers to use the resources of the media center. All supervisors agreed that the graduates had made an impact upon the school in changing the image of the media centers and the attitudes of faculty in using the media center.

For the most part the supervisors could not identify any skills or competencies that were lacking in the graduates' training program. They believed the graduates were well trained in media and reference sources and had acquired abilities to develop excellent rapport with students and teachers. The majority of the graduates did not have to apply cataloging and classification skills extensively due to district-wide processing services, however, some supervisors stated that the graduates could have profited from more training in cataloging and technical skills.

The supervisors' opinions of the current status of media education programs was for the most part favorable, though some did suggest that media education programs need to teach students how to cope with reality. They believed the profession is doing a better job than it did ten years ago in its ability to identify the role of the media specialist. Some supervisors felt that more media education emphasis should be put on media program planning and program development. Media education programs need to stress closer relationship with education and curriculum fields. The majority of supervisors believed that it will be increasingly necessary in the future to provide continuing education programs to keep up with trends and changes as they effect the role of the media specialist.

JULY 15, 1974 GRADUATE RESPONSES (QUESTIONS A,B,C,D,E,F) - BRAC PAGE 1

```
*************************************************************
*                       GROUP ID IS :                        *
*    ARIZONA ST., AUBURN, MANKATO AND MICHIGAN - FIRST AND SECOND YEAR    *
*************************************************************
```

VARIABLE NAME IS   A.01.01 - A   N = 53   MISSING DATA =   0   NUMBER OF VALUES = 5

```
   VALUE         0      1      2      3      4
   FREQUENCY    10      7      6     17     13
   PER CENTS  18.87  13.21  11.33  32.80  24.53
```

MEAN = 2.30;   MEDIAN = 3.00;   STAND DEV = 1.46;   MIN = 0.00;   MAX = 4.00;   RANGE = 4.00

VARIABLE NAME IS   A.01.01 - B   N = 43   MISSING DATA = 10   NUMBER OF VALUES = 3

```
   VALUE         1      2      3
   FREQUENCY     4     18     21
   PER CENTS  9.31  41.87  48.84
```

MEAN = 2.40;   MEDIAN = 2.00;   STAND DEV = 0.66;   MIN = 1.00;   MAX = 3.00;   RANGE = 2.00

VARIABLE NAME IS   A.01.01 - C   N = 43   MISSING DATA = 10   NUMBER OF VALUES = 4

```
   VALUE         1      2      3      4
   FREQUENCY     2      6     15     20
   PER CENTS  4.66  13.96  34.89  46.52
```

MEAN = 3.23;   MEDIAN = 3.00;   STAND DEV = 0.87;   MIN = 1.00;   MAX = 4.00;   RANGE = 3.00

VARIABLE NAME IS   A.01.01 - D   N = 43   MISSING DATA = 10   NUMBER OF VALUES = 3

```
   VALUE         1      2      3
   FREQUENCY     1      8     34
   PER CENTS  2.33  18.61  79.07
```

MEAN = 2.77;   MEDIAN = 3.00;   STAND DEV = 0.48;   MIN = 1.00;   MAX = 3.00;   RANGE = 2.00

VARIABLE NAME IS   A.01.01 - E   N = 43   MISSING DATA = 10   NUMBER OF VALUES = 4

```
   VALUE         0      1      2      3
   FREQUENCY     1      5     30      7
   PER CENTS  2.33  11.63  69.77  16.28
```

MEAN = 2.00;   MEDIAN = 2.00;   STAND DEV = 0.62;   MIN = 0.00;   MAX = 3.00;   RANGE = 3.00

Appendix C

96 Appendix D

Summary of BRAC Questionnaire Graduate Responses by Task and by Program Level[1]

	Q-A	Q-B	Q-C		Q-A	Q-B	Q-C		Q-A	Q-B	Q-C
A. HUMAN BEHAVIOR											
Funct.1				Funct.2				Funct.3			
A.01.01	93.8	1.93	3.27	A.02.02	87.5	2.57	2.86	A.03.08	75.0	2.75	3.33
	81.1	2.40	3.23		94.3	2.41	2.05		90.6	2.90	3.38
	100.0	3.00	3.75		100.0	2.80	3.60		100.0	3.20	3.60
A.01.02	100.0	2.38	3.56	A.02.03	93.8	2.33	3.07	A.03.09	93.8	2.67	3.20
	84.9	2.56	3.27		90.4	2.49	3.23		92.5	3.47	3.47
	100.0	3.00	4.00		100.0	3.00	3.40		100.0	3.20	4.00
A.01.03	93.8	2.53	3.73	A.02.04	75.0	2.50	2.42	**B. LEARNING & LEARNING ENVIRONMENT**			
	90.6	2.69	3.50		84.9	2.42	2.55				
	100.0	3.20	4.00		100.0	2.80	3.20		Q-A	Q-B	Q-C
A.01.04	100.0	2.31	3.06	A.02.05	100.0	3.25	3.56	Funct.1			
	97.6	2.36	3.13		94.3	3.06	3.55	B.01.01	75.0	2.25	2.75
	100.0	3.20	4.00		100.0	3.40	3.80		77.4	2.12	2.90
A.01.05	100.0	2.81	3.50	A.02.06	87.5	2.57	3.50		100.0	3.00	3.40
	92.5	2.96	3.53		90.4	2.51	3.30	B.01.02	93.8	2.27	3.13
	100.0	3.40	4.00		100.0	3.20	3.80		73.6	2.15	3.03
A.01.06	100.0	2.63	3.50	A.02.07	100.0	2.69	3.38		100.0	3.00	3.60
	98.1	2.81	3.33		96.2	2.72	3.34	B.01.03	100.0	2.75	3.63
	100.0	3.40	3.60		100.0	2.80	3.20		90.6	2.48	3.42
A.01.07	93.8	2.67	3.47	A.02.08	93.8	2.53	3.13		100.0	3.40	3.80
	98.1	2.67	3.35		92.2	2.45	2.96	B.01.04	100.0	3.13	3.63
	100.0	3.20	3.80		100.0	2.80	3.80		98.1	2.85	3.62
Funct.2				A.02.09	87.5	2.57	3.07		100.0	3.60	3.80
A.02.01	93.8	2.60	3.67		79.2	2.76	3.41	B.01.05	75.0	2.85	3.42
	98.1	2.71	3.50		100.0	3.00	3.60		82.7	2.60	3.40
	100.0	3.00	3.80	A.02.10	100.0	2.69	3.06		100.0	3.40	3.80
					81.1	2.53	3.00	B.01.06	56.3	2.56	2.89
					100.0	3.20	3.60		71.7	2.61	3.03
									100.0	3.00	3.80
				Funct.2							
				A.02.11	75.0	2.18	2.36				
					72.5	2.32	2.89				
					100.0	2.40	2.80				
				A.02.12	93.8	2.87	3.67				
					83.0	2.61	3.39				
					100.0	2.80	3.80				
				Funct.3							
				A.03.01	100.0	3.25	3.67				
					96.2	2.86	3.69				
					100.0	3.20	3.60				
				A.03.02	93.8	2.87	3.47				
					96.2	2.92	3.49				
					100.0	2.80	3.60				
				A.03.03	100.0	2.88	3.50				
					98.1	2.79	3.48				
					100.0	3.00	3.80				
				A.03.04	100.0	3.19	3.88				
					98.1	3.19	3.57				
					100.0	3.60	4.00				
				A.03.05	100.0	2.56	3.63				
					90.6	2.58	3.38				
					100.0	3.60	4.00				
				A.03.06	100.0	2.69	3.56				
					92.5	2.57	3.31				
					100.0	3.40	4.00				
				A.03.07	93.8	2.60	3.13				
					92.2	2.64	3.36				
					100.0	3.20	4.00				

[1] For each Task the first row of numbers summarizes BA level data, the second row summarizes MA-level data and the third row summarizes sixth-year level data.

Summary of BRAC Questionnaire Graduate Responses by Task and by Program Level
(Continued)

B. LEARNING & LEARNING ENVIRONMENT

Task	Q-A	Q-B	Q-C	Task	Q-A	Q-B	Q-C	Task	Q-A	Q-B	Q-C	Task	Q-A	Q-B	Q-C
Funct.2 B.02.01	37.5 / 60.4 / 100.0	2.33 / 2.48 / 2.80	2.50 / 3.03 / 3.40	Funct.2 B.02.09	93.8 / 92.5 / 100.0	3.06 / 2.90 / 3.40	3.64 / 3.06 / 3.60	Funct.4 B.04.03	87.5 / 82.7 / 100.0	2.71 / 2.60 / 3.20	3.00 / 3.21 / 3.40	Funct.4 B.04.11	37.5 / 58.8 / 60.0	3.17 / 2.93 / 3.00	2.69 / 3.03 / 3.00
B.02.02	75.0 / 84.9 / 100.0	2.58 / 2.58 / 2.80	3.52 / 3.47 / 4.00	Funct.3 B.03.01	25.0 / 61.2 / 80.0	2.25 / 2.27 / 2.50	2.57 / 2.63 / 3.75	B.04.04	75.0 / 75.5 / 100.0	2.67 / 2.54 / 3.20	3.00 / 3.13 / 3.60	B.04.12	81.3 / 75.0 / 80.0	3.00 / 2.67 / 2.50	3.54 / 3.41 / 3.00
B.02.03	25.0 / 45.3 / 80.0	2.25 / 2.56 / 2.75	3.25 / 3.12 / 3.75	B.03.02	56.3 / 53.8 / 80.0	2.78 / 2.79 / 3.25	3.33 / 3.11 / 3.75	B.04.05	75.0 / 67.3 / 100.0	2.58 / 2.46 / 3.40	3.00 / 3.23 / 3.60	Funct.5 B.05.01	68.8 / 79.2 / 80.0	2.73 / 2.57 / 3.50	2.91 / 3.07 / 2.75
B.02.04	62.5 / 67.9 / 80.0	2.80 / 2.81 / 3.20	3.30 / 3.58 / 3.80	B.03.03	68.8 / 75.5 / 80.0	2.45 / 2.59 / 3.00	3.09 / 2.85 / 4.00	B.04.06	93.8 / 84.9 / 100.0	2.87 / 2.73 / 3.40	3.27 / 3.53 / 3.80	B.05.02	43.8 / 58.5 / 80.0	2.57 / 2.65 / 3.00	1.71 / 2.48 / 2.50
B.02.05	81.3 / 92.5 / 100.0	2.54 / 2.55 / 3.40	3.69 / 3.47 / 4.00	B.03.04	87.5 / 86.8 / 100.0	2.50 / 2.61 / 3.40	3.33 / 3.35 / 3.60	B.04.07	93.8 / 84.9 / 100.0	2.60 / 2.53 / 3.20	3.27 / 3.38 / 3.80	B.05.03	6.3 / 24.5 / 80.0	2.00 / 2.43 / 3.25	3.00 / 2.29 / 2.50
B.02.06	50.0 / 71.7 / 80.0	2.63 / 2.45 / 3.25	2.88 / 2.74 / 3.50	B.03.05	68.8 / 71.7 / 80.0	2.55 / 1.83 / 3.00	3.09 / 2.97 / 4.00	B.04.08	25.0 / 67.9 / 80.0	2.50 / 2.50 / 2.75	2.25 / 3.00 / 3.25	B.05.04	93.8 / 81.1 / 100.0	2.60 / 2.60 / 3.00	3.00 / 2.93 / 3.40
B.02.07	87.5 / 88.7 / 80.0	2.64 / 2.68 / 3.50	3.71 / 3.40 / 3.00	Funct.4 B.04.01	75.0 / 65.4 / 100.0	2.50 / 2.68 / 2.80	2.58 / 3.12 / 3.60	B.04.09	43.8 / 56.6 / 100.0	2.57 / 2.27 / 3.00	2.71 / 2.57 / 3.40	B.05.05	62.5 / 75.5 / 80.0	2.60 / 2.55 / 3.25	2.80 / 3.05 / 3.50
B.02.08	68.8 / 86.8 / 100.0	2.45 / 2.59 / 3.20	3.00 / 3.04 / 3.80	B.04.02	87.5 / 86.8 / 100.0	2.79 / 2.59 / 3.40	3.29 / 3.20 / 3.60	B.04.10	31.3 / 54.7 / 100.0	2.60 / 2.34 / 2.60	2.40 / 2.72 / 3.00	Funct.6 B.06.01	18.8 / 43.4 / 60.0	2.00 / 2.29 / 2.00	2.33 / 2.75 / 3.00

Appendix D 97

Appendix D

Summary of BRAC Questionnaire Graduate Responses by Task and by Program Level (Continued)

	Q-A	Q-B	Q-C		Q-A	Q-B	Q-C		Q-A	Q-B	Q-C
B. LEARNING & LEARNING ENVIRONMENT											
Funct.6				**Funct.1**				**Funct.3**			
B.06.02	50.0	2.13	2.13	C.01.03	62.5	2.60	3.60	C.03.04	37.5	2.33	2.83
	45.3	2.29	2.79		60.4	2.58	3.16		60.4	2.41	3.06
	60.0	2.00	2.75		60.0	3.33	3.33		100.0	2.80	3.60
B.06.03	37.5	2.33	2.67	C.01.04	68.8	2.82	3.64	C.03.05	68.8	2.64	2.73
	58.5	2.25	2.81		81.1	2.53	3.30		77.4	2.66	3.00
	80.0	2.50	3.50		100.0	2.60	3.60		80.0	2.75	3.50
B.06.04	56.3	2.63	2.63	C.01.05	81.3	2.75	3.25	**Funct.4**			
	62.3	2.30	3.03		86.8	2.61	3.22	C.04.01	62.5	2.50	2.80
	80.0	2.50	3.25		80.0	3.00	3.75		64.2	2.55	3.18
B.06.05	56.3	2.75	3.00	C.01.06	56.3	2.56	2.89		80.0	2.75	3.75
	50.9	2.30	2.70		77.4	2.61	2.83	C.04.02	81.3	2.69	2.77
	60.0	2.67	3.33		100.0	2.80	3.40		81.1	2.37	3.23
B.06.06	43.8	2.17	2.50	C.01.07	75.0	2.50	2.67		80.0	2.80	3.40
	49.1	2.11	2.63		81.1	2.53	3.14	C.04.03	68.8	2.55	3.00
	80.0	2.50	3.50		100.0	2.80	3.40		77.4	2.46	3.20
C. PLANNING & EVALUATION				C.01.08	87.5	2.64	3.29		80.0	2.75	3.75
					90.6	2.63	3.38	C.04.04	75.0	2.58	2.83
					80.0	3.25	3.75		69.8	2.57	3.19
Funct.1				C.01.09	81.3	2.54	2.92		80.0	3.00	3.75
C.01.01	31.3	1.80	2.80		90.6	2.73	3.27	C.04.05	37.5	2.17	2.83
	39.6	2.24	2.48		100.0	3.40	3.80		56.6	2.60	2.90
	80.0	2.25	3.00	C.01.10	81.3	2.31	2.91		80.0	2.75	3.75
C.01.02	37.5	2.83	3.00		79.2	2.60	3.22	C.04.06	87.5	2.79	3.07
	52.8	2.56	3.33		100.0	3.20	3.80		92.3	2.66	3.38
	60.0	3.00	3.67						100.0	3.00	3.80
				Funct.2							
				C.02.01	81.3	2.23	3.08				
					86.8	2.59	3.33				
					100.0	3.20	3.80				
				C.02.02	68.8	2.64	2.64				
					67.9	3.03	2.78				
					100.0	3.20	3.80				
				C.02.03	81.3	2.69	2.92				
					81.1	2.43	2.98				
					100.0	3.00	3.60				
				C.02.04	81.3	2.31	2.54				
					81.1	2.57	3.19				
					80.0	3.25	3.50				
				C.02.05	62.5	2.70	2.80				
					69.8	2.43	3.08				
					80.0	3.25	3.75				
				Funct.3							
				C.03.01	43.8	2.86	2.86				
					45.3	2.67	3.29				
					60.0	2.33	3.67				
				C.03.02	62.5	2.60	3.40				
					79.2	2.33	3.19				
					100.0	2.80	3.80				
				C.03.03	62.5	2.30	3.10				
					92.5	2.52	3.29				
					100.0	3.00	3.60				

Appendix D 99

Summary of BRAC Questionnaire Graduate Responses by Task and by Program Level
(Continued)

C. PLANNING & EVALUATION	Q-A	Q-B	Q-C		Q-A	Q-B	Q-C	D. MEDIA	Q-A	Q-B	Q-C		Q-A	Q-B	Q-C
Funct.4				Funct.6				Funct.1				Funct.2			
C.04.07	56.3	3.33	3.44	C.06.02	37.5	2.17	3.33	D.01.01	87.5	2.71	3.07	D.02.02	81.3	2.69	2.77
	66.1	2.57	3.09		40.0	2.28	2.56		86.8	2.54	3.30		73.6	2.61	3.18
	80.0	3.00	3.75		40.0	2.50	4.00		80.0	3.00	3.25		80.0	2.75	3.75
C.04.08	37.5	2.67	3.50	C.06.03	18.8	2.33	3.00	D.01.02	75.0	2.58	3.00	D.02.03	87.5	2.61	2.93
	41.5	2.36	3.05		22.6	2.33	2.75		81.1	2.67	3.47		90.6	2.73	2.92
	80.0	2.75	3.75		40.0	2.50	4.00		60.0	3.00	3.33		100.0	3.20	3.60
Funct.5				C.06.04	37.5	2.50	2.83	D.01.03	25.0	2.75	2.75	D.02.04	62.5	2.80	3.00
C.05.01	43.8	2.17	2.50		20.8	2.45	2.64		52.8	2.54	3.14		66.0	2.69	2.91
	62.4	2.16	2.91		40.0	2.50	3.50		60.0	2.67	3.00		80.0	3.50	3.50
	80.0	2.75	3.25	C.06.05	18.8	2.67	2.67	D.01.04	50.0	2.63	3.25	D.02.05	100.0	2.69	2.94
C.05.02	31.3	2.25	2.25		17.0	2.44	2.78		69.8	2.46	3.30		84.9	2.80	3.00
	58.5	2.19	2.71		40.0	2.00	3.50		60.0	2.67	3.33		100.0	3.20	3.60
	60.0	2.67	3.33	C.06.06	6.3	3.00	4.00	D.01.05	68.8	2.91	3.36	D.02.06	62.5	2.44	2.78
C.05.03	100.0	2.80	3.27		18.9	2.40	2.50		69.8	2.62	3.35		84.9	2.49	2.89
	86.8	2.64	3.27		60.0	2.33	3.67		80.0	3.00	3.25		100.0	3.20	3.60
	100.0	3.20	4.00	C.06.07	6.3	--	--	D.01.06	68.8	2.91	3.64	D.02.07	75.0	2.83	2.92
C.05.04	56.3	2.63	3.13		17.0	2.44	2.56		73.6	2.64	3.36		92.5	2.94	3.06
	64.2	2.35	2.91		40.0	2.00	3.50		60.0	3.00	3.67		100.0	3.40	3.80
	100.0	3.00	4.00	C.06.08	0.0	--	--	D.01.07	75.0	2.92	3.67	D.02.08	87.5	2.36	2.71
C.05.05	81.3	2.42	3.00		11.3	2.50	3.00		84.9	2.68	3.48		88.7	2.54	2.98
	71.7	2.46	3.21		20.0	4.00	4.00		80.0	3.00	4.00		80.0	3.00	3.50
	100.0	3.00	4.00	C.06.09	12.5	1.00	4.00	Funct.2				D.02.09	87.5	2.43	2.79
Funct.6					28.3	2.20	2.87	D.02.01	75.0	2.83	2.92		83.0	2.59	2.75
C.06.01	6.3	2.00	2.00		40.0	2.00	4.00		83.0	2.57	3.11		100.0	2.80	3.20
	41.5	2.32	2.77	C.06.10	25.0	2.33	2.67		80.0	3.00	3.75	Funct.3			
	40.0	2.50	4.00		39.6	2.52	2.86					D.03.01	75.0	2.75	3.67
					40.0	2.00	4.00						83.0	2.66	3.25
													80.0	3.00	4.00

100 Appendix D

Summary of BRAC Questionnaire Graduate Responses by Task and by Program Level (Continued)

D. MEDIA

Funct.3	Q-A	Q-B	Q-C
D.03.02	87.5	2.57	3.43
	94.3	2.69	3.24
	100.0	3.20	3.60
D.03.03	6.3	3.00	3.00
	56.6	2.41	3.10
	80.0	2.75	3.75
D.03.04	68.8	3.00	3.00
	88.7	2.67	3.00
	100.0	3.00	3.40
D.03.05	37.5	2.67	2.83
	73.6	2.44	2.72
	100.0	2.80	3.40
D.03.06	37.5	2.67	2.67
	75.5	2.41	2.59
	100.0	3.00	3.60
D.03.07	81.3	2.77	2.92
	92.5	2.80	2.84
	100.0	3.00	3.60
D.03.08	25.0	2.75	2.75
	73.6	2.50	2.68
	100.0	3.20	3.80
D.03.09	18.8	2.33	2.33
	71.7	2.70	2.97
	80.0	3.25	3.50

Funct.3	Q-A	Q-B	Q-C
D.03.10	18.8	2.30	3.00
	50.9	2.89	2.70
	60.0	3.00	3.33
D.03.11	75.0	2.67	2.75
	75.5	2.77	3.15
	100.0	3.20	3.40
D.03.12	75.0	2.75	3.00
	84.9	2.78	3.04
	80.0	3.25	3.50
D.03.13	0.0	--	--
	22.6	2.50	3.17
	60.0	3.33	3.67
D.03.14	62.5	2.70	3.20
	69.8	2.65	3.03
	80.0	3.25	3.25
D.03.15	56.3	2.56	3.33
	66.0	2.54	3.17
	100.0	3.20	3.20
D.03.16	81.3	2.54	3.15
	88.7	2.60	3.09
	100.0	3.00	3.40
D.03.17	87.5	2.57	3.29
	88.7	2.72	3.15
	100.0	3.20	3.60
D.03.18	81.3	2.27	3.08
	84.9	2.71	3.16
	100.0	3.00	3.60

Funct.3	Q-A	Q-B	Q-C
D.03.19	93.8	2.80	3.33
	94.3	2.84	3.12
	100.0	3.20	3.80
D.03.20	75.0	2.58	3.00
	79.2	2.67	3.29
	80.0	3.25	3.50

Funct.4	Q-A	Q-B	Q-C
D.04.01	81.3	2.85	3.15
	94.3	2.64	3.16
	100.0	3.20	3.80
D.04.02	100.0	2.94	3.19
	98.1	2.75	3.19
	100.0	3.20	3.40
D.04.03	81.3	2.77	2.92
	83.0	2.70	2.89
	80.0	3.50	3.00
D.04.04	93.8	2.80	3.20
	92.5	2.63	2.63
	100.0	3.40	3.60
D.04.05	87.5	2.64	3.36
	83.0	2.64	3.18
	100.0	3.20	3.80
D.04.06	100.0	3.00	3.00
	98.1	2.83	3.12
	100.0	3.20	3.80

Funct.4	Q-A	Q-B	Q-C
D.04.07	87.5	2.57	2.93
	88.7	2.65	3.22
	100.0	3.00	3.80
D.04.08	62.5	2.60	3.00
	69.8	2.67	2.83
	80.0	3.00	3.00
D.04.09	81.3	2.69	2.69
	84.9	2.61	2.86
	80.0	3.00	3.00
D.04.10	62.5	2.70	2.80
	71.2	2.49	2.70
	80.0	3.00	2.50
D.04.11	93.8	2.88	2.94
	88.7	2.64	3.17
	100.0	3.40	3.60
D.04.12	93.8	2.73	3.07
	88.7	2.62	3.11
	80.0	3.50	3.75
D.04.13	0.0	--	--
	30.2	2.63	2.63
	40.0	2.50	3.00
D.04.14	87.5	2.79	3.43
	98.1	2.65	3.44
	100.0	3.20	3.60
D.04.15	81.3	2.92	3.42
	83.0	2.61	3.18
	100.0	3.20	3.80

Summary of BRAC Questionnaire Graduate Responses by Task and by Program Level
(Continued)

D. MEDIA	Q-A	Q-B	Q-C		Q-A	Q-B	Q-C		Q-A	Q-B	Q-C		Q-A	Q-B	Q-C
Funct.4				**Funct.5**				**Funct.5**				**Funct.6**			
D.04.16	56.3	2.78	3.22	D.05.03	81.3	2.38	3.08	D.05.12	93.8	2.93	2.67	D.06.05	56.3	2.56	2.67
	75.5	2.50	3.25		79.2	2.62	2.86		88.7	2.91	2.49		66.0	2.54	2.69
	100.0	3.20	3.80		80.0	3.00	3.00		80.0	3.00	2.25		60.0	2.67	3.00
D.04.17	50.0	2.75	2.50	D.05.04	81.3	2.15	2.85	D.05.13	50.0	2.50	2.25	D.06.06	93.8	2.67	3.27
	58.5	2.90	2.10		79.2	2.60	2.55		71.7	2.87	2.42		79.2	2.69	2.90
	40.0	4.00	2.50		80.0	3.00	3.25		80.0	3.00	2.25		100.0	2.80	2.20
D.04.18	93.8	2.73	2.60	D.05.05	68.8	2.00	2.82	D.05.14	87.5	2.71	2.36	D.06.07	93.8	2.73	3.07
	92.5	2.92	2.45		73.6	2.62	2.44		75.5	2.82	2.42		73.6	2.63	2.92
	80.0	3.50	3.00		100.0	3.00	2.80		60.0	2.67	3.33		80.0	2.75	2.50
D.04.19	87.5	2.71	2.79	D.05.06	75.0	2.42	2.92	D.05.15	75.0	2.67	2.33	D.06.08	87.5	2.71	2.93
	86.8	2.74	3.07		71.2	2.70	2.35		73.1	2.79	2.47		69.8	2.59	2.70
	100.0	3.00	3.60		80.0	3.00	2.50		60.0	2.67	2.67		80.0	3.00	2.00
D.04.20	81.3	2.77	2.85	D.05.07	87.5	2.43	2.86	D.05.16	75.0	3.08	2.58	D.06.09	75.0	2.58	3.08
	88.7	2.72	2.89		73.6	2.72	2.28		77.4	2.73	2.37		62.3	2.55	2.70
	80.0	3.25	3.50		80.0	3.00	2.75		80.0	3.00	3.00		80.0	3.00	2.00
D.04.21	68.8	2.45	2.73	D.05.08	68.8	2.55	2.64	**Funct.6**				D.06.10	87.5	2.93	2.93
	58.5	2.48	2.77		79.2	2.83	2.55	D.06.01	87.5	2.54	3.23		63.5	2.67	2.67
	60.0	3.00	3.00		80.0	2.75	2.25		83.0	2.68	3.05		60.0	2.67	1.67
									100.0	3.20	3.60				
Funct.5				D.05.09	68.8	2.73	3.00	D.06.02	81.3	2.62	2.85	D.06.11	75.0	3.00	3.00
D.05.01	87.5	2.64	3.14		79.2	2.81	2.31		79.2	2.62	2.95		61.5	2.56	2.56
	81.1	2.47	3.16		80.0	3.00	2.25		100.0	3.20	3.40		60.0	2.67	1.67
	80.0	3.25	3.50	D.05.10	81.3	2.69	2.46	D.06.03	81.3	2.54	2.46	D.06.12	62.5	3.10	3.40
D.05.02	87.5	2.50	3.00		73.1	2.84	2.53		62.3	2.58	2.73		48.1	2.80	2.68
	73.6	2.38	2.92		80.0	3.00	2.25		60.0	3.00	3.33		60.0	3.00	1.33
	80.0	3.00	3.50	D.05.11	68.8	2.82	2.55	D.06.04	81.3	2.38	2.54	D.06.13	93.8	3.07	3.20
					73.6	2.77	2.47		79.2	2.68	2.78		84.9	2.73	2.91
					80.0	2.75	2.00		80.0	3.00	3.50		60.0	2.67	2.00

Appendix D 101

102 Appendix D

Summary of BRAC Questionnaire Graduate Responses by Task and by Program Level
(Continued)

D. MEDIA

	Q-A	Q-B	Q-C		Q-A	Q-B	Q-C		Q-A	Q-B	Q-C		Q-A	Q-B	Q-C
Funct.6				Funct.6				Funct.7				Funct.7			
D.06.14	81.3	3.08	3.23	D.06.22	0.0	--	--	D.07.03	100.0	3.06	2.94	D.07.11	81.3	2.92	2.46
	83.0	2.80	2.98		3.8	2.50	2.00		90.6	2.75	2.81		86.5	2.76	2.47
	60.0	2.67	2.00		0.0	--	--		80.0	3.25	2.75		100.0	3.00	2.60
D.06.15	43.8	3.00	3.14	D.06.23	87.5	2.79	2.86	D.07.04	81.3	3.15	2.54	D.07.12	93.8	3.00	2.87
	35.8	2.68	2.84		67.9	2.58	2.69		69.8	2.86	2.41		86.5	2.87	2.67
	60.0	3.00	2.00		80.0	2.75	2.25		60.0	3.33	2.67		100.0	3.60	2.60
D.06.16	75.0	2.83	2.67	D.06.24	93.8	2.87	3.07	D.07.05	93.8	2.87	2.73	D.07.13	0.0	--	--
	53.9	2.48	2.41		67.9	2.64	2.58		90.6	2.75	2.27		11.3	2.33	2.00
	60.0	3.00	1.33		80.0	3.50	3.00		80.0	3.50	2.50		40.0	2.00	2.50
D.06.17	81.3	2.77	2.69	D.06.25	100.0	2.81	3.06	D.07.06	100.0	2.94	2.81	D.07.14	0.0	--	--
	47.2	2.44	2.48		92.8	2.63	2.92		90.6	2.92	2.58		3.8	2.50	2.50
	60.0	3.33	1.33		100.0	3.60	3.20		60.0	3.67	2.67		0.0	--	--
D.06.18	62.5	2.80	2.60	D.06.26	100.0	2.88	2.81	D.07.07	93.8	3.00	2.80	D.07.15	0.0	--	--
	39.6	2.43	2.29		96.2	2.74	2.86		92.5	2.76	2.53		9.4	2.33	2.50
	60.0	3.00	1.33		100.0	3.60	3.20		100.0	3.20	2.60		40.0	1.50	1.50
D.06.19	87.5	2.93	2.71	D.06.27	100.0	3.00	2.81	D.07.08	100.0	3.00	2.56	D.07.16	0.0	--	--
	58.5	2.71	2.71		92.5	2.69	2.61		86.8	2.85	2.26		1.9	2.00	2.00
	60.0	3.33	1.33		100.0	3.60	3.20		60.0	3.33	2.67		0.0	--	--
D.06.20	12.5	3.00	3.50	Funct.7				D.07.09	100.0	2.88	2.44	Funct.8			
	15.1	2.50	2.50	D.07.01	87.5	2.86	2.93		84.9	2.76	2.22	D.08.01	62.5	2.80	2.80
	40.0	2.50	1.00		77.4	2.76	2.66		80.0	3.25	2.50		56.6	2.72	2.72
					60.0	3.67	3.33						60.0	2.67	3.00
D.06.21	0.0	--	--	D.07.02	87.5	2.86	2.93	D.07.10	100.0	3.06	2.75	D.08.02	43.8	2.57	2.57
	11.3	2.67	2.67		92.5	2.69	2.49		92.3	2.96	2.40		47.1	2.74	2.83
	20.0	3.00	1.00		80.0	3.50	2.75		80.0	3.25	2.00		60.0	2.33	3.00

Appendix D   103

Summary of BRAC Questionnaire Graduate Responses by Task and by Program Level
(Continued)

D. MEDIA

	Q-A	Q-B	Q-C		Q-A	Q-B	Q-C		Q-A	Q-B	Q-C
Funct.8				**Funct.8**				**Funct.8**			
D.08.03	12.5	2.50	2.00	D.08.11	0.0	--	--	D.08.19	6.3	3.00	3.00
	26.4	2.64	2.57		3.8	2.00	3.00		7.7	2.50	2.75
	40.0	2.00	2.00		0.0	--	--		40.0	1.00	1.00
D.08.04	0.0	--	--	D.08.12	12.5	1.00	2.00	**Funct.9**			
	22.6	2.67	2.58		17.3	2.44	2.78	D.09.01	62.5	2.90	2.80
	40.0	2.00	3.00		60.0	1.67	3.00		64.2	2.35	2.74
D.08.05	12.5	1.50	3.00	D.08.13	12.5	2.00	3.00		100.0	2.80	3.60
	24.5	2.69	2.46		15.1	2.63	2.75	D.09.02	68.8	2.55	3.00
	60.0	2.67	3.33		40.0	1.00	2.00		75.5	2.36	2.72
D.08.06	0.0	--	--	D.08.04	6.3	3.00	4.00		100.0	2.80	3.60
	19.2	2.30	2.40		17.3	2.44	2.22	D.09.03	81.3	2.69	3.08
	40.0	2.50	3.50		40.0	1.00	2.50		84.9	2.42	2.89
D.08.07	0.0	--	--	D.08.15	6.3	2.00	2.00		100.0	3.00	3.60
	22.6	2.75	2.25		20.8	2.09	1.82	D.09.04	75.0	2.58	3.00
	40.0	2.00	3.00		20.0	1.00	3.00		79.2	2.40	2.93
D.08.08	12.5	3.00	3.50	D.08.16	0.0	--	--		80.0	3.00	3.75
	20.8	2.73	2.36		9.4	2.20	2.20	D.09.05	75.0	2.58	2.92
	40.0	2.00	3.00		0.0	--	--		73.6	2.45	2.87
D.08.09	0.0	--	--	D.08.17	6.3	0.00	2.00		80.0	3.00	3.75
	3.8	3.50	3.00		7.5	2.25	2.75	**Funct.10**			
	0.0	--	--		0.0	--	--	D.10.01	62.5	2.60	3.00
D.08.10	0.0	--	--	D.08.18	18.8	2.33	3.00		73.6	2.59	2.82
	3.8	3.00	3.50		20.7	2.82	2.82		80.0	3.25	3.50
	0.0	--	--		20.0	3.00	2.00	D.10.02	75.0	2.75	3.00
									84.9	2.64	2.80
									80.0	3.75	3.50

	Q-A	Q-B	Q-C
Funct.10			
D.10.03	62.5	3.20	3.40
	67.9	2.69	2.77
	80.0	3.50	3.25
D.10.04	81.3	2.92	3.31
	84.9	2.76	2.91
	60.0	3.67	4.00
D.10.05	87.5	2.79	3.14
	79.2	2.62	2.76
	80.0	3.25	3.50
D.10.06	87.5	3.14	3.36
	84.9	2.62	2.98
	80.0	3.50	3.50
Funct.11			
D.11.01	25.0	2.25	2.25
	52.8	2.68	3.21
	80.0	3.00	3.50
D.11.02	12.5	3.00	2.50
	35.8	2.79	3.32
	60.0	3.00	3.33
D.11.03	25.0	3.00	3.00
	50.9	2.69	3.15
	80.0	3.00	3.50
D.11.04	62.5	2.80	3.50
	88.7	2.62	3.11
	100.0	3.20	3.60

Summary of BRAC Questionnaire Graduate Responses by Task and by Program Level
(Continued)

D. MEDIA

	Q-A	Q-B	Q-C		Q-A	Q-B	Q-C		Q-A	Q-B	Q-C
Funct.11				**Funct.12**				**Funct.14**			
D.11.05	87.5	3.00	3.07	D.12.05	87.5	2.71	2.86	D.14.05	25.0	2.25	2.75
	94.3	2.74	3.22		86.8	2.50	3.02		39.6	2.52	2.57
	100.0	3.20	3.60		100.0	3.40	3.60		60.0	3.33	2.67
D.11.06	75.0	3.08	2.92	D.12.06	50.0	2.50	3.25	D.14.06	50.0	2.13	2.75
	81.1	2.70	3.16		58.5	2.42	3.00		75.5	2.67	2.88
	80.0	3.25	3.50		80.0	3.50	3.75		80.0	3.25	2.50
D.11.07	37.5	3.00	2.83	D.12.07	6.3	3.00	4.00	**Funct.15**			
	64.2	2.65	3.00		39.6	2.45	3.16	D.15.01	25.0	2.50	2.50
	80.0	3.00	3.50		80.0	3.00	3.25		43.4	2.64	3.18
									80.0	3.00	3.50
D.11.08	18.8	2.67	2.33	D.12.08	25.0	2.50	2.50	D.15.02	0.0	---	---
	45.3	2.54	2.83		49.1	2.62	3.15		37.7	2.68	2.84
	80.0	2.75	3.50		80.0	3.50	3.75		60.0	3.00	3.33
Funct.12				D.12.09	62.5	2.60	2.70	D.15.03	0.0	---	---
D.12.01	87.5	2.86	3.21		58.5	2.45	2.90		32.1	2.69	2.75
	92.3	2.67	3.14		80.0	3.00	3.75		60.0	2.67	2.67
	100.0	3.20	3.60	D.12.10	43.8	2.43	2.71	D.15.04	31.3	2.60	2.60
D.12.02	87.5	2.86	3.14		54.7	2.43	2.86		47.2	2.67	2.88
	86.7	2.52	3.22		80.0	3.00	3.75		60.0	3.00	3.33
	100.0	3.40	3.60	**Funct.13**				D.15.05	12.5	2.50	3.00
D.12.03	81.3	2.77	3.23	D.13.01	62.5	2.90	3.20		41.5	2.67	3.05
	81.3	2.63	3.14		77.4	2.60	3.17		60.0	3.00	3.33
	100.0	3.40	3.60		100.0	3.20	3.60	D.15.06	50.0	2.38	2.88
D.12.04	50.0	2.63	3.00	D.13.02	50.0	2.75	3.25		43.6	2.67	2.72
	65.4	2.44	3.12		69.8	2.69	3.25		80.0	3.00	3.75
	80.0	3.00	3.75		80.0	3.25	3.60	D.15.07	31.3	2.60	3.00
				D.13.03	56.3	2.78	3.11		62.3	2.53	2.75
					71.7	2.66	3.16		80.0	3.00	3.50
					80.0	3.25	3.75				

	Q-A	Q-B	Q-C
Funct.13			
D.13.04	87.5	2.71	3.07
	84.9	2.71	3.20
	100.0	3.00	3.60
D.13.05	68.8	2.64	2.82
	86.8	2.65	2.96
	100.0	3.20	3.20
D.13.06	87.5	2.71	2.79
	92.5	2.73	2.88
	100.0	3.20	3.20
D.13.07	100.0	2.88	3.13
	92.5	2.80	3.22
	100.0	3.20	3.60
D.13.08	37.5	2.00	2.50
	81.1	2.35	2.79
	100.0	3.40	3.40
Funct.14			
D.14.01	68.8	2.50	2.80
	69.8	2.54	2.92
	80.0	3.25	3.25
D.14.02	37.5	2.67	2.83
	75.5	2.60	2.82
	80.0	3.25	3.25
D.14.03	43.8	2.57	2.71
	64.2	2.71	2.71
	100.0	3.20	2.80
D.14.04	62.5	2.90	2.90
	81.1	2.79	2.91
	100.0	3.20	3.00

Summary of BRAC Questionnaire Graduate Responses by Task and by Program Level
(Continued)

D. MEDIA	Q-A	Q-B	Q-C		Q-A	Q-B	Q-C		Q-A	Q-B	Q-C		Q-A	Q-B	Q-C
Funct.15				Funct.16				Funct.17				Funct.18			
D.15.08	6.3	2.00	4.00	D.16.04	87.5	2.79	3.36	D.17.05	50.0	2.63	2.88	D.18.07	100.0	3.13	3.63
	32.1	2.82	2.65		86.8	2.78	3.17		52.8	2.56	3.15		83.0	2.84	3.34
	80.0	3.00	3.50		100.0	3.20	3.40		80.0	3.25	3.50		100.0	3.20	3.60
D.15.09	6.3	2.00	4.00	D.16.05	100.0	3.00	3.44	D.17.06	56.3	2.78	3.33	D.18.08	68.8	2.82	3.18
	34.0	2.56	2.78		86.8	2.96	3.41		58.5	2.61	3.35		69.8	2.46	3.03
	60.0	3.00	3.33		100.0	3.20	3.60		100.0	3.20	3.60		100.0	3.40	3.60
D.15.10	6.3	2.00	2.00	D.16.06	81.3	2.77	3.00	D.17.07	62.5	2.40	3.00	D.18.09	56.3	3.11	3.89
	28.3	2.25	2.44		62.3	2.70	3.12		49.1	2.58	3.23		58.5	2.77	3.16
	80.0	2.75	3.50		80.0	3.25	3.50		80.0	3.25	3.75		80.0	3.25	3.75
D.15.11	31.3	2.40	2.60	D.16.07	93.8	2.60	2.93	Funct.18				D.18.10	75.0	3.08	3.25
	41.5	2.71	2.52		79.2	2.55	3.31	D.18.01	56.3	3.11	3.33		75.5	2.67	3.13
	60.0	3.00	3.33		100.0	3.20	3.60		77.4	2.71	3.02		100.0	3.20	3.60
									100.0	3.40	3.80				
D.15.12	6.3	3.00	4.00	D.16.08	75.0	2.58	2.92	D.18.02	50.0	2.63	2.75	Funct.19			
	26.4	2.64	2.86		64.2	2.62	3.03		54.7	2.59	2.83	D.19.01	62.5	3.00	3.00
	80.0	3.00	3.50		100.0	3.00	3.80		100.0	3.20	3.60		83.0	2.73	2.98
													100.0	3.20	3.20
Funct.16				Funct.17				D.18.03	62.5	2.70	2.80	D.19.02	93.8	2.73	3.13
D.16.01	87.5	3.07	3.50	D.17.01	18.8	2.33	3.00		56.6	2.60	3.07		77.4	2.80	3.29
	79.2	2.85	3.27		28.3	2.53	3.13		100.0	3.20	3.60		100.0	3.60	3.40
	100.0	3.20	3.20		60.0	3.00	3.67								
D.16.02	87.5	2.93	3.13	D.17.02	87.5	3.21	3.00	D.18.04	93.8	3.20	3.40	D.19.03	100.0	2.88	3.13
	79.2	2.86	3.14		77.4	2.71	2.88		90.6	2.96	3.29		88.7	2.70	3.04
	100.0	3.40	3.60		100.0	2.80	3.60		100.0	3.00	3.40		100.0	3.40	3.40
D.16.03	93.8	2.87	3.53	D.17.03	93.8	3.20	3.40	D.18.05	93.8	3.07	3.33	D.19.04	68.8	3.00	2.36
	75.5	2.80	3.22		81.1	2.70	3.26		88.7	2.89	3.26		86.8	2.67	2.70
	100.0	3.20	3.40		100.0	3.40	3.80		100.0	3.00	3.40		100.0	3.20	3.20
				D.17.04	75.0	2.75	3.42	D.18.06	87.5	3.14	3.14	D.19.05	56.3	3.11	3.00
					56.6	2.60	3.33		81.3	2.70	3.16		67.9	2.81	2.81
					60.0	3.33	3.40		100.0	3.40	3.60		100.0	3.20	2.60

Appendix D   105

106 Appendix D

Summary of BRAC Questionnaire Graduate Responses by Task and by Program Level
(Continued)

D. MEDIA

	Q-A	Q-B	Q-C		Q-A	Q-B	Q-C		Q-A	Q-B	Q-C		Q-A	Q-B	Q-C
Funct.19				Funct.21				Funct.22				Funct.22			
D.19.06	81.3	2.92	2.92	D.21.03	81.3	2.62	3.15	D.22.08	12.5	2.50	3.00	D.22.17	18.8	3.00	2.67
	73.6	2.74	3.08		62.3	2.73	3.18		37.7	2.50	2.55		78.1	2.68	2.88
	100.0	3.40	3.00		60.0	3.00	3.67		60.0	3.00	3.33		60.0	3.00	3.00
D.19.07	75.0	3.17	3.25	Funct.22				D.22.09	75.0	2.83	2.67	Funct.23			
	75.5	2.70	2.90	D.22.01	75.0	2.67	3.00		56.6	2.73	2.67	D.23.01	12.5	3.00	3.00
	80.0	3.25	3.50		67.9	2.61	2.97		80.0	3.00	2.75		40.4	2.62	2.95
Funct.20					100.0	3.20	3.40	D.22.10	43.8	2.71	2.71		40.0	3.00	3.50
D.20.01	93.8	3.27	3.20	D.22.02	75.0	2.50	3.17		62.3	2.79	2.67	D.23.02	0.0	--	--
	88.7	2.94	3.15		71.7	2.61	2.84		60.0	2.67	3.00		26.9	2.43	3.14
	80.0	3.50	3.50		100.0	3.20	3.20	D.22.11	100.0	2.94	3.31		60.0	3.67	3.67
D.20.02	68.8	3.18	2.82	D.22.03	75.0	2.83	3.17		83.0	2.75	3.05	D.23.03	12.5	2.50	2.50
	84.9	2.89	2.89		69.8	2.65	2.89		100.0	3.40	3.20		38.5	2.50	2.90
	80.0	3.75	3.50		100.0	3.20	2.80	D.22.12	81.3	2.85	3.31		20.0	4.00	3.00
D.20.03	56.3	3.00	2.78	D.22.04	75.0	2.67	2.92		78.8	2.83	3.07	D.23.04	18.8	2.67	3.00
	52.8	2.89	3.00		69.8	2.57	2.76		60.0	3.67	3.33		36.5	2.58	2.68
	60.0	4.00	4.00		80.0	3.50	2.75	D.22.13	68.8	2.91	3.18		40.0	4.00	3.50
D.20.04	75.0	3.08	2.92	D.22.05	87.5	2.79	2.79		67.3	2.66	3.09	D.23.05	31.3	2.80	3.00
	73.6	2.95	2.97		66.0	2.69	2.57		80.0	3.25	3.00		44.2	2.52	2.91
	100.0	3.60	3.20		100.0	2.80	2.40	D.22.14	75.0	2.75	3.08		60.0	3.67	3.67
Funct.21				D.22.06	93.8	2.93	2.93		69.2	2.64	2.72	D.23.06	12.5	2.50	2.50
D.21.01	87.5	2.64	2.93		69.8	2.84	2.76		100.0	3.00	2.80		30.8	2.44	2.63
	62.3	2.79	3.12		100.0	3.20	2.80	D.22.15	56.3	2.67	3.00		40.0	3.00	3.50
	80.0	3.25	3.75	D.22.07	18.8	2.67	2.33		63.5	2.76	2.64	D.23.07	18.8	2.67	3.00
D.21.02	87.5	2.57	3.00		60.4	2.78	2.47		100.0	3.20	2.80		32.7	2.53	2.53
	52.8	2.79	3.07		80.0	3.00	2.25	D.22.16	25.0	2.00	2.75		40.0	3.50	3.50
	80.0	3.25	3.75						48.1	2.64	2.68				
									80.0	3.25	2.50				

Appendix D   107

Summary of BRAC Questionnaire Graduate Responses by Task and by Program Level
(Continued)

D. MEDIA	Q-A	Q-B	Q-C		Q-A	Q-B	Q-C		Q-A	Q-B	Q-C		Q-A	Q-B	Q-C
Funct.24				Funct.25				Funct.25				Funct.25			
D.24.01	6.3	2.00	3.00	D.25.02	43.8	2.71	3.14	D.25.11	6.3	3.00	3.00	D.25.19	0.0	--	--
	25.5	2.50	2.83		64.2	2.65	2.88		31.4	2.12	3.81		21.2	2.64	2.73
	60.0	3.33	3.67		80.0	3.00	3.50		80.0	2.75	3.50		60.0	2.33	2.67
D.24.02	6.3	2.00	3.00	D.25.03	18.8	3.00	3.00	D.25.12	25.0	3.00	3.00	D.25.20	0.0	--	--
	25.5	2.58	2.67		39.6	2.57	2.57		34.6	2.41	2.71		13.1	2.64	2.55
	60.0	3.50	3.50		80.0	2.75	3.25		80.0	2.75	3.75		40.0	3.00	3.00
D.24.03	12.5	2.50	3.00	D.25.04	6.3	4.00	3.00	D.25.13	6.3	3.00	3.00	D.25.21	6.3	3.00	3.00
	17.3	2.78	2.78		30.2	2.63	2.38		17.3	3.13	2.88		21.2	2.64	2.82
	40.0	3.00	3.00		60.0	2.67	3.67		60.0	2.33	3.67		60.0	2.33	3.33
D.24.04	25.0	3.25	3.00	D.25.05	6.3	3.00	3.00	D.25.14	18.8	3.00	3.00	D.25.22	18.8	2.00	3.00
	40.4	2.43	2.75		26.4	2.62	3.00		25.0	2.83	2.58		32.3	2.47	2.82
	60.0	3.33	3.67		60.0	2.67	3.67		80.0	2.50	3.50		40.0	3.00	4.00
D.24.05	31.3	2.40	2.63	D.25.06	18.8	3.00	3.00	D.25.15	6.3	3.00	3.00	Funct.26			
	32.7	2.47	2.88		39.6	2.48	3.67		15.4	2.63	3.13	D.26.01	31.3	2.80	2.40
	60.0	3.67	4.00		80.0	2.75	3.50		80.0	2.75	3.50		34.0	2.59	2.94
													60.0	2.33	3.00
D.24.06	25.0	2.50	3.00	D.25.07	6.3	3.00	2.00	D.25.16	0.0	--	--	D.26.02	37.5	2.33	2.50
	51.9	2.70	2.96		28.3	2.79	3.71		13.5	2.57	2.43		34.0	2.40	2.80
	60.0	3.67	4.00		40.0	3.00	3.50		40.0	3.00	3.50		60.0	2.33	2.67
D.24.07	0.0	--	--	D.25.08	18.8	2.67	2.67	D.25.17	0.0	--	--	D.26.03	31.3	2.40	3.00
	19.2	2.50	2.60		34.6	2.67	3.72		19.2	2.50	3.00		41.5	2.48	2.86
	40.0	3.00	3.00		80.0	2.75	3.25		40.0	3.00	3.00		60.0	2.67	2.67
				D.25.09	6.3	2.00	3.00	D.25.18	0.0	--	--	D.26.04	25.0	2.25	3.00
					26.9	2.62	3.85		26.9	2.77	2.92		26.4	2.64	2.86
					80.0	2.75	3.25		80.0	2.50	3.25		60.0	2.33	3.00
Funct.25				D.25.10	0.0	--	--								
D.25.01	25.0	2.50	2.75		35.3	2.33	3.65								
	35.8	2.33	2.61		80.0	2.75	3.25								
	80.0	3.00	3.50												

Appendix D

Summary of BRAC Questionnaire Graduate Responses by Task and by Program Level
(Continued)

D. MEDIA

	Q-A	Q-B	Q-C		Q-A	Q-B	Q-C		Q-A	Q-B	Q-C		Q-A	Q-B	Q-C
Funct. 27				**Funct. 28**				**Funct. 29**				**Funct. 29**			
D.27.01	0.0	--	--	D.28.03	6.3	1.00	1.00	D.29.05	6.3	0.00	3.00	D.29.14	0.0	--	--
	15.1	2.88	3.00		13.2	2.86	2.86		11.5	2.83	3.33		7.8	2.20	3.50
	20.0	3.00	4.00		40.0	2.50	3.50		40.0	2.00	3.00		40.0	2.00	2.50
D.27.02	0.0	--	--	D.28.04	6.3	1.00	3.00	D.29.06	12.5	1.00	2.50	**Funct. 30**			
	11.3	2.83	3.33		15.1	2.63	3.00		9.6	2.80	2.80	D.30.01	43.8	2.29	2.71
	40.0	2.50	4.00		40.0	2.50	3.50		40.0	2.00	3.00		67.3	2.28	2.61
D.27.03	0.0	--	--	D.28.05	0.0	--	--	D.29.07	6.3	0.00	3.00		80.0	2.50	3.75
	11.3	2.83	3.17		13.2	2.86	3.14		9.6	2.60	3.20	D.30.02	62.5	2.30	2.70
	40.0	2.00	4.00		40.0	2.50	3.50		40.0	2.00	2.50		58.5	2.44	2.53
D.27.04	6.3	0.00	3.00	D.28.06	0.0	--	--	D.29.08	6.3	0.00	3.00		80.0	2.50	3.75
	15.1	2.75	3.25		13.2	2.57	3.11		9.6	2.80	3.40	D.30.03	12.5	3.00	2.50
	20.0	2.00	4.00		40.0	2.50	3.50		40.0	2.00	2.50		39.6	2.71	2.76
D.27.05	6.3	0.00	3.00	D.28.07	6.3	0.00	3.00	D.29.09	12.5	1.00	2.50		60.0	3.00	4.00
	17.0	2.78	3.22		17.0	2.56	3.11		9.6	2.80	3.60	D.30.04	12.5	2.50	2.50
	20.0	2.00	3.00		40.0	2.50	3.50		40.0	1.50	2.50		45.3	2.88	2.63
D.27.06	6.3	0.00	3.00	**Funct. 29**				D.29.10	6.3	0.00	3.00		80.0	2.50	3.25
	15.1	2.75	3.38	D.29.01	0.0	--	--		5.8	2.67	3.33	D.30.05	31.3	2.40	3.00
	40.0	2.50	4.00		17.3	2.56	3.11		40.0	1.50	2.50		45.3	2.50	2.50
Funct. 28					40.0	3.00	3.50	D.29.11	6.3	0.00	4.00		80.0	2.50	3.25
D.28.01	12.5	1.00	2.00	D.29.02	6.3	0.00	3.00		13.5	2.86	2.43	D.30.06	31.3	2.00	2.60
	11.3	2.83	2.67		13.5	2.56	3.00		40.0	2.00	2.50		54.7	2.52	2.45
	40.0	2.50	3.50		40.0	2.00	3.00	D.29.12	6.3	0.00	3.00		80.0	2.50	3.25
D.28.02	6.3	2.00	1.00	D.29.03	6.3	0.00	3.00		9.6	2.40	2.80	D.30.07	25.0	1.75	2.75
	24.5	2.46	2.92		13.5	2.71	3.29		40.0	2.00	2.50		41.5	2.55	2.45
	40.0	2.50	3.00		40.0	2.00	3.00	D.29.13	0.0	--	--		80.0	2.50	3.25
				D.29.04	6.3	0.00	3.00		9.6	2.60	3.00	D.30.08	6.3	2.00	3.00
					19.2	2.90	3.20		40.0	2.00	2.50		28.3	2.47	2.67
					40.0	2.00	3.00						60.0	2.33	3.33

Appendix D   109

Summary of BRAC Questionnaire Graduate Responses by Task and by Program Level
(Continued)

D. MEDIA

	Q-A	Q-B	Q-C
Funct.30			
D.30.09	0.0	--	--
	18.9	2.50	2.50
	60.0	2.33	3.00

E. MANAGEMENT

	Q-A	Q-B	Q-C
Funct.1			
E.01.01	100.0	2.44	3.50
	92.5	2.71	3.27
	100.0	3.00	4.00
E.01.02	100.0	2.50	3.38
	88.7	2.64	3.26
	100.0	3.00	3.80
E.01.03	87.5	2.57	3.21
	73.6	2.50	3.13
	80.0	2.75	4.00
E.01.04	37.5	2.67	2.67
	47.2	2.36	2.92
	100.0	2.40	3.60
E.01.05	62.5	2.60	3.00
	55.8	2.34	2.62
	80.0	2.75	4.00
E.01.06	93.8	2.67	3.20
	88.7	2.62	3.13
	100.0	3.20	4.00

	Q-A	Q-B	Q-C
Funct.2			
E.02.01	93.8	2.80	3.47
	86.8	2.65	3.50
	100.0	3.20	3.80
E.02.02	100.0	2.88	3.06
	98.1	2.69	3.37
	100.0	3.00	3.80
E.02.03	93.8	2.73	3.00
	94.3	2.73	3.00
	100.0	3.00	3.40
E.02.04	56.3	2.67	3.00
	62.3	2.59	2.84
	100.0	3.20	3.40
E.02.05	100.0	2.63	2.94
	88.7	2.65	3.13
	100.0	3.00	3.60
E.02.06	93.8	2.40	3.13
	84.9	2.55	3.30
	100.0	3.20	3.80
E.02.07	93.8	2.67	3.07
	90.4	2.68	3.15
	100.0	3.00	3.60
Funct.3			
E.03.01	100.0	2.56	3.06
	86.5	2.60	2.93
	100.0	3.20	4.00

	Q-A	Q-B	Q-C
Funct.3			
E.03.02	93.8	2.47	2.93
	88.5	2.98	2.98
	100.0	3.00	4.00
E.03.03	50.0	2.75	3.38
	61.5	2.77	2.97
	80.0	3.25	4.00
E.03.04	0.0	--	--
	25.0	2.54	2.92
	40.0	2.50	4.00
E.03.05	75.0	2.67	3.33
	73.6	2.56	2.97
	80.0	3.00	4.00
E.03.06	93.8	2.73	3.13
	81.1	2.63	2.86
	100.0	3.00	3.80
E.03.07	93.8	2.93	3.13
	84.9	2.64	2.87
	100.0	3.20	3.40
E.03.08	62.5	2.70	3.10
	62.3	2.66	3.00
	100.0	3.00	3.60
E.03.09	87.5	2.79	3.00
	81.1	2.65	2.95
	100.0	3.00	3.80

	Q-A	Q-B	Q-C
Funct.3			
E.03.10	75.0	2.82	2.91
	69.2	2.61	2.89
	60.0	3.33	4.00
E.03.11	31.3	2.20	2.40
	37.7	2.60	2.00
	60.0	3.00	3.33
E.03.12	75.0	2.25	2.58
	71.7	2.53	2.66
	80.0	3.00	3.50
E.03.13	50.0	2.50	3.00
	67.9	2.58	2.50
	80.0	3.00	3.50
E.03.14	37.5	2.67	3.17
	60.4	2.58	2.71
	80.0	2.75	3.75
E.03.15	50.0	2.63	2.88
	67.9	2.67	2.31
	80.0	2.75	3.00
E.03.16	100.0	2.94	3.44
	83.0	2.68	2.98
	100.0	3.00	3.80
Funct.4			
E.04.01	18.8	2.33	2.67
	28.8	2.80	2.93
	80.0	3.25	3.75

Summary of BRAC Questionnaire Graduate Responses by Task and by Program Level
(Continued)

E. MANAGEMENT

Task	Q-A	Q-B	Q-C
Funct.4			
E.04.02	37.5 / 49.1 / 80.0	2.17 / 2.62 / 3.25	3.00 / 3.00 / 3.75
E.04.03	31.3 / 34.0 / 80.0	2.60 / 2.50 / 2.75	3.00 / 2.56 / 3.25
E.04.04	43.8 / 39.6 / 80.0	2.71 / 2.43 / 2.75	2.86 / 2.76 / 3.50
E.04.05	37.5 / 48.1 / 80.0	2.67 / 2.60 / 2.75	3.00 / 2.88 / 4.00
E.04.06	18.8 / 30.8 / 60.0	2.33 / 2.81 / 3.33	3.00 / 2.88 / 3.67
Funct.5			
E.05.01	6.3 / 46.2 / 60.0	2.00 / 2.75 / 3.00	3.00 / 3.00 / 3.33
E.05.02	6.3 / 34.6 / 60.0	2.00 / 2.89 / 3.00	4.00 / 2.84 / 3.33
E.05.03	0.0 / 11.3 / 20.0	-- / 2.67 / 4.00	-- / 2.67 / 3.00
E.05.04	6.3 / 30.2 / 40.0	2.00 / 2.75 / 2.50	4.00 / 3.00 / 4.00
E.05.05	0.0 / 17.0 / 40.0	-- / 2.78 / 3.50	-- / 2.67 / 3.50
E.05.06	6.3 / 17.0 / 40.0	2.00 / 2.89 / 3.50	3.00 / 2.78 / 3.50
E.05.07	0.0 / 11.3 / 40.0	-- / 2.83 / 3.50	-- / 2.50 / 3.50
E.05.08	6.3 / 26.4 / 20.0	2.00 / 2.71 / 3.00	4.00 / 2.79 / 4.00
E.05.09	6.3 / 26.4 / 40.0	2.00 / 2.86 / 2.50	4.00 / 2.86 / 4.00
E.05.10	6.3 / 28.3 / 20.0	2.00 / 2.73 / 4.00	4.00 / 2.93 / 4.00
E.05.11	37.5 / 50.9 / 80.0	2.67 / 2.52 / 3.00	3.17 / 2.96 / 3.75
E.05.12	68.8 / 62.3 / 80.0	2.55 / 2.70 / 3.00	3.00 / 3.24 / 3.75
E.05.13	50.0 / 49.1 / 80.0	2.50 / 2.65 / 3.00	3.00 / 2.92 / 3.75
E.05.14	12.5 / 26.6 / 80.0	3.00 / 2.67 / 3.00	2.50 / 2.92 / 3.75
E.05.15	18.8 / 43.4 / 60.0	2.67 / 2.57 / 3.00	3.00 / 2.83 / 3.67
E.05.16	0.0 / 11.3 / 60.0	-- / 2.83 / 3.00	-- / 3.00 / 3.67
E.05.17	0.0 / 9.4 / 40.0	-- / 3.00 / 2.00	-- / 2.80 / 3.50
E.05.18	6.3 / 13.2 / 40.0	2.00 / 2.86 / 2.00	3.00 / 2.86 / 3.00
E.05.19	0.0 / 9.4 / 20.0	-- / 2.80 / 3.00	-- / 2.60 / 3.00
Funct.6			
E.06.01	50.0 / 45.3 / 60.0	2.38 / 2.50 / 3.00	2.88 / 2.75 / 3.67
E.06.02	37.5 / 43.4 / 60.0	2.67 / 2.61 / 3.00	3.00 / 2.61 / 3.67
E.06.03	25.0 / 41.5 / 60.0	2.75 / 2.52 / 2.67	3.50 / 2.52 / 3.67
E.06.04	25.0 / 37.7 / 60.0	2.75 / 2.60 / 3.00	3.25 / 2.65 / 3.67
E.06.05	43.8 / 60.4 / 80.0	2.86 / 2.52 / 2.75	3.29 / 2.68 / 3.25
E.06.06	62.5 / 60.4 / 80.0	2.90 / 2.72 / 3.00	3.00 / 2.91 / 3.25
E.06.07	75.0 / 67.9 / 80.0	2.83 / 2.78 / 3.00	3.33 / 3.42 / 3.75
E.06.08	62.5 / 66.0 / 80.0	2.90 / 2.66 / 3.00	3.20 / 3.31 / 3.50
E.06.09	75.0 / 60.4 / 80.0	2.75 / 2.75 / 3.00	3.00 / 3.09 / 3.75
E.06.10	75.0 / 67.9 / 80.0	2.83 / 2.64 / 3.00	3.08 / 3.28 / 3.75
E.06.11	68.8 / 66.0 / 80.0	2.82 / 2.69 / 3.00	2.91 / 3.17 / 3.75

Summary of BRAC Questionnaire Graduate Responses by Task and by Program Level
(Continued)

Appendix D   111

E. MANAGEMENT

	Q-A	Q-B	Q-C
Funct.7 E.07.01	50.0 / 52.8 / 60.0	2.50 / 2.75 / 2.67	2.63 / 2.71 / 2.67
E.07.02	56.3 / 58.5 / 80.0	2.67 / 2.52 / 2.75	2.78 / 2.90 / 3.25
E.07.03	12.5 / 22.6 / 20.0	2.50 / 2.75 / 4.00	3.00 / 2.25 / 2.00
E.07.04	25.0 / 28.3 / 40.0	2.75 / 2.87 / 2.50	2.75 / 2.33 / 3.00
E.07.05	12.5 / 18.9 / 20.0	2.50 / 2.70 / 3.00	3.00 / 2.40 / 3.00
E.07.06	31.3 / 34.0 / 40.0	2.60 / 2.67 / 2.50	3.00 / 2.67 / 3.00
Funct.8 E.08.01	50.0 / 49.1 / 60.0	2.63 / 2.62 / 2.67	2.50 / 2.46 / 3.33
E.08.02	37.5 / 37.7 / 80.0	2.33 / 2.65 / 3.25	2.17 / 2.65 / 3.50

	Q-A	Q-B	Q-C
Funct.8 E.08.03	6.3 / 20.8 / 60.0	3.00 / 2.80 / 3.00	2.00 / 2.50 / 3.33
E.08.04	18.8 / 20.8 / 60.0	2.67 / 2.91 / 3.33	3.00 / 2.55 / 3.33
E.08.05	18.8 / 26.4 / 80.0	2.67 / 2.71 / 3.00	3.00 / 2.57 / 4.00
E.08.06	68.8 / 64.2 / 80.0	2.91 / 2.59 / 3.25	3.00 / 2.79 / 4.00
E.08.07	43.8 / 79.2 / 80.0	2.71 / 2.88 / 3.50	2.71 / 2.93 / 3.25
E.08.08	56.3 / 45.3 / 60.0	2.67 / 2.67 / 3.00	2.44 / 2.63 / 3.33
E.08.09	25.0 / 26.4 / 60.0	2.75 / 2.71 / 3.00	2.75 / 3.00 / 3.67
E.08.10	25.0 / 26.4 / 60.0	2.75 / 2.79 / 3.00	2.50 / 3.00 / 3.67
E.08.11	25.0 / 20.8 / 60.0	2.75 / 2.64 / 3.33	2.50 / 2.82 / 3.67

	Q-A	Q-B	Q-C
Funct.8 E.08.12	18.8 / 28.9 / 60.0	2.67 / 2.60 / 3.00	2.33 / 2.80 / 3.67
E.08.13	6.3 / 32.1 / 60.0	3.00 / 2.71 / 3.00	3.00 / 2.53 / 3.00
Funct.9 E.09.01	81.3 / 45.3 / 80.0	2.31 / 2.33 / 3.25	3.46 / 3.42 / 4.00
E.09.02	87.5 / 50.9 / 60.0	2.14 / 2.41 / 2.67	3.36 / 3.19 / 4.00
E.09.03	62.5 / 43.4 / 80.0	2.10 / 2.48 / 3.00	3.20 / 3.13 / 4.00
E.09.04	62.5 / 43.4 / 60.0	2.20 / 2.70 / 3.00	3.10 / 3.26 / 3.67
E.09.05	68.8 / 37.7 / 60.0	2.09 / 2.60 / 3.00	3.27 / 3.20 / 4.00
E.09.06	50.0 / 43.4 / 80.0	1.88 / 2.43 / 3.00	3.25 / 3.35 / 4.00

	Q-A	Q-B	Q-C
Funct.9 E.09.07	75.0 / 43.4 / 60.0	2.25 / 2.35 / 2.67	3.08 / 3.04 / 4.00
E.09.08	81.3 / 52.8 / 80.0	2.23 / 2.50 / 3.25	3.31 / 3.43 / 4.00
E.09.09	93.8 / 58.5 / 80.0	2.27 / 2.52 / 3.25	3.31 / 3.23 / 4.00
E.09.10	56.3 / 54.7 / 60.0	2.22 / 2.59 / 3.00	3.33 / 3.14 / 4.00
E.09.11	56.3 / 52.8 / 60.0	2.11 / 2.50 / 3.00	3.22 / 2.96 / 4.00
E.09.12	75.0 / 45.3 / 80.0	2.17 / 2.42 / 3.25	3.25 / 2.88 / 3.75
E.09.13	68.8 / 47.1 / 80.0	2.18 / 2.52 / 3.25	3.18 / 2.84 / 3.75
E.09.14	12.5 / 26.4 / 20.0	1.50 / 2.64 / 4.00	3.50 / 3.21 / 4.00
Funct.10 E.10.01	68.8 / 55.8 / 80.0	2.18 / 2.41 / 2.75	3.00 / 2.86 / 3.50

112 Appendix D

Summary of BRAC Questionnaire Graduate Responses by Task and by Program Level
(Continued)

E. MANAGEMENT

	Q-A	Q-B	Q-C		Q-A	Q-B	Q-C		Q-A	Q-B	Q-C
Funct.10				Funct.10				Funct.11			
E.10.02	50.0	2.25	2.38	E.10.10	25.0	1.50	2.50	E.11.05	37.5	2.17	3.17
	38.5	2.50	2.70		26.4	2.86	2.71		26.4	2.57	3.00
	60.0	2.67	3.33		60.0	2.67	2.67		60.0	2.67	3.00
E.10.03	56.3	2.00	2.89	E.10.11	12.5	2.00	2.00	Funct.12			
	48.1	2.48	2.84		35.8	2.84	2.68	E.12.01	43.8	2.14	2.86
	80.0	2.75	3.50		40.0	2.00	2.50		51.9	2.78	3.04
									80.0	2.75	3.25
E.10.04	25.0	1.75	2.75	E.10.12	68.8	2.36	2.55	E.12.02	18.8	3.00	3.00
	34.0	2.50	2.61		52.8	2.68	2.39		36.5	2.89	3.11
	40.0	2.50	3.50		60.0	3.00	2.67		60.0	3.00	3.67
E.10.05	56.3	2.11	2.78	E.10.13	56.3	2.33	2.89	E.12.03	6.3	2.00	3.00
	41.5	2.55	2.64		45.3	2.58	2.79		20.8	2.45	2.82
	60.0	2.67	3.00		60.0	3.00	3.25		20.0	4.00	4.00
E.10.06	18.8	1.00	3.00	Funct.11				E.12.04	6.3	2.00	3.00
	39.6	2.62	2.95	E.11.01	31.3	2.20	3.20		28.3	2.80	2.93
	40.0	3.50	3.00		37.7	2.45	2.90		60.0	3.00	3.67
					60.0	3.00	3.33				
E.10.07	68.8	2.10	3.10	E.11.02	43.8	2.14	3.00	E.12.05	6.3	2.00	3.00
	49.1	2.58	2.77		30.2	2.38	3.06		18.9	2.80	3.40
	60.0	3.67	3.00		60.0	3.00	3.33		20.0	4.00	4.00
E.10.08	62.5	2.30	3.20	E.11.03	0.0	--	--	E.12.06	6.3	2.00	3.00
	52.8	2.64	2.71		13.2	2.71	3.00		35.8	2.63	3.05
	40.0	2.50	3.50		20.0	2.00	3.00		60.0	3.00	3.67
E.10.09	68.8	2.36	2.91	E.11.04	31.3	2.80	3.20	E.12.07	12.5	1.50	2.50
	62.3	2.61	2.76		32.1	2.53	3.00		35.8	2.63	3.11
	80.0	3.25	3.25		60.0	2.67	3.00		60.0	3.00	3.67

	Q-A	Q-B	Q-C
Funct.12			
E.12.08	6.3	2.00	3.00
	15.1	2.88	3.50
	40.0	2.50	3.50
E.12.09	0.0	--	--
	9.4	2.60	3.20
	40.0	2.00	3.50
E.12.10	31.3	2.40	2.80
	52.8	2.64	2.89
	40.0	3.00	3.50
Funct.13			
E.13.01	6.3	2.00	2.00
	20.8	2.82	3.18
	60.0	3.00	3.33
E.13.02	18.8	3.00	2.67
	52.8	2.64	3.11
	80.0	3.25	3.50
E.13.03	31.3	2.80	3.20
	39.6	2.38	2.76
	40.0	3.00	3.50
E.13.04	18.8	2.67	3.00
	30.2	2.50	2.63
	40.0	2.50	3.50
E.13.05	6.3	3.00	3.00
	17.0	2.67	2.89
	40.0	2.50	3.50

Summary of BRAC Questionnaire Graduate Responses by Task and by Program Level
(Continued)

E. MANAGEMENT

	Q-A	Q-B	Q-C		Q-A	Q-B	Q-C		Q-A	Q-B	Q-C
Funct.13				Funct.14				Funct.15			
E.13.06	43.8	2.71	3.29	E.14.06	31.3	2.80	3.00	E.15.08	56.3	2.44	2.44
	49.1	2.62	2.69		37.7	2.75	2.85		71.7	2.65	2.78
	40.0	3.00	3.50		60.0	2.67	3.00		60.0	3.33	2.67
E.13.07	18.8	2.67	3.67	E.14.07	50.0	2.88	2.25	E.15.09	25.0	2.75	2.75
	35.8	2.74	2.89		79.2	2.64	2.43		47.2	2.65	2.83
	40.0	2.50	3.50		60.0	3.00	3.00		100.0	3.20	3.40
E.13.08	43.8	2.57	2.71	Funct.15				E.15.10	37.5	2.50	3.00
	71.7	2.63	2.61	E.15.01	50.0	2.63	2.50		41.5	2.36	2.64
	60.0	3.00	3.00		60.4	2.47	2.50		60.0	3.00	3.33
Funct.14					80.0	3.00	3.50	E.15.11	18.8	2.67	3.00
E.14.01	75.0	2.67	2.58	E.15.02	6.3	2.00	2.00		28.3	2.57	2.79
	69.2	2.61	2.56		39.6	2.48	2.67		60.0	3.00	3.00
	100.0	3.00	2.60		60.0	3.00	2.67	E.15.12	6.3	3.00	4.00
E.14.02	68.8	2.60	2.40	E.15.03	50.0	2.75	3.38		32.2	2.65	2.82
	66.0	2.66	2.34		50.9	2.78	2.41		60.0	3.33	3.00
	60.0	2.67	2.67		20.0	4.00	3.00	E.15.13	25.0	2.75	2.57
E.15.03	37.5	2.17	2.33	E.15.04	100.0	3.06	2.69		49.1	2.60	2.50
	49.1	2.65	2.15		79.2	2.74	2.52		60.0	3.33	3.00
	40.0	2.50	3.00		100.0	3.00	2.80	E.15.14	43.8	2.71	2.57
E.14.04	75.0	2.42	2.58	E.15.05	50.0	2.88	2.75		69.8	2.75	2.50
	59.6	2.71	2.45		54.7	2.66	2.45		80.0	3.25	3.00
	80.0	2.75	2.50		80.0	3.25	2.50	E.15.15	6.3	3.00	2.00
E.14.05	56.3	2.44	2.67	E.15.06	31.3	2.40	2.60		20.8	2.64	2.82
	66.0	2.66	2.63		39.6	2.57	2.67		60.0	3.00	2.67
	60.0	2.67	3.00		100.0	3.40	3.40	Funct.16			
				E.15.07	62.5	2.80	2.80	E.16.01	81.3	2.75	3.00
					64.2	2.59	2.71		86.8	2.60	2.87
					80.0	3.25	3.75		80.0	3.00	3.00

	Q-A	Q-B	Q-C
Funct.16			
E.16.02	81.3	2.75	2.92
	84.9	2.64	2.82
	80.0	3.00	2.50
E.16.03	75.0	2.73	2.82
	94.3	2.60	2.80
	80.0	3.00	2.75
E.16.04	62.5	2.67	2.89
	73.6	2.67	2.64
	80.0	3.00	2.75
E.16.05	68.8	2.70	2.90
	77.4	2.65	2.55
	80.0	3.00	3.25
E.16.06	50.0	2.29	2.71
	75.5	2.63	2.67
	100.0	3.20	2.60
E.16.07	93.8	2.53	2.86
	86.8	2.78	2.78
	60.0	3.33	4.00
E.16.08	81.3	2.92	2.83
	78.4	2.77	2.42
	40.0	3.50	2.50
E.16.09	68.8	2.80	2.70
	69.8	2.78	2.46
	40.0	3.50	2.50
E.16.10	37.5	3.00	2.60
	34.0	2.67	2.28
	20.0	4.00	4.00

Appendix D 113

Summary of BRAC Questionnaire Graduate Responses by Task and by Program Level
(Continued)

E. MANAGEMENT

Task	Q-A	Q-B	Q-C	Task	Q-A	Q-B	Q-C	Task	Q-A	Q-B	Q-C
Funct.16				**Funct.17**				**Funct.2**			
E.16.11	50.0	2.71	2.57	E.17.07	12.5	3.00	3.00	F.02.03	18.8	2.00	2.50
	67.3	2.63	2.60		27.1	2.50	3.00		24.5	2.46	2.38
	80.0	3.25	2.75		40.0	3.50	4.00		80.0	2.50	2.75
E.16.12	81.3	2.67	2.58	**F. RESEARCH**				F.02.04	12.5	1.00	2.00
	82.1	2.33	2.42		Q-A	Q-B	Q-C		15.1	2.50	2.50
	80.0	3.25	2.75						60.0	2.33	2.67
Funct.17				**Funct.1**				**Funct.3**			
E.17.01	43.8	2.33	2.50	F.01.01	25.0	2.00	2.67	F.03.01	6.3	--	--
	24.5	2.54	2.77		49.1	2.46	2.58		20.8	2.45	2.45
	40.0	3.00	2.50		100.0	2.60	2.80		60.0	2.00	2.67
E.17.02	25.0	2.33	2.33	F.01.02	18.8	2.00	2.50	F.03.02	6.3	--	--
	24.5	2.38	2.31		22.6	2.42	2.42		18.9	2.50	2.40
	100.0	2.80	2.60		80.0	2.50	2.75		80.0	2.25	2.75
E.17.03	18.8	2.50	3.00	F.01.03	18.8	2.00	2.50	F.03.03	6.3	--	--
	23.1	2.33	2.42		28.3	2.33	2.67		24.5	2.46	2.46
	60.0	2.67	3.67		100.0	2.60	2.80		80.0	2.25	2.75
E.17.04	37.5	2.60	2.80	F.01.04	25.0	2.00	2.33	**Funct.4**			
	40.4	2.48	2.33		32.1	2.71	2.71	F.04.01	18.8	2.00	2.00
	60.0	3.33	3.00		100.0	2.60	2.80		32.1	2.29	2.41
									80.0	2.25	2.75
E.17.05	12.5	3.00	3.00	**Funct.2**				F.04.02	12.5	2.00	2.00
	26.9	2.50	2.29	F.02.01	25.0	2.00	2.33		32.1	2.35	2.47
	40.0	2.50	1.50		35.8	2.58	2.53		80.0	2.25	2.75
					80.0	2.50	2.75				
E.17.06	12.5	3.00	3.00	F.02.02	18.8	2.50	2.50	F.04.03	18.8	2.00	2.00
	15.4	2.75	3.13		32.1	2.53	2.59		43.4	2.52	2.48
	20.0	4.00	4.00		80.0	2.50	2.75		80.0	2.50	3.00

Task	Q-A	Q-B	Q-C
Funct.4			
F.04.04	18.8	2.00	2.00
	35.8	2.53	2.53
	80.0	2.50	3.00
F.04.05	12.5	2.00	2.00
	35.8	2.58	2.58
	80.0	2.50	3.00
Funct.5			
F.05.01	6.3	--	--
	24.5	2.38	2.69
	80.0	2.75	3.00
F.05.02	6.3	--	--
	26.4	2.36	2.64
	80.0	2.75	3.00
F.05.03	6.3	--	--
	17.0	2.33	2.33
	60.0	2.33	3.00
Funct.6			
F.06.01	6.3	--	--
	17.0	2.44	2.78
	60.0	2.67	3.33
F.06.02	18.8	2.00	2.50
	22.6	2.75	2.58
	80.0	2.75	3.25
F.06.03	18.8	2.00	2.50
	17.0	2.78	3.22
	80.0	2.75	3.25

Summary of BRAC Questionnaire Graduate Responses by Task and by Program Level
(Continued)

F. RESEARCH	Q-A	Q-B	Q-C		Q-A	Q-B	Q-C		Q-A	Q-B	Q-C		Q-A	Q-B	Q-C
Funct.6				Funct.7				Funct.1				Funct.3			
F.06.04	12.5	2.00	2.00	F.07.03	12.5	4.00	4.00	G.01.03	81.3	2.33	2.83	G.03.01	87.5	2.54	2.77
	20.8	2.45	2.73		24.5	2.62	2.54		73.6	2.54	2.97		92.5	2.65	2.65
	80.0	2.75	3.25		60.0	2.67	3.33		100.0	3.20	3.60		100.0	3.60	3.60
F.06.05	12.5	2.00	2.00	F.07.04	12.5	3.00	3.00	G.01.04	37.5	2.00	3.00	G.03.02	62.5	2.56	3.00
	18.9	2.70	2.80		30.2	2.50	2.38		45.3	2.65	2.70		69.8	2.69	2.50
	80.0	2.75	3.25		80.0	2.75	3.25		80.0	3.50	3.50		100.0	3.60	3.60
F.06.06	6.3	---	---	F.07.05	12.5	3.00	3.00	G.01.05	56.3	2.50	3.13	G.03.03	93.8	2.93	3.21
	18.9	2.60	2.80		26.4	2.50	2.57		71.7	2.66	2.58		96.2	2.89	3.30
	60.0	2.67	3.33		60.0	3.33	3.00		100.0	3.40	3.50		100.0	3.60	3.80
F.06.07	12.5	2.00	2.00	F.07.06	18.8	3.00	2.00	Funct.2				G.03.04	50.0	2.71	2.57
	17.0	2.67	2.67		33.9	2.56	2.39	G.02.01	100.0	2.87	3.13		52.8	2.68	2.89
	80.0	2.75	3.25		80.0	2.50	3.25		96.2	2.94	3.39		80.0	3.00	3.50
									100.0	3.80	4.00				
F.06.08	12.5	2.00	2.00	F.07.07	31.3	2.75	2.75	G.02.02	43.8	2.83	3.17	G.03.05	18.8	3.00	2.00
	18.9	2.60	2.60		28.3	2.60	2.67		39.6	2.52	2.43		49.1	2.73	2.65
	60.0	2.67	3.33		60.0	2.67	3.33		100.0	2.60	2.80		80.0	3.00	3.50
Funct.7				G. PROFESSIONALISM				G.02.03	100.0	3.00	3.07	G.03.06	18.8	2.00	2.50
F.07.01	43.8	2.67	2.67		Q-A	Q-B	Q-C		94.3	2.92	3.34		38.5	2.65	2.75
	45.3	2.50	2.29	Funct.1					100.0	3.80	4.00		80.0	3.50	3.25
	60.0	2.67	3.00	G.01.01	50.0	2.57	3.00	G.02.04	100.0	3.07	3.13	G.03.07	75.0	2.55	2.73
					66.0	2.31	2.94		94.3	2.94	3.24		73.6	2.58	2.97
					100.0	3.20	3.60		100.0	3.80	4.00		100.0	3.00	3.40
F.07.02	37.5	2.80	2.80	G.01.02	25.0	2.00	2.67					G.03.08	12.5	2.00	3.00
	45.3	2.58	2.38		54.7	2.66	2.62						24.5	2.92	3.14
	60.0	2.67	3.00		100.0	2.80	3.00						40.0	4.00	4.00

Appendix D 115

116 Appendix D

Summary of BRAC Questionnaire Graduate Responses by Task and by Program Level
(Continued)

	Q-A	Q-B	Q-C		Q-A	Q-B	Q-C		Q-A	Q-B	Q-C
G. PROFESSIONALISM											
Funct.3				Funct.5							
G.03.09	18.8	2.50	3.00	G.05.03	87.5	2.67	3.00				
	35.8	2.79	2.63		88.7	2.74	2.96				
	100.0	2.80	3.00		100.0	3.40	3.20				
Funct.4				G.05.04	50.0	2.43	2.71				
G.04.01	68.8	2.60	2.90		56.6	2.47	2.57				
	86.8	2.80	3.02		100.0	3.00	2.80				
	100.0	3.40	3.60	G.05.05	6.3	--	--				
G.04.02	93.8	2.64	2.93		26.4	2.79	2.71				
	94.3	2.84	3.08		100.0	2.80	3.00				
	100.0	3.60	3.80	Funct.6							
G.04.03	100.0	2.67	2.87	G.06.01	50.0	2.57	3.14				
	98.1	2.87	3.13		71.2	2.78	3.16				
	100.0	3.40	4.00		80.0	3.50	4.00				
G.04.04	50.0	2.83	3.17	G.06.02	87.5	2.77	3.38				
	37.7	2.85	3.05		88.7	2.85	3.43				
	100.0	3.20	3.40		100.0	3.60	4.00				
Funct.5				G.06.03	93.8	2.79	3.57				
G.05.01	93.8	2.64	2.93		90.6	2.73	3.46				
	90.6	2.81	3.00		100.0	3.40	4.00				
	80.0	3.50	3.50	G.06.04	93.8	2.64	3.43				
G.05.02	81.3	2.58	3.00		92.5	2.80	3.29				
	88.7	2.80	2.93		100.0	3.60	4.00				
	100.0	3.20	3.00								

Summary of BRAC Questionnaire Graduate Responses by Competency Area and Function[1]

A. HUMAN BEHAVIOR

Funct.	Q-A	Q-B	Q-C		Funct.	Q-A	Q-B	Q-C
01	97.3	2.47	3.44		04	67.2	2.71	2.92
	91.9	2.64	3.34			71.7	2.57	3.13
	100.0	3.20	3.88			93.3	3.04	3.42
02	90.6	2.61	3.15		05	55.0	2.50	2.68
	88.1	2.58	3.10			63.8	2.56	2.76
	100.0	2.93	3.53			84.0	3.20	2.93
03	95.3	2.83	3.49		06	43.7	2.34	2.54
	94.1	2.88	3.46			51.6	2.26	2.79
	100.0	3.24	3.84			70.0	2.36	3.22
C.A. Av.	94.0	2.65	3.33			63.5	2.57	2.98
	91.0	2.69	3.26			70.3	2.50	3.05
	100.0	3.12	3.75			87.0	3.00	3.46

B. LEARNING AND LEARNING ENVIRONMENT

Funct.	Q-A	Q-B	Q-C		Funct.	Q-A	Q-B	Q-C
01	83.3	2.64	3.24		04	63.3	2.66	3.03
	82.3	2.47	3.23			68.6	2.52	3.15
	100.0	3.23	3.70			85.0	2.85	3.71
02	64.6	2.59	3.28		05	62.5	2.45	2.83
	76.7	2.62	3.21			68.7	2.36	3.00
	91.1	3.14	3.65			88.0	2.92	3.72
03	61.2	2.51	3.08		06	16.9	2.25	3.06
	69.8	2.42	2.98			25.7	2.39	2.73
	84.0	3.03	3.82			40.0	2.43	3.82
					C.A. Av.	53.5	2.49	2.99
						61.2	2.49	3.02
						79.8	2.85	3.69

C. PLANNING & EVALUATION

Funct.	Q-A	Q-B	Q-C
01	66.2	2.54	3.10
	73.9	2.56	3.13
	86.0	2.96	3.55
02	75.0	2.51	2.80
	71.4	2.61	3.07
	92.0	3.18	3.69
03	55.0	2.55	2.98
	70.9	2.52	3.17
	88.0	2.73	3.63

D. MEDIA

Funct.	Q-A	Q-B	Q-C
01	64.3	2.77	3.25
	74.1	2.59	3.34
	68.6	2.91	3.40
02	79.9	2.63	2.86
	83.0	2.66	2.99
	91.1	3.12	3.59
03	57.2	2.64	3.04
	75.8	2.65	3.02
	90.0	3.10	3.55

Funct.	Q-A	Q-B	Q-C
04	77.7	2.75	2.99
	91.6	2.67	2.95
	85.7	3.21	3.37
05	77.3	2.58	2.72
	76.4	2.72	2.54
	78.7	2.94	2.72
06	73.4	2.81	2.95
	62.2	2.62	2.70
	68.9	3.02	2.25
07	69.9	2.97	2.73
	68.1	2.68	2.42
	63.7	3.15	2.55
08	11.2	2.14	2.74
	19.3	2.45	2.62
	31.6	1.92	2.67
09	72.5	2.66	2.96
	75.5	2.40	2.83
	92.0	2.92	3.66
10	76.0	2.90	3.20
	79.2	2.65	2.84
	76.7	3.49	3.54
11	43.0	2.85	2.80
	64.2	2.68	3.13
	82.5	3.05	3.50

[1] For each Function the first row of numbers summarizes BA-level data; the second row summarizes MA-level data; and the third row summarizes sixth-year level data.

Summary of BRAC Questionnaire Graduate Responses by Competency Area and Function (Continued)

D. MEDIA

Funct.	Q-A	Q-B	Q-C	Funct.	Q-A	Q-B	Q-C	Funct.	Q-A	Q-B	Q-C
12	58.1	2.69	3.06	21	85.4	2.61	3.03	07	31.2	2.59	2.86
	67.3	2.51	3.07		40.5	2.77	3.12		35.9	2.71	2.54
	88.0	3.24	3.64		73.7	3.17	3.72		43.3	2.90	2.82
13	68.7	2.67	2.98	22	62.1	2.72	2.94	08	30.8	2.73	2.61
	82.1	2.65	3.08		65.9	2.69	2.78		36.8	2.71	2.71
	95.0	3.21	3.51		84.7	3.15	2.90		66.2	3.10	3.52
14	47.9	2.50	2.79	23	15.2	2.69	2.83	09	66.5	2.12	3.27
	67.6	2.64	2.80		35.1	2.52	2.82		42.1	2.50	3.16
	83.3	3.25	2.91		42.9	3.55	3.48		67.1	3.11	3.94
15	17.2	2.40	3.06	24	15.2	2.44	2.94	10	49.0	2.02	2.77
	35.0	2.63	2.79		30.4	2.57	2.78		44.8	2.60	2.72
	73.3	2.95	3.38		54.3	3.36	3.55		60.0	2.84	3.13
16	88.3	2.83	3.23	25	10.8	2.87	2.91	11	28.7	2.33	3.14
	76.7	2.77	3.21		28.7	2.59	3.02		27.9	2.53	2.99
	97.5	3.21	3.51		66.4	2.74	3.41		52.0	2.67	3.13
17	63.4	2.76	3.15	26	31.2	2.45	2.73	12	13.7	2.12	2.91
	57.7	2.61	3.19		33.9	2.53	2.87		30.5	2.71	3.11
	82.9	3.18	3.62		60.0	2.42	2.84		48.0	3.03	3.64
18	74.4	3.00	3.27	27	31.0	0.00	3.00	13	23.4	2.68	2.94
	73.6	2.72	3.13		14.2	2.80	3.23		43.4	2.63	2.85
	98.0	3.23	3.60		30.0	2.33	3.83		50.0	2.84	3.42
19	76.8	2.97	2.97	28	5.4	1.00	2.00	14	56.4	2.57	2.54
	79.0	2.74	2.97		14.3	2.68	2.96		61.0	2.67	2.49
	97.1	3.32	3.19		40.0	2.50	3.43		65.7	2.75	2.82
20	73.4	3.13	2.93	29	5.8	0.18	3.33	15	37.9	2.69	2.75
	75.0	2.92	3.00		11.4	2.66	3.21		50.0	2.61	2.65
	80.0	3.71	3.55		40.0	2.00	2.75		70.7	3.22	3.05

Funct.	Q-A	Q-B	Q-C
30	25.0	2.28	2.72
	44.4	2.54	2.57
	73.3	2.52	3.43
C.A. Av.	50.5	2.54	2.93
	56.7	2.64	2.89
	72.8	3.00	3.30

E. MANAGEMENT

Funct.	Q-A	Q-B	Q-C
01	80.2	2.58	3.16
	74.4	2.53	3.06
	93.3	2.85	3.90
02	90.2	2.68	3.10
	86.5	2.65	3.18
	100.0	3.09	3.63
03	67.2	2.64	3.03
	66.0	2.64	2.78
	83.7	3.00	3.72
04	31.2	2.47	2.92
	38.4	2.63	2.84
	76.7	3.01	3.65
05	12.5	2.26	3.36
	27.6	2.76	2.85
	25.7	3.03	3.58
06	54.5	2.77	3.13
	56.1	2.64	2.95
	72.7	2.95	3.61

Summary of BRAC Questionnaire Graduate Responses by Competency Area and Function
(Continued)

E. MANAGEMENT

	Q-A	Q-B	Q-C
Funct. 16	69.3	2.71	2.78
	75.9	2.65	2.61
	68.3	3.25	2.95
17	23.2	2.68	2.80
	26.0	2.50	2.61
	51.4	3.11	3.04
C.A. Av.	44.5	2.49	2.96
	48.3	2.50	2.82
	64.4	2.99	3.39

F. RESEARCH

	Q-A	Q-B	Q-C
Funct. 01	21.9	2.00	2.50
	33.0	2.48	2.60
	95.0	2.58	2.79
02	18.7	1.88	2.33
	26.9	2.52	2.50
	75.0	2.46	2.73
03	6.2	0.00	0.00
	11.4	2.47	2.44
	73.3	2.17	2.72
04	16.2	2.00	2.00
	35.9	2.45	2.49
	80.0	2.40	2.90
05	6.2	0.00	0.00
	22.7	2.36	2.55
	73.3	2.61	3.00
06	12.5	2.00	2.17
	14.4	2.62	2.77
	72.5	2.72	3.28
07	24.1	3.03	2.89
	33.4	2.55	2.46
	65.7	2.75	3.17
C.A. Av.	16.2	2.26	2.41
	28.4	2.52	2.57
	76.4	2.53	2.94

G. PROFESSIONALISM

	Q-A	Q-B	Q-C
Funct. 01	50.0	2.28	2.93
	62.3	2.56	2.76
	96.0	3.22	3.44
02	85.9	2.94	3.13
	81.1	2.83	3.10
	100.0	3.50	3.70
03	48.6	2.53	2.75
	59.1	2.73	2.83
	86.7	3.34	3.52
Funct. 04	78.1	2.69	2.97
	79.2	2.84	3.07
	100.0	3.40	3.70
05	63.7	2.58	2.91
	70.2	2.72	2.83
	96.0	3.18	3.10
06	81.2	2.69	3.38
	85.7	2.79	2.34
	95.0	3.53	4.00
C.A. Av.	64.1	2.59	2.96
	70.3	2.74	2.95
	95.6	3.36	3.58

Appendix E

Phase III Summative Evaluation:
Items to Cover in Statue Report

General Instructions. Please review the Phase II report discussion of your Program's components before answering the following questions regarding your 3rd year program. Please support your answers with a brief discussion of the reasons for any changes you describe.

PROGRAM GOALS AND OBJECTIVES

I-1 At the beginning of the 3rd year of your program, were the goals and objectives of the program different from those of the prior 2 years?

I-2 In view of what happened during the 3rd year of your program, do you contemplate modifying the goals and objectives of your program?

I-3 During the third year of your program you received no program support by the SLMP. Were you able to obtain offsetting funds? If so, where did you obtain these funds? If you did not receive offsetting funds, how did you adjust your program to make up for this loss? Did this loss have a major impact on your program?

PROGRAM PARTICIPANTS

II-1 Was there a marked increase or decrease in the enrollment in your experimental program during its 3rd year? If so, please explain the reason for this.

II-2 Do you anticipate a marked increase or decrease in enrollment during the next academic year? If so, please provide an explanation for this.

II-3 During the 3rd year of your program was your advisory board utilized? Please explain.

II-4 In preparation for the 3rd year of program implementation, what changes in staffing patterns did you make? Why did you make these changes? What impact did these changes have on your program?

II-5 What staffing changes do you anticipate making prior to the beginning of the 4th year of your program? Please explain the reasons for these anticipated changes

II-6 Do you feel that your experimental program now is attracting students who have personal and/or academic characteristics <u>different</u> from those of students who applied to your program prior to experimentation, or who are applying to current non-experimental programs conducted by your department? If yes, do you feel that these differences can be related to the nature of your experimental program, or are they more apt to be related to the general changes which seem to be occurring in the student body at your University?

PROGRAM COMPONENTS

III-1 What curriculum content changes were made?

III-2 What changes were made in instructional practices (e.g., individualization, self-instruction, special program features)?

III-3 What changes were made in the implementation of your field-work component?

III-4 To what extent have you maintained the interdisciplinary aspects of your program?

III-5 To what extent were you able to maintain open communication channels for obtaining information from students, staff and from the field for the purpose of evaluating and/or modifying your program?

PROGRAM RESULTS

IV-1 Identify and describe the key successes and/or difficulties which emerged during the 3rd year of your program.

IV-2 To what extent were you able to achieve the 3rd year program goals and objectives?

IV-3 During the first 2 years of your program, you developed various quality control procedures for evaluating and modifying your program. Did you maintain or change these procedures during the 3rd year of your program? Please explain.

PROGRAM IMPACT

V-1 Do you feel that your program has led to any systemic changes in various departments in your University?

Appendix F-1

V-2 To what extent do you feel that your program has had an impact within your State? For example:

    a. Did your program effect the characteristics of other library media educational programs within your State?

    b. Did your program have any effect on the development of media center programs in the field?

    c. Did your program have any effect on certification procedures?

    d. Did your program have any effect on program approval criteria?

CONCLUSIONS AND RECOMMENDATION

VI-1 Will the program be maintained and/or adopted as the standard program for the education of school library media personnel in your institution?

VI-2 In view of your experiences with the SLMP, what do you feel are the most important issues facing school library media education programs?

VI-3 In view of your experiences and the issues which you have identified, what would you recommend to other institutions engaged in developing and improving school library media education programs?

Appendix F-2

ARIZONA STATE UNIVERSITY
COLLEGE OF EDUCATION
Dr. Del Weber, Dean

AN EXPERIMENTAL PROGRAM IN
SCHOOL LIBRARY MEDIA EDUCATION
1971–1973

1974 Status Report by
HOWARD J. SULLIVAN

Contents

PROGRAM GOALS AND OBJECTIVES 124	PROGRAM RESULTS 126
PROGRAM PARTICIPANTS 125	PROGRAM IMPACT 127
PROGRAM COMPONENTS 126	CONCLUSIONS AND RECOMMENDATIONS 128

PROGRAM GOALS AND OBJECTIVES

I-1. The goals and objectives at the beginning of the third year of our program were identical to those of the prior two years. Our program was intentionally developed during this period of support by SLMP so that we would have a continuing (and improved) library-media program at the conclusion of the two-year period.

I-2. We made minor modifications in the program during the third year, and we anticipate other modifications in future years. However, the modifications will not be of the magnitude of those made during the two-year period of the SLMP project. During the third year, we added one newly developed course (Compentency-based Instruction) as a requirement at the M.A. level. Audiovisual Production Techniques in Education was developed because of the need for a production course in common media for library-media majors. This course is now a recommended elective for students in the B.A. and M.A. programs. Both of these courses were designed to enable students to acquire sets of skills identified during the project as being important for students to possess.

A change that we plan to make during 1974-75 is the adoption of a screening procedure after students have completed several courses but prior to the time that they are scheduled for their workshop. We plan to attempt to formally identify students whom we think have a low probability of success in their internship and subsequently as library-media specialists, and to counsel these students into a field in which they are likely to be more successful.

I-3. We developed the program during the two experimental years in a manner that we could subsequently continue it with our regular staff. That is, we developed courses, course modules and course objectives that constituted what in our opinion was a strong library-media program. The largest part of the SLMP money went toward the support of personnel engaged in this development effort. Nearly all of the development was completed during the two-year period. Thus, the program structure and materials developed during the two-year period were now available for use by the faculty and students, and additional money was not needed for development purposes.

Development of the new courses referred to above (Item I-2) did require faculty and graduate student time, but on a much smaller scale than the efforts of the preceding two years. This development effort was assumed as a normal part of the load of the faculty members involved, although we received several thousand dollars in graduate student support for it from the university and from a U.S. Office of Education sponsored project.

The greater emphasis on non-print media that occurred in our program as a result of the School Library Manpower Project has increased considerably the requests from faculty members for non-print materials to use in training library-media students. Through re-allocation of resources within our Department and some additional funding from the College, we were able to

Appendix F-2   125

allocate an additional $3000 for such materials in 1973-74. This amount will be increased to approximately $5000 in 1974-75, and it is likely that we will be able to maintain this higher level of support for materials in future years.

PROGRAM PARTICIPANTS

II-1. The number of students taking regular course work toward a B.A. or M.A. degree in Library Science during the second year of the project was 33, of whom 29 were enrolled in the experimental program. During the third year, 49 students took regular course work toward the B.A. or M.A. degree in Library Science. Because the program developed during the experimental phase subsequently became our regular program, all 49 students participated in this program during the third year. It seems probable that the visibility which the program received during the experimental phase accounted for some of the increased enrollment. It is difficult to isolate the other factors which contributed to the enrollment growth.

II-2. We anticipate a rather large, but steady, increase in enrollment in the program over the next several years. This is due to a number of factors: (1) our program has become more popular because of the joint library-media emphasis; (2) there has been in recent years a marked increase in the number of instructional material centers being built in the schools in Arizona and school districts are seeking persons with both print and non-print training; (3) we have been very successful in placing our graduates during the past three years; and (4) we will move the Children's Literature courses into the Library Science area in 1975-76. These are high-enrollment courses for elementary education majors. The courses will serve as an excellent recruitment base for the library-media program.

II-3. The Advisory Board was not retained as an official body during 1973-74. Individual members of the former board were contacted frequently for advice and assistance.

II-4. For the third year, we lost two faculty members who were employed on SLMP funds during the second year of the experimental program. However, the two additional faculty positions during the project were allocated primarily to development of modules, objectives and materials, rather than to instruction per se. Thus, we retained three full-time faculty positions for instruction in the Library Science area. In addition, the offering of new courses for Library Science students in both the Audiovisual Education and Educational Technology areas of the Department has increased the number of non-Library Science staff offering courses in the program.

II-5. One faculty member, who was initially employed with SLMP funds, was retained on a temporary basis (on a regular University line) during the third year. This person will not be returning during 1974-75. As her replacement, we have employed a recent recipient of a Ph.D. in education with a library-media emphasis.

II-6. The students who have applied for entry into our program during the past two years have been better qualified academically than previous applicants. This is not due to general changes occurring in the University student body. It may be related to the increased visibility, both in Arizona and nationally, that our program has received. We really are unable to identify the reasons for the improvement in academic qualifications of our applicants.

PROGRAM COMPONENTS

III-1. The curriculum content changes reflect directly the modified goals and objectives referred to under Item I-2. The Competency-based Instruction course was added as a requirement for the M.A. program, and the Audiovisual Production course was added as a recommended elective in both the B.A. and M.A. programs. No other significant changes were made in the curriculum.

III-2. No major changes were made in instructional practices. However, completion of the entire curriculum outline for the program at the end of the second year made it possible to use this outline as the basis for planning and conducting the instructional program.

III-3. There were two important changes in the field-work component. One change was to place interns in a wider geographic and socio-economic range of schools during the third year of the program. This was due to a conscious effort by the individual in charge of the field-work program to work with a large number of school districts throughout the Phoenix metropolitan area. A second change was to provide several of the interns with an internship experience at both the elementary and secondary levels, rather than at only one level.

III-4. The interdisciplinary aspects of the program have been extended with the addition of an Educational Technology course and another Audiovisual Education course to the curriculum.

III-5. We have continued to receive information from students, staff and from the field at about the same level as during the second year of the experimental program. Through use of an anonymous evaluation form, we solicit ratings and suggestions for improvements from students on every course in the program. We also request comments from each field-work supervisor, both officially and informally, on the weaknesses of the intern with whom she works. While feedback from the students and supervisors has been generally favorable, we have through these procedures identified certain weaknesses in the program which we are working to correct.

PROGRAM RESULTS

IV-1. There were no major difficulties during the third year of the program. The changes instigated during the experimental program itself resulted in some confusion and discontent among students and some faculty members, particularly during the first year of the program. However, the new program was well enough established and installed by the third year that these problems no longer existed.

The major success associated with the program is the increasing demand for our students because they have library-media training. The demand for our library-media graduates during the third year had exceeded the supply of available graduates by mid-June, even though a number of positions typically open up later in the summer. This situation contrasts sharply with the general job market in education in Arizona. Relatively few jobs are available for graduating teachers, and a very large number of both experienced and inexperienced teachers are unable to find employment.

IV-2. We did not employ any direct program-wide assessment procedures with respect to the program goals and objectives during the past year. We are, however, pleased with the results of the program on the following criteria: (1) number of students enrolled, (2) placement of graduates, and (3) overall attitudes of students in the program and general acceptance in the school library community in Arizona.

IV-3. We maintained the procedures for regular student evaluation of the program during the third year and we will continue to maintain them. Although we developed assessment items for each module during the two years of the experimental program, we did not employ module-by-module assessment on a program-wide basis during the past year. Use of the materials and assessment items within each module was at the discretion of the individual faculty members.

PROGRAM IMPACT

V-1. The program has not led to systemic changes in other Departments in our University, but it has produced major changes in our own Department. The most significant change has been the strengthening of the Library Science area within the Department. Following the two-year period of the project, one new faculty position (which previously was filled by a staff member in Educational Technology) was assigned to the Library Science area. By moving the Children's Literature courses into Library Science, one or more additional faculty positions will be created in Library Science. The increase in number of faculty members is particularly important because it results in a diversification of courses and instructors for Library Science students. The program also was responsible for (1) bringing about a much closer working relationship among the three curriculum areas in the Department and (2) a considerably greater allocation of financial resources within the Department to the Library Science area.

V-2. It is our judgment that our program has had its greatest effect within the state on the attitudes toward the development of media center programs at the local level. We receive a large number of requests from school districts for library-media specialists, in contrast to three years ago when the typical request was for a school librarian without reference to media skills or training. Instructional materials centers are a feature of nearly all of the new schools being built in this area, and this was not the case a few years ago. It is, of course, not possible to determine the extent to which the publicity and personnel associated with our program influenced this change. There is no doubt, however, that they did have some positive effect on it.

An interesting correlary of the library-media movement in Arizona has been the sharp increase in the number of audiovisual specialists who are either returning to school to take Library Science courses or who are including such courses in their graduate program in Audiovisual Education. This is due in large part to the fact that it is becoming increasingly difficult to obtain a professional position in a school media center without training in both areas. Again, there is no accurate way to determine the impact of our program with respect to this situation.

Our program has not had any direct effect on certification procedures in the state. The program meets the state requirements for endorsement as a school librarian. Although we have held talks with the key State Department of Education personnel regarding a library-media endorsement, we do not feel that the adoption of such an endorsement would serve a particularly useful purpose in Arizona at this time. Given the nature of our program, this may seem to be an anomaly, but we feel that we are able to provide adequate library-media training under our newly developed program, even though no library-media endorsement exists and its graduates receive a school librarian endorsement instead. Since this is our only program and the only other school library program in the state is much smaller than ours, we do not see the present lack of a library-media endorsement or credential in Arizona as a serious handicap.

CONCLUSIONS AND RECOMMENDATIONS

VI-1. The program developed under the School Library Manpower Project has been adopted as the school library media training program at Arizona State University.

VI-2. In my opinion, the most important issues facing school library media education programs are:

1. Recruitment of bright and personable individuals for entry into the library-media field at all levels from elementary schools through universities. (I think that far too many school librarians and library-media specialists are more interested in the technical aspects related to books and other media than in either their students or the content of the books and other media.)

2. The financial pressures on the schools and the resulting trend toward eliminating or downgrading non-administrative positions other than classroom teaching positions.

3. Development of training programs that are practical and appealing enough that the most capable students will remain in the programs and will identify with the library-media field.

VI-3. Recommendations:

      1. Establish and maintain both a vigorous program for recuritment of students and high standards for admission into the program. If possible, entry standards should relate to both academic ability and interpersonal skills. (The same recruitment concerns obviously apply for faculty members.)

      2. Establish a public relations and public information campaign aimed at promoting the image of the school library and/or media center as a lively, student-oriented learning center that is an essential part of a good educational program and a place where students like to pursue their educational interests.

      3. Avoid the reasonably common practice of attempting to make the trainees into library academicians or scholars. In addition to the basic skills needed for operation of a school library media center, attempt to develop favorable attitudes in the trainees toward working closely with students and teachers. Give them sets of procedures for working with teachers and as much practice as possible in working with classroom teachers in a school setting, so that they develop their skills in working with the teachers and so that they create an important constituency that desires the services they provide.

Appendix F-3

AUBURN UNIVERSITY
SCHOOL OF EDUCATION
Dr. Truman M. Pierce, Dean

AN EXPERIMENTAL PROGRAM IN
SCHOOL LIBRARY MEDIA EDUCATION
1971–1973

1974 Status Report by
WILLIAM E. HUG

Contents

PROGRAM GOALS AND OBJECTIVES 132	PROGRAM RESULTS 134
PROGRAM PARTICIPANTS 133	PROGRAM IMPACT 137
PROGRAM COMPONENTS 134	CONCLUSIONS AND RECOMMENDATIONS 138

PROGRAM GOALS AND OBJECTIVES

I-1. At the beginning of the third year of the Auburn program the goals and objectives of the media specialist curriculum remained the same. However, the <u>Behavioral Requirements Analysis Checklist</u> furnished information that was used to modify, delete, and add to the specific objectives under the general program goals and objectives. In other words, the primary thrust of the program remained the same while specific components were refined as the staff gained experience.

I-2. A concentrated effort to revise the curriculum is now under way. The original thirteen objectives of the program were hard to remember and were difficult to articulate with the curriculum. Four criteria have been developed to help select different organizers for the media specialist curriculum. They are: (1) each topic or heading should make visible the unique contribution that media specialists make to the educational program; (2) topics should be brief enough to be remembered and specific enough to have meaning; (3) topics were not to include competencies considered as prerequisite; and (4) the combination of topics should allow the reader to conceptualize the role media specialists play. It is now proposed that the following list of topics be used to organize competencies.

MEDIA PROGRAM OPERATIONS COMPETENCIES

    selection
    acquisition
    technical processing
    production
    maintenance
    circulation
    equipment operations
    reference
    personnel supervision

MEDIA PROGRAM PLANNING COMPETENCIES

    personnel
    facilities
    finance
    purposes
    policies
    priorities
    criteria
    evaluation
    curriculum
    in-service

CONSULTATIVE COMPETENCIES

    public information
    instructional development
    interpersonal communication
    curriculum development
    assisting users

I-3. After program support ended from SLMP, the University awarded the Department a new position plus additional operating capital. The SLMP Program remained essentially the same as it did during the funding period. The major cutback affected the number of materials that could be provided at no cost to students and the money available for student travel.

PROGRAM PARTICIPANTS

II-1. Enrollment increased by eight percent during the third year of the program. This is the smallest increase the Department has had in the past five years and is viewed as a normal tapering off of a new program. When the award was granted the Department was then only one year old.

II-2. The media specialist curriculum in the Department of Educational Media is expected to grow at the rate of between five and ten percent for the next five years. This growth rate is anticipated because of the increased emphasis that schools in the Southeast are placing on accreditation and, consequently, on media program development.

II-3. Because of the inability of the Department to pay travel expenses, the advisory board was not utilized during the third year of the program. The advisory board has been kept informed of the program, publications and activities of SLMP. Each advisory board member received a copy of the final report and the <u>Behavioral Requirements Analysis Checklist</u>.

II-4. Because of increased University support no basic changes in staffing patterns were required. During the third year of the program a committee of three was named to manage the field experiences of our students. This required some shifting of academic load. This change, however, was considered minor.

II-5. One staff member is leaving the Department to manage one of our more active field centers. The new member added to the faculty has competencies in instructional design and development. It is anticipated that this will free some of our more experienced personnel to work with students in the field.

II-6. The percentage of students enrolling in the media specialist program with both experience and school library training is decreasing. More students are coming into the graduate program as soon as they finish their undergraduate work. This is probably not related to the nature of the program but rather to the geographical location of Auburn. The visibility that the experimental program had on the surrounding community was great. Practitioners with traditional library backgrounds were attracted to the Auburn program for retraining. Most of these professionals came from within a fifty mile radius. Since those professionals within close geographic range of Auburn with the highest motivation have now completed their degrees, the increase in enrollment is noticeable among inexperienced personnel.

PROGRAM COMPONENTS

III-1. Several content changes were needed as perceived by both staff and students. Notable among these was the need for a more comprehensive view of technical processing, a more reality-oriented basic practicum, and a more sophisticated production sequence. The delay in moving into curriculum renewal this past year related to two activities that the School of Education and the Department of Educational Media were involved. First, a general study of all programs in the School of Education was being made during the 1973-74 academic year. Generally speaking, curriculum revision was delayed until this work had been completed. Secondly, Auburn University has an experimental program for working with first-year teachers. The faculty of the Department of Educational Media have been working extensively with first-year media specialists. It was hoped that a year working in the field with these individuals would indicate other areas for curriculum revision. Information from both of these projects is now being applied in efforts to reorganize.

III-2. Instructional practices have remained essentially the same.

III-3. During the 1973-74 academic year, field work was handled by a committee. Four graduate courses were identified for field work. The committee managed the identification of field centers, the articulation between the field center and the Department of Educational Media, and the identification and monitoring of field experiences.

III-4. The Department is now, as it was in the beginning, composed of personnel with various backgrounds. The faculty hold doctorates in librarianship, instructional technology, audio-visual education, educational administration, curriculum, and instructional product development.

III-5. The individualized field experience remains as one of the best channels for communication among faculty and students. Valuable information is also obtained during the hour-long final oral examination given to each student during the last quarter of his program. The first-year teacher program has also provided additional information to the Department from practitioners in the field.

PROGRAM RESULTS

IV-1. Perhaps the best way to describe the third year of the Auburn program is one of maintenance but not of major change. Although, the year has been filled with discussion concerning changes that need to be made.

Appendix F-3   135

During the Spring quarter weekly planning sessions by the faculty have begun to transform this dialogue into plans of action. As mentioned before, the difficulty of getting started resulted from the involvement of the Department in other activities of the School of Education. Although not usually thought of as success, perhaps the most valuable outcome of the third year has been the general dialogue between both staff and students.

IV-2. Although many of our evaluation procedures are subjective and defy quantification, one effort to sample the achievement of objectives was made of all School of Education interns during their student teaching quarter. This population included students who had no course work in educational media to those who had more than three courses in the Department. This population included those students minoring in educational media and expecting to complete the media specialist program at the Master's level. In this sense, the study suggested the strength of the Department's foundation courses. These included Learning Resources, Media for Children, Media for Young Adults, Organization and Administration, and Cataloging and Classification.

An instrument was developed to: (1) sample levels of competency of AU interns in media utilization and instructional development; (2) test for significant differences between and among interns having one, two, three, or more courses in educational media; and (3) test for significant differences between and among interns' self-appraisal of their competency levels and actual performance.

Instrument Development. Twenty multiple choice questions were constructed in order to sample competencies in media utilization, and twenty-one questions were developed to sample competencies in instructional development. Interns were asked for self-appraisal of competencies they believed they possessed in five aspects of media utilization and four aspects of instructional development. Questions were collected, developed, and screened by the faculty of the Department of Educational Media. Selection was based on the belief that each item represented a competency that an intern should possess. Items used to sample competencies related to: (1) identifying strengths and limitations of media; (2) locating materials; (3) evaluating and selecting media; (4) media production; (5) machine operation; (6) identifying performance objectives; (7) classifying objectives according to one of the accepted taxonomies; (8) identifying teaching/learning strategies and materials congruent with a performance objective; and (9) selecting criterion measures that are congruent with a performance objective.

Analysis of Results. Scores ranged from 1 to 32 (41 possible); the mean was 17.48 with a standard deviation of 5.67. The bell-shaped nature of the scores determined the appropriateness of utilizing a one-way analysis of variance in order to test for significant differences at the .05 level.

Significant differences were found between and among those having no course work in educational media and those with one course; those with one course and those with two courses; those with two courses and those with three courses; and those with three courses and those with more than three courses. In all cases the findings were in favor of interns with the most course work in educational media.

COMPARISON OF ACHIEVEMENT WITH NUMBER OF COURSES INTERNS COMPLETED IN EDUCATIONAL MEDIA (N=142)	
CHOICE	GROUP MEAN
1 Media Utilization	
No course	7.35
One course	8.10
Two courses	10.28
Three courses	13.00
More than three courses	13.11
2 Instructional Development	
No course	7.29
One course	8.54
Two courses	8.78
Three courses	10.67
More than three courses	12.00
3 Groups 1 and 2 Above	
No course	16.13
One course	16.65
Two courses	17.57
Three courses	23.67
More than three courses	25.11

The more confidence an intern expressed in media utilization and instructional development, the less he was able to perform; conversely, the more competent reflected the least amount of confidence in their preparation in media utilization and instructional development. Similar results were found between scores on the total number of multiple choice items and between scores that related specifically to the area of media utilization or instructional development.

Significant differences existed between and among interns having one, two, three, or more courses in educational media in favor of interns with the most course work in media. Also, significant differences existed between and among interns' self-appraisal of their competency levels and actual performances. The less an intern knew the more he thought he knew. The probability that these findings occurred by chance was less than one in 10,000.

Appendix F-3   137

COMPARISON OF ACTUAL ACHIEVEMENT AND
SELF-APPRAISAL OF MEDIA COMPETENCY
(N=142)

CHOICE	GROUP MEAN
1 Media Utilization	
Well prepared	6.75
Adequate	7.18
Very little preparation	8.94
No preparation	11.20
Blank	
2 Instructional Development	
Well prepared	7.25
Adequate	8.61
Very little preparation	9.00
No preparation	9.07
Blank	
3 Groups 1 and 2 Above	
Well prepared	14.00
Adequate	15.80
Very little preparation	18.01
No preparation	20.20
Blank	

IV-3. The study described in IV-2 represents the prototype of a procedure the Department would like to expand in the near future. Although the usual evaluation procedures were used for courses and modules of instruction, a more comprehensive program for evaluating the total effort is being developed along the lines of the study described.

PROGRAM IMPACT

V-1. Results of the study described in IV-2 have contributed to the request for a required course in educational media for all interns. The results of this study have sensitized the general faculty in the School of Education to both the need for media specialists and the need for a greater degree of competency in general teacher education.

V-2. The media specialist program has had an impact within the State. Representatives from other media programs within Alabama as well as other states in the Southeast came to Auburn to study the program and to discuss their plans for curriculum revision. Media centers in elementary, secondary, and junior colleges have been invited to draw upon assistance of the faculty and staff in conceptualizing and building media programs. The Department extends an open invitation to help practitioners in the field whenever it can. In addition, staff from the Department has been actively involved in rewriting certification procedures for the State of Alabama.

CONCLUSIONS AND RECOMMENDATIONS

VI-1. The media specialist program at Auburn has been adopted as generally conceived in the original proposal.

VI-2. Perhaps the most important issue facing school library media education programs relates to internal factors that are obstructing the development of programs to train the kind of personnel needed in the field. Our observation is that administrators seem unanimous in their desire for media specialists with preparation broader than formerly associated with school librarianship. Personal and political obstacles within the institutions themselves seem to be blocking program development to a greater extent than factors such as finance or acceptance by schools.

VI-3. Auburn's recommendation to institutions developing programs for school library media personnel would include several obvious steps. First, a task force representing the disciplines from the various departments and schools involved should be appointed for the purpose of directing program development. Conceptualization of the role of the media program and identification of the competencies required should proceed independently and apart from the courses available. Although interested factions including school personnel should be represented in the task force, they should refrain from referring to this course or that course and from the natural tendency to defend current programs. Unless the personnel involved can stand away from what they are currently doing and develop an integrated program based on the real and perceived needs of schools, the resources of the training institution can never be thoroughly assessed. In other words, the strength of a training institution has to be assessed in relation to what it intends to do. Unless intent is explicated with some degree of clarity, determination of the actual capacity of the institution to build a media specialist program is difficult. The belief is that commitment to a role and a plan will help eliminate the barriers to change.

Appendix F-4

MANKATO STATE COLLEGE

SCHOOL OF EDUCATION

Dr. Benjamin A. Buck, Dean

AN EXPERIMENTAL PROGRAM IN
SCHOOL LIBRARY MEDIA EDUCATION
1971–1973

1974 Status Report by

FRANK R. BIRMINGHAM

Contents

PROGRAM GOALS AND OBJECTIVES 140	PROGRAM RESULTS 141
PROGRAM PARTICIPANTS 140	PROGRAM IMPACT 141
PROGRAM COMPONENTS 140	CONCLUSIONS AND RECOMMENDATIONS 141

PROGRAM GOALS AND OBJECTIVES

I-1. No, not substantially. We were involved in a goal setting exercise for the State College Board and a self-study project, and the original project goals were essentially the basis of our final report.

I-2. I believe the goals and objectives will remain essentially the same.

I-3. We received no supporting funds. The program was adjusted substantially. The field trips, conventions, meetings, and observations were all eliminated.

PROGRAM PARTICIPANTS

II-1. We no longer maintained a separate experimental program so there were no students enrolled. In the regular full-time M.S. in Media Program the number of full-time students was about the same as previously.

II-2. No. (Unless we are accredited, then I expect a doubling.)

II-3. No. We had no funds to offset these expenses (we previously paid for their on-campus meal).

II-4. We lost the full-time staff person funded by the project. As we were not administering the same type program, it was not a substantial loss. We kept the secretary, and this was a substantial gain.

II-5. None, We are hiring one full-time Ph.D. to replace a staff member who resigned Fall Quarter, 1973.

II-6. I feel the publicity of the School Library Media Program is definitely responsible for our attracting a higher caliber of student.

PROGRAM COMPONENTS

III-1. Curriculum development on going as part of the experimental program was continued. I don't know of any substantial changes that were made.

III-2. None - cut back.

III-3. None - cut back.

III-4. The Curriculum and Instruction unit continued to offer curriculum courses in our building for our students.

Appendix F-4   141

III-5. We were not able to keep these open as well as we had during the project, as students were no longer in "blocks" and not as easy to reach, etc.

PROGRAM RESULTS

IV-1. We survived in a situation where staff and funds were being drastically reduced. Also, we were permitted to hire a new staff member--above institution salary averages. These may seem small successes but they were definitely significant. We also were given one of the few available graduate assistantships for 74-75.

IV-2. See above.

IV-3. We did not really maintain these as we did not continue the program in the same form.

PROGRAM IMPACT

V-1. No.

V-2 a. No.

b. I would think so, but could not support such a statement.

c. No. The new certifications were developed before the experimental program.

d. No.

CONCLUSIONS AND RECOMMENDATIONS

VI-1. We are "regrouping". Next fall we will begin re-offering one set of blocked courses each quarter. This will allow us to re-establish the field observation components (students paying their own mileage). The following year we will introduce a second set of blocks, and I look for the full set of blocks to be re-established if these sections work.

[In an October 1974 comminique, Dr. Birmingham reported that "The re-instituted blocked course this fall has fifteen students -- enough for it to survive. There seems to be no student resistance to paying for field trips so these are also proceeding excellently."]

VI-2. The need to develop criteria for selecting students interning in the school library media field.

VI-3. I would suggest more planning time than Mankato had -- also a more stable funding basis than the quarter hour count formula used in Minnesota.

Appendix F-5

MILLERSVILLE STATE COLLEGE
DIVISION OF EDUCATION
Dr. James E. Maurey, Dean

AN EXPERIMENTAL PROGRAM IN
SCHOOL LIBRARY MEDIA EDUCATION
1971–1973

1974 Status Report by
JOSEPH F. BLAKE

Contents

PROGRAM GOALS AND
OBJECTIVES 144

PROGRAM PARTICIPANTS 145

PROGRAM COMPONENTS 145

PROGRAM RESULTS 146

PROGRAM IMPACT 148

CONCLUSIONS AND
RECOMMENDATIONS 149

PROGRAM GOALS AND OBJECTIVES

I-1. During the third year Millersville's three major goals were revised. This revision was significant because it provided the staff with local definitions of key terms. These definitions were not available at the beginning of the program. They had to evolve as the faculty moved toward new ways of thinking and acting.

The program is now focused on three major goals: (1) development of a competency-based, field-centered, and performance-oriented undergraduate program for the beginning school library media specialist; (2) provision of learning activities in a variety of modes and settings; (3) education of media specialists as teachers who function as instructional leaders in their schools.

Definitions of three terms in the first objective are as follows:

Competencies are considered to be presently identifiable knowledges and skills found to be essential to successful administration of school library media centers and programs.

Field-centered means that the curriculum is directed to media programs of the schools.

Performance-orientation refers to professional activity that is greater than the sum of known, identifiable occupationally-related competencies. It includes aspects of professional decision-making, educational philosophy, and service that distinguish one individual from another. In particular, it goes beyond what is to be done in present schools by suggesting what "should" be done theoretically and idealistically. In this respect, it illustrates how departments of educational media may progress beyond the "status-quo" of occupational task analyses.

The "Millersville Checklist of Tasks Performed by Beginning Librarians in School Media Centers", the product of a local occupational task analysis, has remained the program constant. Enabling objectives and activities designed to prepare students to perform these tasks have been set in modules. These objectives and their activities are frequently revised as faculty improve their program development skills.

I-2. There are no plans to modify the three long-range program goals. The objectives designed to achieve these goals are undergoing constant revision toward specificity and validity in relation to the role of the beginning school library media specialist.

I-3. After the first year the experimental program design was adopted for the total program. Regular staff had key roles from the beginning and at no time was there any dependency on outside or new expertise.

Appendix F-5   145

PROGRAM PARTICIPANTS

II-1. No, there was not a marked increase or decrease in the enrollment of the program during its third year.

II-2. No, a marked increase or decrease in the enrollment of the program is not anticipated during the next academic year.

II-3. No. We are evaluating this experience in an attempt to determine new ways of obtaining assistance in program development from outside sources, e.g., local schools, state department of education, other institutions of higher learning.

II-4. Two staff members were given part-time assignments in the Division of Education to work on program development for the College's teacher preparation program. This was a natural extension of the Department's commitment to teacher education and belief that students of educational media should be encouraged to establish professional identity with educational goals and responsibilities that are shared by teachers in other fields. The impact of these changes per se had little impact on the Millersville Program, however, cast in the context of the Department's commitment to teacher education we have a continuing concern for media specialists who are concerned with learning first and media second, and classroom teachers who are proficient in basic media competencies that are vital to instruction. We are trying to model behavior suggesting that common loyalties help both groups plan and develop programs together.

II-5. We do not anticipate making staffing changes prior to the beginning of the fourth year of the program.

II-6. It seems to me that we are attracting more students who consciously declare that they are more interested in working with people than with "books." These students are more outgoing, flexible, and aggressive. I'm not sure whether the program has anything to do with this, for this seems to be true of teacher education in general at Millersville.

PROGRAM COMPONENTS

III-1. The curricular outline has been revised. At the present time the curriculum is divided into five contexts representing subject content for: Communication Behavior, Learning Processes, Media, Administration, Professionalism. Each context is divided into a number of organizers, e.g., in the Learning Processes Context, the organizers are: Ecology, Principles, Systems, Design, Implementation, and Evaluation. Each context and organizer has a local definition. This represents the department's attempt to move toward more careful explanations of what we are trying to achieve and a coherent conceptualization of the total program.

III-2. No changes, but a continuing attempt to provide a variety of modes and settings.

III-3. No changes.

III-4. Relationships within the Division of Education have been maintained. An important extension of interdisciplinary effort has been a collaboration with the College's Departments of English and Speech and Drama in the development of a new secondary certification program in communications.

III-5. Channels as described in our final report are functioning and being maintained.

PROGRAM RESULTS

IV-1. Key successes of the third year include:

- continuation of program development activities and increased staff involvement.

- adoption of many program features by other departments in the College's Division of Education.

- preparation for and completion of program approval review by the Pennsylvania Department of Education. The program received a full five year approval and an exemplary designation. This review employed a new approach to program review which focused major attention on program objectives and assessment.

A lingering problem is student assessment. It is common to all competency-based programs. Some reflections follow:

• Since the Millersville program is in transition student progress is assessed through a mix of instrumentation and judgment. In its modularized approach to teaching and learning, the department is seriously attempting to make assessment procedures known to students before instructional activities are begun. In each module, assessment is directly related to stated expectations of the student. The responsibility of module writers is to employ assessment procedures with as high a degree of objectivity and reliability as possible.

• The difficulties of assessing behavior in this respect are well known by the staff. Nevertheless, several advantages have already been found as a result of this approach. Modules with activities for independent study, small groups, and field-settings enable the staff to assess student progress in situations that occur outside classroom walls. Modules provide opportunities for more frequent assessment than in the former program and encourage staff members to plan together in establishing policies and attempting new methods of assessment. Students must furnish satisfactory evidence

Appendix F-5   147

of completion of a module if it is a prerequisite for another related but more advanced module. As students progress through modules at individual rates, the staff is able to follow their progress at various stages in a sequence or block of modules.

● The department finds that assessment is easiest for areas in which basic competencies are readily identifiable. These areas include operation of equipment and certain aspects of instructional design, local production, cataloging, and information-retrieval. Assessment is more complex for areas in which original and personal solutions are sought. These areas include evaluation and selection of media for designated instructional purposes, activities for which a number and variety of materials may be equally appropriate. They also include solutions to problems of administering media centers, such as the planning and implementation of services for newer types of school programs. In these instances, decision and solutions of students cannot be said to be either right or wrong without consideration of supporting rationale and evidence. To provide a better standard of objectivity in assessing these behaviors, judgments by more than one staff member or by teachers and media specialists in schools are often required, as is personal consultation with the individual student.

● In student-teaching, assessment of basic tasks for the routine administration of media centers is relatively simple. For performance-oriented responsibilities in which student-teachers interact in the ongoing instructional process with teachers and young people, collective professional judgments of the field-supervisor, classroom teachers, and cooperating media specialists seem to furnish the only available means of assessment.

● Certain authorities claim that competency-based programs should be designed only for those student behaviors that may be measured with scientific precision. Pursuit of this idea to its logical end might mean that teacher-preparation programs at present would be confined to limited numbers of readily identifiable and measurable behaviors in the psychomotor and at the lower levels of the cognitive domains. Given the present state of the art of competency identification and assessment, Millersville would be content if it could identify as high as, say, forty percent of needed occupational competencies that might presently be measured with some precision.

● The performance-orientation of the program is needed to prepare media specialists for more elusive but essential professional responsibilities that are required in individual and collective inquiry into new problems as encountered in school settings. As professional workers know, evidence of satisfactory professional performance in these respects is still likely to be based, as a rule, on judgments made by one's colleagues.

● A fundamental aim of competency-based programs is to make the time needed for completion of a program a variable rather than a constant for all students. Students are offered opportunities to repeat activities or to undertake alternate remedial activities until satisfactory achievement is demonstrated. The recommended practice is to assess student behavior whenever possible on a pass-fail basis. In terms of customary college grading systems, this implies that all students will receive high grades upon satisfactory completion of the program. This has been the policy of the department with the students in its experimental program, a policy that has been a matter of concern to many persons when appraising undergraduate programs, but not always of equal concern when considering graduate programs.

- At this time, the policy of grading is unresolved in view of the fact that the body of competencies needed for successful administration of school media programs has yet to be identified in its entirety. Nevertheless, the staff has given more careful consideration to the matter than it did in the former program. It remains evident that performance of pre-service students and also of in-service teachers varies considerably from one individual to another. The question inevitably arises: "Can a common standard of performance possibly apply to the individual with original as contrasted to routine solutions or to the individual who contributes well beyond minimal expectations of his campus department or his school?"

- In retrospect, it appears that grading on a pass-fail basis may be sufficient for areas in which competencies are readily identified and specified, whereas grading on a relative basis may remain necessary for performances of a high professional order. If this is the case at present, judgments by professionals are likely to remain necessary in the years ahead; at least until that time in which scientific measures are found that may be applied to activities involving interaction in collective endeavor, decision-making and problem-solving in creative ways, and perhaps in personal commitment to the advancement of teaching and learning.

IV-2. The third year program goals and objectives centered on the continuation of program development activities and preparation for the Pennsylvania Department of Education program review. Achievements are reflected in other parts of this document.

IV-3. The quality control procedures developed during the first two years for evaluating and modifying the program have been maintained. Outcomes of these procedures have lead to refinement of elements in the program, increased cooperation with other departments, and expansion of student experiences that occur off-campus. It is planned to use the data from the HumRRO study to revise the "Millersville Checklist of Tasks to be Performed" and conduct another occupational task analysis of recent graduates.

PROGRAM IMPACT

V-1. Other certification programs in the College have adopted and/or adapted many of the objectives, procedures, formats, and activities developed by the Department of Educational Media. Department members have assumed strong leadership roles in the teacher preparation program at all levels.

V-2 a. It is difficult to determine our impact on other library media education programs within Pennsylvania. More obvious is our impact on teacher preparation programs on this and other campuses within the growing competency-based teacher education movement. Maybe we've demonstrated that a faculty can work toward these things.

b. and c. It's too early to respond to this and I'm not a very good judge. Certification procedures are legal matters.

d. Questions regarding certification procedures and program approval criteria should be directed to the people in the Teacher Education Section of the Pennsylvania Department of Education. The only thing relevant I can mention is that our program was the first in Pennsylvania to be reviewed for program approval with a set of competency-based procedures.

CONCLUSIONS AND RECOMMENDATIONS

VI-1. Yes!

VI-2. - The establishment of direct relationships between school library media education and teacher preparation at all levels.

- Articulation between undergraduate and graduate programs.

- Continued support for research and experimentation.

VI-3. The Department of Educational Media believes that a competency-based and performance-oriented program can be developed without substantially altering traditional college requirements pertaining to course sequences, semester hours, student-faculty ratios and the like.

Several recommendations are given here concerning program development that could be useful for other institutions.

On the basis of the philosophy and assumptions given for the program, the department recommends that programs for school library media specialists be coordinated with other departments of education. It is believed that students of educational media should be encouraged to establish professional identity with educational goals and responsibilities that are shared by teachers in other fields.

The department has endeavored to implement a competency-based, field-centered, and performance-oriented program that meets needs of contemporary schools. To identify present needs, the department studied occupational task analyses from outside sources and conducted a local analysis involving its graduates of two years. Because of the value of the information obtained from its graduates, the department recommends the use of occupational task analyses in curricular and instructional planning. Whenever feasible, it is recommended that local task analyses be conducted in cooperation with graduates in their schools. Acknowledging the immediate value of task analysis, it is evident that local task analyses must be periodically updated to provide experiences that remain current with duties performed on the job.

Millersville students continue to enter the program at various stages of undergraduate preparation and represent diversity in motivation, interests, and abilities. The policy of admissions followed in this respect is compatible with an essential feature of competency-based programs, i.e., emphasis on terminal rather than entry requirements. This emphasis calls for a high degree of flexibility and a considerable amount of faculty attention to the personal development of the individual student. To accommodate these approaches, it is recommended that students be encouraged to evaluate prescribed activities and be allowed to design alternate avenues in learning that will result equally well in the attainment of basic competencies and professional responsibilities. Accommodations of this nature can serve as a major base in program design for flexibility, one from which students can progress on an individualized pattern toward successful achievement of exit requirements.

Emphasis has been given to staff involvement in program planning, a principle that is fundamental to competency-based programs as instruction is brought into view for study by others. Accepting the proposition that program development may be equated with staff development, it is recommended that staff participation be encouraged during early stages of conceptualizing and implementing a new program.

Assistance in program development may be obtained from outside sources through a variety of systematic strategies, one of which is the advisory board. It is recommended that outside assistance be obtained and coordinated by this or other means for both new and established media programs to help identify necessary competencies, extend learning activities to off-campus settings, and assess program objectives and accomplishments.

A systematic process of curricular change can establish local guidelines for members of a department. At present, competency-based programs are in early stages of development with few guidelines available from outside sources. Changes from tradiational programs to those that seek to specify competencies and performance responsibilities with greater precision and to establish identity with school programs must draw upon the unique contributions of each staff member. Departmental study is needed to establish primary goals, plan curricular components, develop instructional methodology, identify appropriate instructional media, provide learning activities on and off campus, and apply adequate assessment procedures. The multi-dimensions of the study require time for development and maturation that will extend over a long period. For these reasons, the Department of Educational Media recommends that primary emphasis should be given to staff development during a gradual process of program change. The development of instructional products is an outcome of the process and a necessary element in program review and revision.

On the basis of its experience in competency-based education, the department endorses the principles involved in this approach to instruction. At present the theory underlying the identification and specification of competencies for teacher-education programs is far in advance of the state of the art. Initial attempts to specify competencies, design appropriate instructional activities, and plan assessment techniques will likely prove unsatisfactory to the individual writer, as revealed to him in products such as the instructional module. Nevertheless, the potential of competency-based programs is promising enough to suggest that precision in instructional design is not a temporary educational fad but a beginning in academic effort to make campus programs compatible with present and future requirements of schools, a beginning that will evolve in strength and importance. The department believes that identification and specification of competencies should be a total faculty effort. It also believes in giving serious consideration to Millersville's performance-oriented dimension for activities and responsibilities that are likely to remain, for some time to come, subject to professional judgment rather than objective assessment.

Appendix F-6   153

UNIVERSITY OF DENVER
GRADUATE SCHOOL OF LIBRARIANSHIP
Dr. Margaret Knox Goggin, Dean

AN EXPERIMENTAL PROGRAM IN
SCHOOL LIBRARY MEDIA EDUCATION
1971–1973

1974 Status Report by
CHOW LOY TOM

Contents

PROGRAM GOALS AND OBJECTIVES 154	PROGRAM RESULTS 159
PROGRAM PARTICIPANTS 154	PROGRAM IMPACT 161
PROGRAM COMPONENTS 156	CONCLUSIONS AND RECOMMENDATIONS 162

PROGRAM GOALS AND OBJECTIVES

I-1. The goals and objectives of the program were similar to those of the prior two years.

I-2. There are presently no plans to modify the goals and objectives of the program.

I-3. The University of Denver supported the program during the third year. Plans were made during the second year of the program to incorporate it, effective the third year, as an identifiable component or area of the Advanced Studies or Sixth-Year Program of the Graduate School of Librarianship. In addition to this program for District School Library Media Directors, there are currently three other areas of post-master's or sixth-year study in the Advanced Studies Program at the University of Denver: Students completing any one of the areas are awarded a Certificate of Advanced Studies.

Incorporation of the program into the Advanced Studies Program was made with one stipulation regarding the assignment of staff, namely that enrollment in the program would determine the assignment of program faculty. Limited enrollment would necessitate part-time assignment of one experimental program faculty member who would also be assigned other teaching responsibilities. This third year there was only one student in the program and only one faculty member was assigned to the program on a half-time basis. It should be noted that the position of full-time media consultant made possible through SLMP funding was not continued as a University position. However, the University continues to support the Technology Laboratory.

These limitations affected the program in three major areas: (1) there was less emphasis in the program on instruction on media production; (2) the student paid for multi-media materials used; and (3) there was less time for the recruitment program for the fourth year. However, the University of Denver provided a full tuition scholarship to the student in the third year program.

PROGRAM PARTICIPANTS

II-1. There was a marked decrease in the enrollment in the program. There was one student as opposed to seven during the second year. This may be attributed to a number of inter-related reasons: the general economy, the market for the position of district school library media director, the shift in attitude of the necessity of formal education and the fact that some individuals may be considered "over-qualified" or "overly educated"; the fact that unless there is funding beyond full tuition during the academic year, there is often limited enrollment of full-time students in some of the advanced studies or continuing education programs for mid-career librarians; the high tuition at the University of Denver which is a private institution; the limited recruitment program; and nationally, enrollment in programs on the sixth-year level is generally low.

Appendix F-6   155

II-2. Due to limited recruitment activities, inquiries concerning the program were minimal during the third year. At this writing there is only one prospective applicant. The individual expects to apply for a University of Denver full tuition scholarship, but as all scholarships available for students in the Advanced Studies Program for the next academic year have been awarded, this fact may affect the individual's decision to apply. See II-1 for explanation.

II-3. The Advisory Board was replaced by the Advanced Studies Program Committee of the Graduate School of Librarianship during the third year of the program. The suggestions for program development obtained from students and faculty during the prior two years were considered by the Advanced Studies Program Committee in modifying the program as an identifiable area of the Advanced Studies Program.

The faculty member assigned to the program was also a member of the Advanced Studies Program and kept the group informed of the program in both scheduled meetings of the Committee and through informal means.

II-4. As noted in I-3, when the program was incorporated as an area of the Advanced Studies Program, the administration of the Graduate School of Librarianship recognized that enrollment in the program would determine the staffing pattern. With only one student in the program the third year, the School found it possible to assign only one of the faculty members of the experimental program on a half-time basis specifically to the program. It should be noted that this assignment covered the administrative aspects of the program, some specific components of the case study and the advising of the study itself. This means that the experimental program staff of 2-1/2 positions was reduced to a one-half time position. Except for the limitations identified in I-3 above, the curriculum content of the program was not generally affected by these changes.

II-5. Enrollment in the program would affect staffing assignment during the fourth year of the program. The administration and the experimental program staff members who are regular members of the faculty are flexible in this regard. Should it develop that there are no students in the program during the fourth year, there are plans for an active recruitment program for the fifth year. It is quite likely that this would be part of the responsibilities of one of the faculty members who was on the staff of the experimental program.

II-6. Students attracted to the present program must now meet the established requirements of the Advanced Studies Program in two specific areas which were not required during the experimental program: (a) have a master's degree in librarianship from a program approved by the American Library Association Committee on Accreditation, and (b) have a minimum of three years of experience in a School Library Media Center.

Students were accepted in the experimental program who had master's degrees in either librarianship or education, but the program did not require

156 Appendix F-6

that their library, education or audio-visual backgrounds be in programs approved by the ALA Committee on Accreditation. These academic differences are due to the general requirements of the Advanced Studies Program of the Graduate School of Librarianship. It should be noted that the experimental program was planned with the requirements of the Advanced Studies Program in mind, but permission to "relax" the requirements was granted because of the experimental nature of the program.

PROGRAM COMPONENTS

III-1. The program components for the third year are shown in Figure 1. A comparison of Figure 1 with Appendix A (Phase II Final Report) will bring out these differences in the third year program: (1) the field case study was assigned a block of 16-19 quarter hours, as contrasted with 24; (2) the mini or concentrated courses totalled 4 hours, instead of 6; (3) 8-12 hours of electives, instead of 15; (4) the seminar in advanced studies was added for a total of 9 hours; (5) the course Research Methods in Librarianship: Introduction (3 hours) replaced the informal "research consultation" component of the experimental program; and (6) the course Library Architecture (3 hours) replaced the 2 hour mini course on the experimental program.

The field case study of 16-19 quarter hours was divided into 5, 9, and 2-5 quarter hour blocks for the Fall, Winter, and Spring quarters respectively. The hours informally assigned to the several components within the blocks are shown in parentheses in Figure 1.

The Fall Quarter: The 5 hour case study block was divided into three parts: (a) orientation, (b) tutorial/research consultation, and (c) media production. An examination of Figure 1 indicates that continuity in two of the three components of the Fall field case study (tutorial/research consultation and media production) was provided in the two remaining quarters of the program.

Due to the limited enrollment and reduction in the hours assigned to the field case study, two phases of the orientation component of the experimental program were not formally developed during the third year: (1) the formal phase of the pre-program inventory, and (2) lectures on interpersonal communication, sociology, education, national assessment, and mass communications.

Program evaluation during the second year indicated the need to strengthen the research component. Although the research methods course replaced the informal research-consultation component of the experimental program, the tutorial/research consultation component was retained to give the student an opportunity to consult with other program faculty members.

Since the University of Denver was unable to fund the position of the full-time media consultant of the program, instruction in the media production phase of the program was not as fully developed as in the previous years. However, the Director and the personnel of the Technology Laboratory of the Graduate School of Librarianship and the program faculty member were able to assist the

Figure 1

UNIVERSITY OF DENVER
GRADUATE SCHOOL OF LIBRARIANSHIP

DISTRICT SCHOOL LIBRARY MEDIA DIRECTOR PROGRAM*
1973-74

	FALL Quarter Hours	WINTER Quarter Hours	SPRING Quarter Hours	TOTAL
FIELD CASE STUDY**	5	9	2-5	16-19
Orientation	(1)			
Tutorial/Consultation	(3)	(3)	(1-3)	
Media Production	(1)	(1)	(1-2)	
Field Survey		(5)		
Research Methods in Librarianship	3			3
Seminar in Advanced Studies	3	3	3	9
Library Architecture			3	3
MINI COURSES***		4		4
ELECTIVES	4-5		4-7	8-12
TOTAL	15-16	16	15-16	46 +/-

*A post-master's program designed for practicing and potential district school library media directors using the methodology of directed field case study. Students completing the program will be awarded a Certificate of Advanced Studies.

**The field case study of 16-19 quarter hours is divided into 5,9 and 2-5 quarter hour blocks. The quarter hours informally assigned to the several components within these blocks are shown in parentheses.

***Two mini or concentrated courses of 2 quarter hours each are of financial and legal aspects of district school library media programs.

student with the aspects of media production on which the student needed assistance in each of the quarters.

The Winter Quarter: Although the Winter quarter on-site or field survey is still assigned 9 hours, it was informally divided into three parts: 5 hours for the field survey (which was limited to three weeks), 3 hours of tutorial/research consultation for the preparation of the preliminary report of the study, and 1 hour for the planning of the multi-media presentation.

The Spring Quarter: During the Spring quarter the case study was set up for 2-5 hours. The student elected it for 3 hours. Informal time designations for these hours were 2 hours for tutorial/research consultation for the preparation of the Final Report and one hour for the production of materials and preparation of the multi-media presentation.

The year-long seminar in advanced studies (3 hours each of the 3 quarters) concentrated on current theories, trends, issues, and research in library and information sciences and technologies. Major areas of concern were administration, service, and resources in the Fall, Winter, and Spring quarters respectively.

The Fall seminar concentrated on such topics as management by objectives, participatory management, unionization, equal opportunity and affirmative action, personnel administration, and library financing.

Two aspects of the experimental Fall quarter program were "absorbed" by the seminar during the third year: (1) the administration clinic and (2) sessions on standards for school library media programs and certification. Since the seminar stressed administration, the clinic was not held. As the student had extensive experience with standards for School Library Media Programs and elected to study certification of librarians and district library media directors as her seminar report, special sessions on these topics were not conducted.

The Winter quarter seminar examined the service role of libraries with emphasis on non-traditional aspects of librarianship. The student's seminar paper was entitled, "Philosophy of Library Service in Theory and Practice."

The Spring seminar stressed such areas as international standards for bibliographic control, mechanical information banks and information retrieval systems in the social sciences and humanities, publishing (reprints, text books, micropublications) and its impact on libraries. The seminar group project dealt with the establishment of a community information center.

III-2. Except for their 15 hours of electives, students attended specially designed classes for the program during the first two years. Program revision for the third year resulted in the substitution of regular library school courses (the seminar in advanced studies, the research methods, and library architecture) for the special classes of the experimental program. In addition, the student received tutorial help in the mini course on the financial aspects of district school library media programs.

The three week field work component or on-site survey of the Winter quarter necessitated adjustments on the part of professors of both the seminar in advanced studies and the legal aspects course. In the former course the student was given a seminar assignment which she worked on during the period she was in her school district; in the latter course the student joined the regular class of the professor upon her return to campus and was then given a special assignment.

III-3. Two major changes were made in the implementation of the field work component: (a) the period for the field survey was reduced from five to three weeks, and (b) the faculty advisor was not required to visit the student during the field survey. The expense of the on-site visit and the fact that the faculty advisor had other teaching responsibilities were two reasons for the elimination of the provision of an on-site visit of the student by a faculty member. However, the program is flexible enough to permit faculty on-site visits whenever feasible.

III-4. The interdisciplinary aspects of the program were maintained in the two mini courses and in encouraging the student to elect courses outside the Graduate School of Librarianship. The student elected courses in mass communications and education, but was unable due to the scheduling of courses to take work in art and speech communication.

III-5. The channels of communication were open between the student and program faculty. The student was objective in her evaluation of her program as well as her course work and discussed her recommendations with faculty concerned during the course of the year. For example, she observed that there should be greater coordination between the assignments in the research methods course and her field case study. The suggestion was also made that students be encouraged to design their questionnaires for use with specific computer programs. After graduation, the students' written evaluation of the strengths and limitations of the program corroborated statements made in prior discussion.

PROGRAM RESULTS

IV-1. The key success of the 3rd year program was the multi-district study completed by the student. This involved careful analysis of data obtained from administrators, instructional teaching personnel and students of seven georgraphically adjacent school districts; in addition, the public librarians in the area were willing participants in the study. The recommendations of the study have much potential for cooperative services in the improvement of the instructional programs of the seven small school districts studied.

Difficulties during the third year were similar to those of the experimental program: (1) during the Fall quarter the need to further coordinate the content of the research methods course with the field case study was recognized by both the student and faculty member assigned to the program;

(2) even with attempts to modify the program and to accomodate the student, the latter still found it difficult to complete the program at the end of the third quarter. This may indicate that the ramifications of the case study are too broad for a three-quarter program; and (3) external problems (as illness in the family) affected the adjustment of the mid-career graduate student.

IV-2. In general, student program goals and objectives of the third year were achieved "very well". Although external circumstances affected the rate at which the student worked on the case study, the student persevered and was able to complete program requirements within the time limits of the program.

It should be noted that the program emphasizes the process of learning or conducting a study of a school district. Student achievement described above would indicate that this was achieved to an acceptable level. However, the program could have provided a richer learning experience for the student if there were more students in the program the third year. Since there was only one student in the program there was no peer interaction of field case study experiences. However, modifications in the program planned for the third year (III-2) gave the student opportunity for much peer interaction in other program related experiences in the library school and in other departments of the University.

See related discussion under I-3, II-1, II-4, and IV-3. Even though these sections point up the degree in which the program was implemented, the student had access to the resources of the University and program goals were met, as evidenced by the student's completion of the program.

IV-3. Quality control procedures for evaluating and modifying the program were maintained to the degree possible with one student and faculty time equivalent to a one-half time position:

1. Although the field or on-site survey was reduced from 5 to 3 weeks and the faculty on-site visit to the school district was eliminated, weekly progress reports and telephone conversations helped maintain good contact between the student and the program faculty member.

2. During the experimental program the multimedia presentations were given to invited groups which included individuals in the Library School, other departments of the University, school districts involved in the program and those in the metropolitan area of the University and to members of the Advisory Board. A somewhat modified multimedia presentation was planned for the third year, but factors beyond the control of the student and program faculty member made it impossible to schedule the multimedia presentation before a large group.

This year while there was less emphasis on the instructional aspects of the media production component, the student was required to use appropriate media in presenting the results of the study and to defend recommendations of the study to students in one class. Course objectives of the the class concerned effective communication and the use of multimedia in the teaching-learning process. Although the group was small, the questions raised in the discussion period were, in some respects, of a higher quality than was possible in the larger groups of the experimental program. The written comments from the audience were evaluative with regard to the strengths and limitations of the research reported in the presentation.

The immediate feedback was appreciated by the student. The experience of the multimedia presentation gave the student insights for reporting the study to the different school districts involved in the study. As a footnote, the knowledge and interest of the audience, their critical comments and suggestions contributed to a worthwhile learning experience for both the student in the program and students in the audience.

3. Tutorials were used to identify areas of strengths and limitations during and at the end of each quarter.

4. As in the experimental program, the student was evaluated by instructors of the mini-courses, program related courses, and electives.

5. Since the channels of communication were open between the student and the faculty of the Library School and other cooperating program faculty, only one end-of-the year written evaluation was requested.

PROGRAM IMPACT

V-1. There was no change, but there is an increased awareness of the field of librarianship in departments in the University where faculty were/are involved as lecturers or instructors in the program; this is also true among faculty (and departments) who taught electives taken by the students.

V-2. There is no evidence that other library media educational programs within the State of Colorado (University of Colorado and Colorado State University) have been changed.

The impact of the type of case study of the program which involves long-range plans cannot be readily assessed because of the long-range character of some of the recommendations of individual studies. See discussion on "Program Impact" in the final report of the program for some of the results of the program (See Attachment 1). It may be pointed out that items 2,3, and 4 refer specifically to school districts in the State of Colorado. One of the school districts mentioned in item #1 is in Colorado. It should be noted that the program had certain effects on some school districts during the period of the case study (items #3 and #7). Undoubtedly, the effect of the program will be felt in the school districts and the students who studied them for some time.

To date the program has had no effect on certification procedures for Directors of School Library Media Programs within the State of Colorado. It should be noted that the program objective concerning certification was to "enable students to work toward state certification for the position of district school library media director" in states where there is certification for this position.

See discussion under Question II-6. Note especially that one important change was made in the admission requirement of students -- they must have a degree in librarianship from a program approved by the ALA Committee on Accreditation. Since the seminar in advanced studies is a requirement of the Advanced Studies Program, it is unfeasible for students in the program to participate effectively in the seminar without the broad background in librarianship that the others have.

CONCLUSIONS AND RECOMMENDATION

VI-1. The program will not be maintained or adopted as the standard program for school library media education, not for the standard or fifth year program of studies. This is a post-master's or sixth year program and, as indicated above and in responses to other questions, the experimental program was modified and incorporated, effective September, 1973, as an identifiable area of the Advanced Studies Program of the Library School.

VI-2. Relative to the standard or fifth year program, the most important issues facing school library media education programs are:

1. Is field work experience (practicum) as a segment of a graduate program valid?

2. Is there a recommended ratio of theory to library skills in a graduate program?

3. Is it possible for school library media specialists to be competent in both print and non-print areas?

4. Is a knowledge of a foreign language necessary in the preparation of a school library media specialist?

5. Is the inclusion of education courses valid in the fifth year program?

VI-3. Recommendations relative to the issues identified above are:

1. A strong media centered program should include field work experience.

2. Theory must undergird all learnings and be made understandable by appropriate practical applications.

Appendix F-6   163

3. School library media specialists should have competencies in both print and non-print areas with specialization in one.

4. Knowledge of a foreign language is not necessary in the preparation of a school library media specialist.

5. Education courses should be included in a well-rounded program for the school library media specialist.

Attachment 1
Results - School Districts

The impact of the program will undoubtedly continue for sometime for each participant, whether student or school district. Although preliminary, field reports by participants and school district personnel of the first year program and school district plans reported by several participants in the second year program appear encouraging. The following are some of the program results:

1. The position of district school library media director was established in two school districts which did not have designated directors at the time of the studies.

2. In one school district where there was an established director, the program participant developed models of personnel, materials, and facilities for the elementary schools in her district. As a direct result of the study, each of the eleven new elementary schools in the district benefited over a two year period in the following manner: (a) a professional school library media specialist was employed; (b) $15,000 was budgeted for library materials the first year of operation; (c) building specifications, including furniture, were adapted for these media centers from the model plan; and (d) full or half-time aides were provided for all new elementary media specialists.

3. Curriculum planning has been implemented in one school district on a K-12 grade level. Prior to the study, principals in the elementary and secondary schools did not meet together to discuss curriculum matters. During the study administrators and teachers began meeting to consider the total educational program. One apparent outcome was the establishment of the position of director of school library media programs for grades K-12.

4. One participant was able to implement some of the recommendations of her study in the development of a model media center in a new open space concept school in the district. This individual also used data gathered on staff, materials, facilities, and programs of her case study to submit a proposal to the state library for a special purpose grant, funded by ESEA,

Title II. This model elementary media center was designated as an examplary school library media program by the ESEA, Title II Board and was granted $18,000 for further expansion and development as a demonstration center for the state. This grant was one of 24 selected from 127 proposals submitted.

5. Remodeling plans developed during the program were considered in the remodeling of a specific library in another district.

6. One district is planning a workshop on communication for library media personnel and is moving toward PPBS in developing library media programs.

7. As a direct result of questions asked in interviews of school library media personnel during the field survey, several media specialists in one district have indicated that they have implemented some of the ideas brought out in the interviews.

These program results reflect a statement by a participant, that "the district sent me to get ideas and new ways to approach school library media programs".

Appendix F-7

UNIVERSITY OF MICHIGAN
SCHOOL OF LIBRARY SCIENCE
Dr. Russell E. Bidlack, Dean

AN EXPERIMENTAL PROGRAM IN
SCHOOL LIBRARY MEDIA EDUCATION
1971–1973

1974 Status Report by
HELEN D. LLOYD

Contents

PROGRAM GOALS AND OBJECTIVES 166	PROGRAM RESULTS 169
PROGRAM PARTICIPANTS 166	PROGRAM IMPACT 171
PROGRAM COMPONENTS 167	CONCLUSIONS AND RECOMMENDATIONS 172

Appendix F-7

PROGRAM GOALS AND OBJECTIVES

I-1. Program goals and objectives as stated in the University of Michigan Proposal for an Experimental Program in the School Library Manpower Project and in the Final Report of Phase II were carefully reviewed and revised in the Fall of 1973. Major consideration was given to the twelve "Objectives of the School Library Media Specialist", and to the discrepancy analysis relating course objectives to these. The Core Faculty also used BRAC and feedback both formal and informal from students, cooperating school library media specialists, and the Advisory Board for the Program in preparing the revised set of Program Objectives attached.

Only one of these, number twelve, is entirely new. The Core Faculty felt it essential to note that only beginning level competencies could be achieved by most students within the one year Master's degree program and that, in fact, professional development must be viewed as a lifetime endeavor with each person assuming responsibility for realistic self-assessment and growth.

I-2. The revised statement of goals and objectives has been adopted by the Curriculum Committee and the Faculty of the School of Library Science and distributed to new and prospective students. Although all curriculum is subject to continuous review and revision, another comprehensive appraisal will be made when the results of the Phase III evaluation are available.

I-3. A major portion of the grant funds awarded to the University of Michigan were allocated for new personnel, two faculty positions and one technician. In the Summer, 1973, the State Legislature approved the University's recommendation to continue this new program and agreed to provide funds for that purpose. Further support was provided internally by the University for additional media equipment and materials for instruction.

PROGRAM PARTICIPANTS

II-1. The University of Michigan is committed to a policy of controlled growth, which means that total enrollment will be limited to the present level although some programs may expand slightly during the next decade. The School of Library Science will continue to limit its total admissions, but within the school no restrictions have been placed as yet on a student's choice of program specialization. The number of students completing the school library media program during the third year was larger than in the two preceding years, thirty-nine. However, some of these students had entered the program before September, 1973. The School of Library Science policy which permits entrance at three times during a year, was discussed in the Final Report of Phase II.

Interest in the school library media specialization remains high. Most graduates have found jobs and reports of their success have influenced current and prospective students. Job descriptions which emphasize broad media and education competencies and interpersonal communication skills have encouraged bright humanistic young people to enter the program.

Appendix F-7   167

II-2. In the future, the potential for internship placement during a single term may cause limits to be placed on enrollment in the School Library Media Program. Thirty students were placed in cooperating schools for either an internship or student teaching experience during the Winter, 1974 term. This proved somewhat difficult for the Core Faculty members who supervised these students and the cooperating school systems through which they were placed.

II-3. The Program's Advisory Board has continued to be involved in its activities, meeting in December, 1973, to hear a summary of the Final Report of Phase II and to review revised Program Objectives, "A Guide for Planning Individual Programs for the School Library Media Specialist," and "Guidelines for Internship Experience." (All are attached to this report.) "Guidelines" revision was done by a Board subcommittee working with the results of the internship evaluation in the Final Report of Phase II.

The Board expressed continuing support for the Program and a willingness to advise as needed, either individually or as a group. Members agreed to meet again when Phase III evaluation results are available. At that time further program changes may be recommended.

II-4. Staffing pattern has not changed much during the third year of the program, nor are changes anticipated in the near future. A new person was employed as media technician for the School of Library Science when the resignation of the former technician occurred. At that time, the job description was reviewed and modified slightly to place greater emphasis on assistance to faculty members in the production and classroom utilization of media.

PROGRAM COMPONENTS

III-1. Changes in curriculum content were based on formative evaluation measures discussed in the Final Report of Phase II, some of which had already been decided during the Spring of 1973; e.g., changes in the required cataloging course to include Dewey classification and the cataloging of non-print media. The Seminar in Media Design and Production, formerly an elective, became a standard element in the Program for most students during the third year and will remain so in the future. This, the Core Faculty decided, was an essential step to bring Program graduates up to an acceptable level of competency in instructional design.

Fewer students during the third year needed to take the pre-program course in Instructional Media: Methods and Materials (formerly Audiovisual Methods) or the basic literature courses for children and young adults. This allowed a number of them to elect some of the newly developed courses within the School of Education in video production and film making. In the future, all students in the school media specialization will be required to demonstrate basic video production skills acquired through regular courses or special workshops and practice in the Self-instructional Laboratory of the Educational Media Center.

Another curriculum content change was the result of a change in the core requirements for all students in the AMLS degree program. The Contemporary Library Development course, no longer required of other library science students, became an elective for students in the School Library Media Program. The Core Faculty still believes that the rationale for such an overview of trends and issues in all types of libraries is sound. It is supported by the increased interest in cooperative efforts with other libraries which was revealed by the "Inventory of Interest and Competency" used with students in Phase II. A number of students continue to elect this course, however, and aspects of networking are being incorporated into other required courses such as Cataloging and Classification, Reference, and the Teaching Role of the School Library Media Specialist (formerly, Teaching with Media).

Changes have occurred and continue to occur in the objectives and content of individual courses. These changes have been influenced by course evaluations, a review of the Program using BRAC, a school-wide self-study in preparation for a visit by the ALA Committee on Accreditation in the Fall, 1974, the availability of new materials, and individual faculty members' review of their courses' content and methodology.

III-2. No major changes have been made in instructional practices during the past year. Rather, there has been a gradual but consistent increase in the use of newer media and in self-instructional programming. Students in the Seminar in Design and Production and the media technician have worked with several faculty members to develop new materials and instructional strategies to meet course objectives specified by the faculty members. Field trips and student-selected projects continue to be used frequently as means to acquaint students with current practices and problems to be solved.

Students elected to the Advisory Board and Core Faculty members planned several informal meetings in addition to the Library Science Convocations and LSSO (Library Science Student Organization) meetings. Although some noon-time Knapp-sack lunches, popular with earlier students, were tried during the third year, evening meetings in the new Library Science Student-Faculty Lounge seemed more satisfactory. A session on placement opportunities and procedures was especially well-attended, as one might have predicted.

Counseling students to plan programs according to individual needs and interests has been a vital part of the U-M Program. The time involved for three faculty members to meet with each student every term was a problem, however, and during the third year a viable alternative to this successful but time-consuming method was sought. Planning guides were developed and distributed along with Program goals and objectives and class schedules at a general counseling meeting for all students entering the Program. Core Faculty and student representatives on the Advisory Board discussed all aspects of the Program including requirements and electives. They allowed time to answer questions and to get acquainted over coffee and cookies. Students were asked to study the planning guide sheets and class schedule and to come to an appointment with one of the Core Faculty members prepared to

Appendix F-7 169

ask questions and make programming decisions. These decisions could be modified later if either student or faculty advisor felt the need to do so. Response from students and faculty was positive and this procedure will be continued during the coming year.

III-3. The fieldwork component continues to incorporate visitations and field-based individual projects as well as an internship experience for students in the Program. A seminar, held in connection with the internship, offered students a chance to discuss the fieldwork with the cooperating library media specialists on some occasions and, on others, to discuss problems, solutions, and high points in the field experience among themselves and with faculty supervisors. At the final session, graduates of the Program were invited to exchange ideas and share on-the-job experiences with current students.

The revised "Guidelines for Internship Experiences" stressed interaction with students and teachers and problem solving projects. Examples of student projects initiated during the third year include a "Booked for Lunch" discussion for elementary school students and a slide-tape program on vocations illustrating the fifteen job clusters with local work situations.

For three students who had had considerable experience in media centers (one was a media supervisor on leave) an alternate field experience was planned. These students visited a number of different kinds of media centers with the program director and worked out solutions to problems posed by the media specialists visited. This involved campus meetings to discuss alternatives and to decide upon recommendations to be made. While this seemed a worthwhile experience for the students, it was very time-consuming for the director who handled this in addition to a full course load.

III-4. All interdisciplinary aspects of the program have been continued including membership on the Core Faculty and the Advisory Board representing both library science and education; required courses from both schools; elective courses from these and other schools within the University; and the use of classrooms, laboratories, and the Educational Media Center in the School of Education.

III-5. Informal meetings with students and the internship seminars discussed above provided valuable channels of communication. Conferences with all cooperating school library media specialists; review of Program by the Advisory Board, the School of Library Science Curriculum Committee, and the Library Science Faculty; and review of joint listed courses by the School of Education Curriculum Committee and Executive Board were initiated by the Program's Core Faculty. Student course evaluations continue to provide valuable feedback for each faculty member on the reactions to course content and instructional methods.

PROGRAM RESULTS

IV-1. Successes and problems were not greatly different during the third year from those reported earlier. Student, faculty, and Program strengths

170   Appendix F-7

noted in the Final Report of Phase II were continued with the modification in counseling procedure noted in Section III above. Most problems continue to be those related to time and limitations of physical resources.

Developments during the past year which might well be noted are: (1) decisions to continue the Program, (2) role of Program students in the self-study activities of the School of Library Science, (3) use of trigger films, (4) growth of the Seminar in Media Design and Production, and (5) decisions regarding the internship.

Action of the University administration and the Michigan State Legislature to provide funding for continuation of the program was reported earlier. During the past year, however, the Core Faculty successfully implemented a series of steps toward the adoption of the experimental program as the approved school library media specialization for the University. After revisions were made by the Core Faculty, incorporating recommendations of students, Advisory Board, and others, and the results of the Phase II evaluation, the Program was reviewed by the School of Library Science Curriculum Committee and, with their endorsement, sent to the faculty of the School who also approved it.

During the extensive self-study activities this past year, several students in the School Library Media Program took leadership roles on student-faculty-alumni committees. They used their knowledge of curriculum development, media facilities and equipment, and counseling to help in the evaluation and revision of the Library Science Master's degree program.

Trigger films developed in the Experimental Program have been used in several University of Michigan classes. Screenings this past year at several state and regional meetings as well as at the national AECT and ALA meetings have stimulated interest throughout the country in these films and in the method.

The Seminar in Media Design and Production has become an integral rather than an elective part of the School Library Media Program. As the course has expanded, more students have had the experience of systematic instructional design, including pre- and post-testing, within the School or University setting.

IV-2. During the third year it became increasingly evident that more time should be spent in the internship situation. Following recommendations of students and cooperating media specialists, the Core Faculty plans to extend the number of hours each student is expected to spend in a school to 120 rather than the present 90. Many students within the past three years have voluntarily extended their assignments and have thus had more opportunity to follow through with projects and to have additional experiences with students and teachers.

Plans have been made for each Core Faculty member who supervises students in the internship to receive credit for this as an official part of faculty course load, in keeping with recommendations in the Final Report of Phase II.

Another recommendation concerning the internship could not be implemented. Although requests were made through proper University channels to provide remuneration for the media specialists cooperating in the internship, this was not approved. The University position remains firm. It provides for paying a stipend for field-based supervision of student teachers, but will not allow payment in the case of graduates with teaching certificates. Most of the School Media Program students fall into the latter category.

Revised Program goals and objectives describe competencies graduates should be expected to perform. All these are receiving attention within the Program and are thus, in one sense, being achieved. Action has been taken on all the recommendations in the Phase II Final Report. These recommendations could well be considered process objectives for the continuing Program. Only one, as noted above, has not been achieved to some degree.

IV-3. Special questionnaires developed for use with students and faculty during Phase II were not used during the third year because of the general self-study activities. Student evaluation of individual courses was continued. The "Inventory of Interest and Competency" and the "Semantic Differential Scale" were used and discussed in the course, Seminar in School Library Media Problems, rather than administered pre and post to students as during Phase II. Students were asked to complete the BRAC in cooperation with the Phase III Evaluation. The Core Faculty completed BRAC jointly as a part of the program revision process during the past year. They have discussed use of portions of BRAC with several courses in the Program next year. The Phase III Evaluation, when results are available, is expected to be very helpful in Program modification.

PROGRAM IMPACT

V-1. Impact upon the School of Library Science has been discussed in other parts of this report. It can be summarized as affecting content, method, and media available for many courses; affecting students other than those in the Program through their contacts with school media program students and Core Faculty, particularly if they have elected any of the media program courses. Faculty has been affected in many ways, especially through review of the School Media Program, through access to the media technician, and through availability of media equipment and materials.

Impact upon the School of Education is more difficult to specify. Certainly, those education faculty members who have participated in Advisory Board or Plan-In activities and those who have had media Program students in their classes have been influenced by the Program and the role school library media specialists are preparing to take. The review of joint-listed courses and approval of several new media courses by School of Education Curriculum Committee and Executive Board has added to that School's awareness of changes in media education. Education students electing media courses are also influenced directly or indirectly by the program.

Finally, the Educational Media Center has expanded considerably since the beginning of the School Library Media Program. New media equipment and materials have been provided by both the Schools of Education and Library Science and an advisory committee for the Center includes two of the Program's Core Faculty members. The Associate Director of the Program who is the Director of the EMC has worked closely with the School of Library Science in developing new media courses in television and film-making as well as in revision of existing media courses offered through the School of Education.

V-2. There has been impact within the State, especially in development of media center programs in the field and on certification. Participation by media supervisors and school principals on the Advisory Board and interaction among cooperating media specialists, interns, and Core Faculty members have been effective influences. Media specialists from the field have participated regularly in seminars and convocations since the beginning of the School Library Media Program. Further impact on the field has resulted because practicing library media specialists have returned to take new courses developed for the Program.

Revised, competency-based certification plans for the State are being developed primarily through the professional organization Michigan Association for Media in Education. Two members of the Core Faculty are on the MAME certification committee, and another Core Faculty member is on the certification committee of the American Association of School Librarians.

CONCLUSIONS AND RECOMMENDATIONS

VI-1. As has been explained earlier, the School Library Media Program has been adopted as the standard program for this specialization at the University of Michigan and will therefore be maintained.

VI-2. The School Library Manpower Project has analyzed and defined the role of a school media specialist as increasingly complex and has listed a wide range of competencies which a person should possess to do this job well. Through our experimental programs we have attempted to expand the content of school library media education. No longer can we certify as fully-prepared professionals those persons who cannot demonstrate skills in designing, producing, selecting, organizing, and utilizing all forms of educational media, but we are also expecting knowledge of curriculum and learning, skills in communicating with others and in leadership. Finally, these skills must rest upon a broad foundation of general knowledge and of the philosophic and theoretical bases from which practices evolve.

The experimental programs have tried to employ methods which are both efficient and effective and which also become content as they illustrate processes the learner must incorporate in his own professional role. Skills must be observed and tried, problems must be detected before they can be solved. Practical experiences in the field and in laboratory and case study situations are essential to effective school library media education.

Appendix F-7   173

    An important issue for library media education is how can these skills be taught most efficiently without loss of effectiveness? Furthermore, how can we best determine that these skills have been learned and will be used appropriately on the job?

    VI-3. Specification of competencies is necessary if we would know what our students can and must be prepared to do as professionals. But we must not be so specific that we neglect the broader vision, the longer range, the links from one process or bit of knowledge to another.

    Nor can we know, let alone teach all that may be important to media professionals in the future. Education for school library media specialists must be on a professional lifetime continuum. One of the essentials for the present Master's level program must be to teach students to appraise their own competencies and the educational environment in which they operate to determine their needs for continuing professional development.

THE UNIVERSITY OF MICHIGAN
SCHOOL OF LIBRARY SCIENCE

Objectives for the School Library Media Program

The School Library Media Program is designed to provide students with beginning level competencies necessary to perform the role of a library media specialist in an elementary and/or secondary school. The program includes courses in media, management, human relations, curriculum and learning and research. Objectives stated below describe competencies expected upon completion of the program.

1. To develop, promote, and evaluate a program of media services within a school.

2. To contribute regularly to curriculum development through one's knowledge of available media and the ability to apply research findings in learning, human development and educational technology.

3. To plan and arrange facilities which support an effective media program.

4. To communicate regularly with media staff, faculty and administration, parents, public library and other community agencies in planning and interpreting programs and activities.

5. To communicate to faculty and students a knowledge of materials and equipment available and their appropriate uses.

6. To recommend to students a wide range of materials suitable for their developmental level.

7. To interpret the content of print or non-print materials within the media collection.

8. To design and produce media for instruction using resources available.

9. To locate information needed by students and teachers who are using the School Library Media Center when necessary.

10. To provide and use suitable criteria for evaluation and selection of materials and equipment.

11. To organize the media collection for easy accessibility.

12. To appraise one's own competencies in terms of continuing professional development.

Appendix F-7

THE UNIVERSITY OF MICHIGAN
SCHOOL OF LIBRARY SCIENCE
A Guide for Planning Individual Programs for the School Library Media Specialist

Name of Student: _____

Interest Level: ____ Ele.   ____ Jr. High/Middle School   ____ Sec.

Date of beginning program: _____   Expected completion: _____

Prerequisites, these courses or their equivalents:

    Ed.D400 Instructional Media: Methods and Materials _____

    L.S.465/Ed.D465 Literature for Children _____

    L.S.470/Ed.D470 Literature for Young Adults _____

Library Science:

    444 - Teaching Role of the Library Media Specialist _____

    502 - Design and Production of Media _____

    517 - Cataloging and Classification _____

    529 - Reference _____

    576 - Administration of the School Library Media Center _____

    690 - Field Experience _____

    700 - Seminar in School Library Media Problems _____

    703 - Seminar in Media for Children and Young Adults _____

    704 - Seminar in Media Production _____

Education: Competencies in each of these areas (Curriculum, Learning & Human Relations) are necessary to fulfill the requirements of the program. In general, such competencies must be obtained through graduate level work with at least one course in each area.

Curriculum:

    Ed.D531 - Jr. High-Middle School Curriculum _____

    Ed.D605 - Elementary School Curriculum _____

    Ed.D632 - Secondary School Curriculum _____

Learning:

    Ed.C510 - Psychology & Teaching of Reading, Writing & Spelling _____

    Ed.C515 - Technology of Learning _____

    Ed.C516 - Instructional Gaming _____

    Ed.C600 - Educational Psychology _____

    Ed.C642 - Language and Cognitive Development in Children _____

A Guide for Planning - page 2

    Learning (continued):

        Ed.C701 - Psychology of Learning _____

        Ed.D540 - Improving Reading in the Content Areas _____

    Human Relations:

        Ed.C530 - Mental Hygiene of Childhood and Adolescence _____

        Ed.C606 - Education & Socio-Cultural Change (see prerequisites)_____

        Ed.C700 - Growth of Self _____

        Ed.D505 - Multicultural Education (see prerequisites)_____

Additional Courses for Consideration as Electives:

    English - Speech - Education:

        English 436 - Art of the Film _____

        Speech 421 - Introduction to Radio and Television _____

        Speech 522 - Film Theory _____

        Ed.D503 - Television in Teaching _____

    Library Science:

    **L.S.550 - Introduction to Documentation & Information Retrieval _____

    **L.S.620 - Bibliography of the Social Sciences _____

    **L.S.623 - Bibliography of the Sciences _____

    **L.S.626 - Bibliography of the Humanities _____

** *L.S.636 - Contemporary Library Developments _____

  *L.S.688 - Story-telling _____

  *L.S.691 - History of Children's Literature _____

    *pertinent to those interested in working at the elementary level
   **pertinent to those interested in working at the secondary level

The number of hours necessary to complete this program ranges from thirty to thirty-six, depending upon the student's previous preparation.

Certification. In Michigan, thirty semester hours of library media courses constitute a major, which is recommended for certification as a librarian (media specialist) on a Kindergarten through Grade 12 basis. Students who plan to seek certification in another state are advised to check requirements with that state's department of education. Keep in mind that courses taken at the undergraduate level may also be counted toward a certification major or minor.

Revised, December 1973

Appendix F-7   177

U-M EXPERIMENTAL PROGRAM
SCHOOL LIBRARY MANPOWER PROJECT
"Guidelines For Internship Experience"

Orientation Experiences

In so far as possible, interns should:

1. Receive orientation to the area and/or school district media program.

2. Observe and/or participate in area and/or district level meetings for media personnel.

3. Observe and/or assist at a media processing center.

4. Receive orientation at the building level, including introduction to administrators, teachers, and students; community characteristics; school regulations and policies; media program status and needs.

5. Attend school, departmental, subject area, grade level, or team faculty meetings in order to learn ways in which the media center might provide services.

6. Attend other special group meetings; i.e., curriculum study group sessions, special interest pupil groups, building PTO meetings, etc.

Media Service Experiences

In so far as possible, interns should have opportunities to:

1. Cooperate closely and plan with the School Media Specialist.

2. Consult with pupils, teachers, and administrators in order to provide media services to meet their personal and curricular needs.

3. Become informed about existing media center policies in order to interpret them for effective utilization of the media program.

4. Encourage the use of media and the media center, publicize new media, et cetera.

5. Develop an awareness of and encourage the utilization of community resources.

6. Contribute to the maintenance of an atmosphere conducive to learning.

7. Provide reference service.

8. Contribute unique talents to special projects.

9. Train pupils and staff in the use of media equipment.

10. Work intensively with groups of pupils; i.e., storytelling, book talks, developing media research skills, working with student media assistants.

U-M EXPERIMENTAL PROGRAM
SCHOOL LIBRARY MANPOWER PROJECT
"Guidelines for Internship Experience"

Media Service Experiences

11. Design and produce media for special instructional needs.

12. Supervise circulation and retrieval of materials and equipment.

13. Evaluate and select media in cooperation with pupils and staff.

14. Attend in-service programs for faculty, when appropriate, suggesting creative and innovative uses of various media.

15. Become aware of the various reports made by the media specialist each year; e.g., Title II report, annual report to the principal.

16. Develop, in cooperation with the media specialist, criteria for evaluation of the media program.

17. Study the selection, arrangement, and utilization of media center furnishing and equipment.

18. Take inventory as a quality control factor -- perhaps of one small part of the collection --, analyze the strengths, weaknesses, and relevance of items in the collection in light of needs of the pupils, teachers, and curricular offerings.

19. Identify the administrative structure and staffing relationships of the School Media Program.

20. Cooperate with the school media specialist in analyzing and, where advisable, redesigning a specific work procedure (e.g., acquisition, processing, or circulation.)

U-M EXPERIMENTAL PROGRAM
SCHOOL LIBRARY MANPOWER PROJECT
"Guidelines for Internship Experience"

Media Service Experiences

21. Participate in media activities within the classroom environment as appropriate.

22. Maintain and improve professional skills.

23. Participate in professional organization activities or meetings.

Appendix G

Revised BRAC Survey Questionnaires
GRADUATE QUESTIONNAIRE

A. How frequently do you perform this task in your job?

   X - Not applicable or appropriate.
   0 - Never.
   1 - Less than monthly.
   2 - Monthly (1 to 3 times per month).
   3 - Weekly (1 to 4 times per week).
   4 - Daily

B. How would you judge the importance of this task relative to the other tasks performed in your job?

   0 - Minor importance (one of the least important tasks of my job).
   1 - Less than average importance.
   2 - Average importance.
   3 - More than average importance.
   4 - Major importance (one of the most important tasks of my job).

C. How would you judge your capability to perform this task the first few times you had to perform it on your job after graduation?

   0 - I had little or no capability and had to learn task from scratch.
   1 - I needed fairly close guidance to perform this task.
   2 - I could perform this task adequately with general supervision.
   3 - I could perform this task well with little or no supervision.
   4 - I could perform this task with unusually high skill and without supervision.

D. As part of your pre-service education as a school library media specialist, did you take courses, field work, practicums, etc. when you learned how to perform this task or at least learned something about the task?

   0 - No, task not covered in courses I took.
   1 - No, but I learned it elsewhere.
   2 - Yes, but task received only brief coverage/emphasis.
   3 - Yes, and task received same emphasis as most other tasks/topics.
   4 - Yes, and task received very heavy emphasis in course(s) I took.

Appendix G   181

Revised BRAC Survey Questionnaires
SUPERVISOR QUESTIONNAIRE

A. You have under your supervision a recent graduate of a school library media education program. To the best of your knowledge, how frequently does this person perform this task in his/her job?

   X - Not applicable or appropriate.
   0 - Never.
   1 - Less than monthly.
   2 - Monthly (1 to 3 times per month).
   3 - Weekly (1 to 4 times per week).
   4 - Daily.

B. How would you judge the importance of this task relative to the other tasks performed by this person?

   X - I am not knowledgeable enough about school library media personnel to answer this question.
   0 - Minor importance (one of the least important tasks of the job).
   1 - Less than average importance.
   2 - Average importance.
   3 - More than average importance.
   4 - Major importance (one of the most important tasks of the job).

C. How would you judge this person's capability to perform this task when he/she first began working for you following his/her graduation?

   X - I am not knowledgeable enough about this person to answer this question.
   0 - Person had little or no capability and had to learn task from scratch.
   1 - Person needed fairly close guidance to perform this task.
   2 - Person could perform task adequately with general supervision.
   3 - Person could perform task well with little or no supervision.
   4 - Person could perform task with unusually high skill and without supervision.

D. Do you consider this to be a task which a recent graduate of a school library media education program should be able to perform well almost immediately after assuming his/her job?

   0 - No. Usually takes considerable experience and/or further education.
   1 - No, but should be familiar with the task.
   2 - No, can learn this task on the job.
   3 - Yes. Should possess minimally acceptable skills and knowledges and be prepared to acquire additional capability on the job or through continuing education.
   4 - Yes. Should possess completely acceptable professional skills and knowledges.

Revised BRAC Survey Questionnaires
PROGRAM DIRECTOR QUESTIONNAIRE

A. Does this task receive coverage in your school library media education program?

    0 - No.
    1 - Yes, but receives less than average emphasis.
    2 - Yes, receives average emphasis.
    3 - Yes, and receives above average emphasis.
    4 - Yes, and is one of the most heavily emphasized tasks in our program.

B. How would you judge the importance of this task relative to other tasks performed by school library media personnel?

    0 - Minor importance (one of the least important tasks).
    1 - Less than average importance.
    2 - Average importance.
    3 - More than average importance.
    4 - Major importance (one of the most important tasks).

C. At the time of graduation from your program what would you judge the capability of a typical graduate to be on this task? (Assume that graduate had taken that part of your program which covered the task).

    0 - Very low. Would have little or no capability and would have to learn from scratch.
    1 - Quite low. Would need fairly close guidance to perform task.
    2 - Adequate. Could perform task adequately with general supervision.
    3 - Quite high. Could perform task well with little or no supervision.
    4 - **Very** high. Could perform task with unusually high skill and without supervision.

D. Do you consider this to be a task which a recent graduate of a school library media education program should be able to perform well almost immediately after assuming his/her job?

    0 - No. (Can perform task only after considerable experience and/or further education.)
    1 - No. (But should be familiar with the task.)
    2 - No. (Can learn this task on the job.)
    3 - Yes. (Should possess minimally acceptable skills and knowledges and be prepared to acquire additional capability on the job or through continuing education.)
    4 - Yes. (Should ossess completely acceptable professional skills and knowledges.)

Appendix G

Revised BRAC Survey Questionnaires
STUDENT QUESTIONNAIRE

A. As part of your current education as a school library media specialist, have you taken or are you now taking courses, field work, practicums, etc., where you learn how to perform this task or at least learn something about the task?

   0 - No, task not covered in courses I am taking or have taken.
   1 - No, but I learned it elsewhere.
   2 - Yes, but task received only brief coverage/emphasis.
   3 - Yes, and task received same emphasis as most other tasks/topics.
   4 - Yes, and task received very heavy emphasis in my course(s).

B. How would you judge your present capability to perform this task?

   0 - I have little or no capability to perform this task.
   1 - I would need fairly close guidance to perform this task.
   2 - I could perform this task adequately with some general supervision.
   3 - I could perform this task well with little or no supervision.
   4 - I could perform this task with very high skill and without supervision.

Z
675
S3
S356
1975

APR 8 1975